Fútbol in the Park

FIELDWORK ENCOUNTERS AND DISCOVERIES
A series edited by Stefan Timmermans

Fútbol in the Park

*Immigrants, Soccer, and
the Creation of Social Ties*

DAVID TROUILLE

The University of Chicago Press   Chicago and London

The University of Chicago Press, Chicago 60637
The University of Chicago Press, Ltd., London
© 2021 by The University of Chicago
Published 2021
Printed in the United States of America

30 29 28 27 26 25 24 23 22 21   1 2 3 4 5

ISBN-13: 978-0-226-74874-0 (cloth)
ISBN-13: 978-0-226-74888-7 (paper)
ISBN-13: 978-0-226-74891-7 (e-book)
DOI: https://doi.org/10.7208/chicago/9780226748917.001.0001

Library of Congress Cataloging-in-Publication Data

Names: Trouille, David, author.
Title: Fútbol in the park : immigrants, soccer, and the creation of social ties / David Trouille.
Other titles: Fieldwork encounters and discoveries.
Description: Chicago : University of Chicago Press, 2021. | Series: Fieldwork encounters and discoveries | Includes bibliographical references and index.
Identifiers: LCCN 2020024734 | ISBN 9780226748740 (cloth) | ISBN 9780226748887 (paperback) | ISBN 9780226748917 (ebook)
Subjects: LCSH: Hispanic Americans—Socialization—California, Southern. | Hispanic American men—California, Southern—Social life and customs. | Hispanic American men—Social networks—California, Southern. | Soccer—Social aspects—California, Southern. | Social interaction—California, Southern.
Classification: LCC E184.S75 T76 2020 | DDC 305.868/07949—dc23
LC record available at https://lccn.loc.gov/2020024734

For los jugadores del parque and immigrants everywhere trying to find a place to call home.

CONTENTS

INTRODUCTION

The ball bounces toward Polo with the mouth of the goal wide open in front of him. His team is down by one goal and time is running out in the pickup soccer game in a West Los Angeles park. He winds up to smash the ball into the back of the net. But perhaps reveling in his game-tying goal just a little too soon, he pulls back and sends the ball flying over the crossbar.

"¡Basura!" (Garbage!)
"¡Estúpido!" (Stupid!)
"¡Viejito!" (Old-timer!)
"¡Jugador del parque!" (Park player!)

Calls ring out from the bleachers mocking the forty-one-year-old from Veracruz, Mexico. But the men aren't only interested in shaming Polo. They have an ulterior motive in seeing a tie game. Recently, a rule had been established that if a game ended in a tie, both teams had to leave the playing field in order to give more playing opportunities to men on the sidelines.

As the sun blazes overhead, thoughts turn from the games to the beer drinking that often follows. Addressing Polo, Motor quips: "Mejor vaya por las chelas." (Better go for the beers.) Never one to avoid confrontations, Polo fires back at the Salvadoran: "No me hables ni mierda con tu equipo de maletas." (Don't talk shit to me with your team of lousy players.) Titi, also from El Salvador, softly jokes that Polo was mad because "nadie lo quiere" (no wants him) for the various league teams that drew players from these daily pickup games, further proof that he was merely a "park player." Motor—coach of the most-celebrated league team—smiles and slaps hands with Titi to express his approval. Both ignore the fact that Titi had also been dropped from Motor's team in favor of the younger talent that continually flocked to the park.

Roberto, whose playing days are also winding down, blows his whistle to signal the end of the loosely timed match. As the next group of players enters the field, Polo brushes off his teammates' complaints and joins his most vocal critics standing on the bleachers. The men continue to chide Polo for his disastrous miss, invoking his nickname Apocalypto (from a film about Mayan warriors that called to mind his facial features and long black hair). Head held high, Polo blames a mistimed pass for his bungled goal. He adds that he has nothing to prove, since he had scored countless "golazos" (stellar goals) over the years. Then, going on the offensive, he singles out several of his detractors who had rarely, if ever, put the ball into the net. Caballo (Horse)—a sturdy, aptly nicknamed Honduran—begins to question whether Polo had ever really scored these golazos when the men's attention abruptly shifts to a small skirmish at midfield. As two men battle over the ball, one player takes offense to his opponent's aggressive tactics. Play stops as the two men argue nose to nose, but they relent when their teammates gently pull them apart. A few men whistle from the sidelines to make light of the confrontation. One man shouts out: "¡Arriba los novios!" (Long live the boyfriends!) As the match resumes, the men on the bleachers return to debating their legacies as players.

At the conclusion of the sixth and final game of the day, many of the players and spectators relocate to picnic tables by the field, eager to continue the fun over shared beers. Ignoring Motor's call to buy beer for everyone as penance for his botched goal, Polo shares the cost with several others for an eighteen-pack of Modelo. The arrival of the cold Mexican beer re-invigorates banter about Polo's earlier miss and his delusions of grandeur. References to other park heroes and villains enliven the discussions, as do comparisons to professional players.

On a break from a home-remodeling job a few miles from the park, Valderrama pulls his battered truck into the parking lot, followed by several others who arrive from their shifts in nearby restaurants. Approaching the men, Valderrama pulls out a few dollars from his dusty pocket and jokes that it's for the "borrachos del parque" (park drunks). Like the rest of the group, he comes with a thirst for beer and conviviality. Their money and spirited presence lead to several additional beer runs. Since no one is willing to drive, Mi Chavo bikes the half-dozen well-traveled blocks to the convenience store and earns a free beer for his efforts. A bit down on his luck, he's one of several men who drink without putting in money.

The atmosphere remains lively and jovial, but the men take care to conceal the beer cans for fear of receiving expensive drinking citations from the police, who regularly patrol the park. Other issues weigh on the men's minds as well. Titi declines an offered beer, stating that he has to meet a client for a potential painting job, but Polo jokes that the real reason was that his wife would scold him ("lo regaña"). When Roberto wonders aloud why Polo hasn't yet left for his restaurant shift, Polo smiles and claims that he's "on vacation." Although some hurry home or moderate their consumption, these outside concerns remain largely unspoken as the men drink and converse into the early evening.

*

Most readers will have some awareness of Latino men playing soccer and socializing in public parks. This is a familiar scene in Los Angeles and in many places throughout the country. Over the past half century, immigration from Latin America has transformed the public landscape in the United States.[1] Numerous communities are witnessing one of the hallmarks of this transformation: the emergence of park soccer.[2]

Soccer may "explain the world"—to quote the title of a popular book—but most people have little understanding of how socializing around the game actually works and what it really means for the participants and those around them.[3] For some, the increased presence of Latino men in public parks is cause for pride and celebration. To others, their presence feels disruptive—an unwelcome symbol of demographic change. In fact, the park first came to my attention after hearing about a group of local residents who were upset about a new soccer field that had been installed five miles south of UCLA, where I was a first-year graduate student. They circulated a flyer which claimed that the field at the Mar Vista Recreation Center had turned the predominately White and affluent neighborhood into a giant sports arena, trapping residents in a "lawless, Wild West environment."[4] Yet from my first visit to the park in January 2008, I saw signs of an intriguing world that would have been entirely unrecognizable to anybody who read the flyer. This book sheds much-needed light on a scene many people only glimpse from afar.

Based on over a decade of ethnographic research, *Fútbol in the Park: Immigrants, Soccer, and the Creation of Social Ties* explores how a group of predominately Latino immigrant men could feel such passion—even fight—about a world they created around playing soccer in a park. The men wanted to live rich, meaningful lives, and what they did together in the park helped them achieve this. Here they built relationships and a sense of who they are, separate from their identities elsewhere or their country of origin. Together on the soccer field, sharing beers after the games, and occasionally exchanging taunts or blows, the men worked on the meaning of their lives. And through these engrossing, revealing, and at times immortalizing activities, they forged new identities and connections, giving themselves a renewed sense of self-worth and community. In short, the park became a place to anchor and enrich their lives in a new country.

Yet time in the park created a dual dilemma for the men. On the one hand, they needed to meet at the park in order to feel at home and network; but, on the other hand, their time on the field sometimes conflicted with their jobs and family obligations. Moreover, their presence in the park was sometimes viewed in a negative light by local residents. The catch-22 of the men's situation became all the more problematic given the increased stigmatization of Latino immigrants—a decisive factor in the election of Donald Trump in 2016, eight years after I first visited the park.

"Bad Hombres"

In the third and final presidential debate, Republican presidential candidate Donald Trump proclaimed on national television that "we have some bad hombres here and we're going to get them out." His deliberate use of Spanish capped a series of attacks by Trump and his supporters on Latino immigrant men as inherently criminal, violent, and illegal. A year earlier, Trump had launched his campaign by invoking this "Latino threat"[5] in the starkest terms:

> When Mexico sends its people, they're not sending their best. They're not sending you. They're not sending you. They're sending people that have lots of problems, and they're bringing those problems with us. They're bringing drugs. They're bringing crime. They're rapists. And some, I assume, are good people.

Although the demonization of Latino immigrant men predated Trump's candidacy, his election added greater urgency to my project. The men I interacted with for eleven years at the park are not hardened criminals; but when outsiders believe they are—against all evidence—they are reacting to external cues that make them feel unsafe.[6] For some park neighbors, the Mar Vista soccer players came to embody the "bad hombres" vilified by Trump, and they resembled the men rounded up and deported under his leadership, including many in Los Angeles.[7] Yet while resentments are real, they often result from unfamiliarity and distorted impressions. Trump's condemnation of Latino immigrant men as "bad hombres" persists and gains credence in part due to a lack of understanding about these men's experiences. Even Trump's attempt at moderation during his campaign launch was rooted in an *assumption* that some Latinos might be "good people."

As I would later learn, similar dynamics were at play in the park. While Latinos were often brought into the neighborhood as gardeners, handymen, and nannies, there was little interaction between local residents and users of the field. Most observed them from afar playing soccer, socializing, and occasionally drinking beer or coming into conflict with one another. I rarely observed the mostly White neighbors coming into contact with the men, including those who disparaged them and attempted to restrict their access to the soccer field. In fact, local residents resisted participation by the players and their advocates in community meetings about the field. Like the author of the flyer that first introduced me to tension at the field, park neighbors seem to have sensed that there was something "Wild West" about these men and what they were up to in the park.

By studying a group of men who came to be labeled in similar ways to Trump's "bad hombres," this book aims to bring much-needed clarity and empathy to contentious debates concerning immigration.[8] At this turbulent time in US immigration history, the immigrant men at the Mar Vista soccer field are finding their way as so many generations before them have, but with notable differences. In their need for community and sociability, as well as physical exercise in a sport they love, they have created a particular version of street-corner conviviality and a social context in which they can feel comfortable with others and with themselves. Yet in making foreign territory familiar, they also generated grounds for conflict with residents of the surrounding community and even among themselves.

In these changing, often tumultuous times, we need a deeper, more genuine understanding of how Latino immigrant men cultivate a sense of self and belonging in a new, sometimes hostile environment. *Fútbol in the Park* tells a version of this story. Drawing on the men's voices and experiences, I try to understand them on their own terms as they carve out a space to socialize and build relations in a public park. The point is not to pass judgment on these men, but to understand what happens in these "alien places" within public space. In this way, my book offers a dynamic, multidimensional portrait rarely granted to Latino immigrants.

This is a challenging time to write about Latino men. There is a danger of stigmatizing, sensationalizing, even of sentimentalizing the subject.[9] Yet much of the academic and popular literature on Latino immigrant men tends to represent them as workers devoid of social value beyond the work they do or as part of the "Latino threat" narrative centered around criminality and moral corruption.[10] As such, it says little about how Latino immigrant men bond with others and the kinds of companionship they crave. Conversely, Latina immigrants are often portrayed as more fully human—as workers, but also as mothers, spouses, and friends.[11]

By showing the context, meaning, and value of the very activities that sometimes serve to marginalize and criminalize this population, I offer the book as a rejoinder to those who may view these men and their behavior through the prism of narrow and dehumanizing stereotypes. Now, more than ever, is the time to write honestly and holistically about Latino immigrant men, who too often have been portrayed as suffering laborers or dangerous

criminals. The men I describe in my book are not one-dimensional carica-
tures deserving sympathy or scorn, but people living full and complex lives
amid challenging circumstances. To capture how they imbue their lives
with meaning, an ethnographic approach seemed the best way forward.

Street-Corner Ethnography

Pockets of interaction and sociability have intrigued urban ethnographers
for over a century. This follows an abiding interest among US sociologists
in identifying how people seek out and build community in the modern
city. Ethnographic methods have proven highly effective in understanding
and capturing these enduring forms of social life. For pioneering sociologist Robert Park, this was about getting "the seat of your pants dirty in
real research."[12] Indeed, with their commitment to observe people in their
everyday contexts over an extended period of time, ethnographers have
provided invaluable insights into how people construct and make sense
of their lives.[13]

   Some of sociology's most memorable texts have been ethnographic studies of small groups of people socializing on the proverbial street corner.[14]
By integrating the human dimensions and sociological ramifications of
the worlds under study, classic works such as *Street Corner Society*, *Tally's
Corner*, or *A Place on the Corner* show how individuals and groups create
order and meaning in their everyday lives. In many cases, these studies
challenge what the research site looks like from the outside, serving as
a bridge connecting subjects with readers. Through careful, comparative
analyses, ethnographers also show how invisible or indistinct factors—such
as other aspects of the subjects' lives or broader structural and historical
forces—affect the sites and people they study.[15] Although firmly rooted
in the contours of the situation and the historical moment, these studies
often shine a light on more universal social processes, such as how status
hierarchies are made and remade or how individuals maintain respectability
in the face of broader stigmatization.[16] And while their orientations and
emphases may differ, ethnographers strive to represent everyday experience and local knowledge in a form others can comprehend.[17]

   Fútbol in the Park draws on this well-established practice, but focuses
on a population that has not received the same ethnographic attention as
other groups.[18] Following in the footsteps of ethnographers who studied
street corners and bars, I examine the social world of the park and, through
it, the lived experience of the immigrants who played there. From the out-
set, I sensed that the men were continuing a long tradition of immigrants
building a place for themselves in their new home. As I developed a deeper
understanding of the setting and activities at the park, my research fo-

cused on the dynamic formation of relationships there. I became especially interested in how socializing and playing soccer together facilitated connections and the exchange of resources, particularly through job referrals. The men seemed to be creating a familiar and supportive environment that diminished the dislocation associated with migration. But as is often the case with ethnography, my study also broadened as I recognized something more commonplace, universal, and enigmatic in the men's interactions. My book explores how gathering together in the park to socialize and play soccer—an activity outsiders may view as frivolous, even childish—has become so richly meaningful to this group of immigrant men.[19]

Immigrants and Social Networks

As I became aware of the rhythms of park life, my thoughts turned to a foundational sociological insight. The men seemed to be engaged in the "networking" that migration scholars identify as key to the survival and success of newcomers.[20] Following patterns outlined in previous studies, these men presumably shared information, exchanged resources, and provided emotional support for one another. I also assumed that the men's ties were stable, long-standing, and likely originating from their countries of birth, as past researchers have claimed. In any case, initially I was more interested in the meaning and impact of the men's relationships than in their history or how those relationships were sustained. However, this distinction between what networks provide and how they are formed proved shortsighted. Over time, I came to see how the creation, maintenance, and meaning of these relationships were part of the same story.

*

Networks are essential sources of social organization and resource mobilization; prospective migrants draw on them in order to leave home, to cross borders, and to establish themselves in new destinations. These connections provide access to jobs, housing, and loans, as well as to more intangible help in adapting to often strange and difficult circumstances.[21] However, in their adherence to the sociological truism that networks matter, many researchers have taken for granted the processes from which social ties arise. There is a tendency to attach too much importance to place of origin in explaining migrant networking, given that preexisting ties and credentials can quickly deteriorate or become impractical in new places.[22]

Moreover, much of the seminal research on migrant networks was conducted at an earlier point in the history of Mexican migration in the late twentieth century. It focused on rural Mexican communities with long histories of US-bound migration.[23] In the intervening years, migration has multiplied severalfold from all over Mexico and Central America, including from urban areas. As sociologist Rubén Hernández-León and others have shown, these migrants are unlikely to have equally tight networks at their place of origin.[24] As migration becomes more massive, leading everyone to have at least some contact with someone in the United States, those close, dense contacts are less important than they used to be for getting to the United States. Yet the weaker contacts drawing people north are unlikely to provide the same level of support or to sustain that support over time. Network instability can also create tensions between givers and receivers, leading in some cases to conflict and abuse, as sociologist Cecilia Menjívar and others have revealed.[25] The loosening of these traditional ties makes the type of community building I observed at the park all the more important.

This shift in migration histories was true for many of the men at the park. Take, for example, Polo—the principal organizer of the midday soccer games—who was in his late thirties when I first met him in 2008. At the urging of one of his closest friends, he had come to Los Angeles in 1988 from Veracruz, Mexico, at the age of nineteen. Polo had had a decent job working for an oil company in Mexico. However, impressed by the home his friend had built in his hometown with earnings from north of the border, he wanted to try his luck in the United States. Single and childless, Polo was the ninth of ten children. Other than his childhood friend, Polo knew no one in Los Angeles and had only a few distant relatives in other parts of the country. Although his friend helped him find work in a restaurant, the two men soon had a falling-out. But as political economist Michael Piore might have predicted, the nineteen-year-old's need for community grew as he settled and shifted his perspectives beyond work and the Spartan existence that initial dreams of return might have entailed.[26]

To his delight, within several months of his arrival, he found a new community of friends at nearby Penmar Park, before gravitating to Mar Vista a few years later.[27] Like Polo, many men told me that they knew few people when they first arrived in Los Angeles and gradually grew apart from their initial contacts, including relatives and hometown friends. I also learned that most of the men had become acquainted in the park, rather than arriving together as preexisting units.

Migrant networks remain essential but emerge under changing, often disruptive conditions. People come and go; things happen: relationships change, priorities shift, resources dissolve, opportunities surface, and so on. This was certainly the case for many of the men I came to know at the park. Pre-migration ties helped them emigrate, but became less available for helping them take the next steps in a new world. Yet, despite the fact that theories of migration assume the existence and utility of these networks, the day-to-day processes by which social networks erode, change, and develop over time are generally overlooked in the study of migration.

Analyses that use networks as a kind of capital to help explain outcomes often treat social ties as something people simply "have." But this approach limits and freezes what is an inherently dynamic concept.[28] A network is sociological shorthand for the work that people do through interaction to build, sustain, and occasionally capitalize on their relationships. Instead of viewing networks as automatically "there" or passively reproduced, my book shows how migrants actively build a foundation for making new ties in their everyday lives. In contrast to research that employs a passive language of "social ties," my study emphasizes "social tying"—the dynamic, daily construction of connections.

Fútbol in the Park

While there are certainly many ways that Latino immigrants meet new people, playing soccer and gathering in parks are frequently cited as central to the development of social ties, especially for working-class men. For example, in *Return to Aztlan*, a foundational text on the social organization of migration, Douglas Massey and his coauthors point to "Los Patos" park as a primary meeting place in Los Angeles for a dispersed community of Mexican immigrants.[29] Although only briefly described in their study, these sociable interactions in the park are shown to help the migrants sustain community and develop new connections. According to the authors, soccer is "probably the most important" voluntary organization. Moreover, in migration studies more generally, soccer frequently surfaces as a principal organizing activity in the lives of Latino immigrants[30]—a key element in a robust nexus of sports, parks, and integration also found in the experiences of previous newcomers to the United States.[31]

While the work of Massey and others on this subject is noteworthy, it is only suggestive. Despite frequent references in academic and more popular writings to the popularity and perceived importance of soccer and public parks, we have little sociological understanding of *how* they facilitate network formation and galvanize group life.[32] How is it that playing soccer and socializing in public parks appear so conducive to the development of social ties? How are park and game interactions made meaningful and compelling in ways that foster interpersonal relationships and enrich participants' sense of self? What do these encounters mean in the men's everyday lives, given their limited leisure and networking options?

Whereas casual observations provide superficial explanations, extended participant observation reveals the continual work that goes into forming and sustaining social ties. Rather than dictated by some higher authority or organizational script, the networking I observed at the Mar Vista Recreation Center needed to be done by the men on their own. The formation of social relationships through group activity was neither automatic nor straightforward, but emerged over time in complex and sometimes paradoxical, problematic ways. A focus on daily park interactions helps us see network development not only as relational, but also as a contingent and transformative social process. Unlike the immigrants in *Return to Aztlan* who retained their ties to "paisanos" (compatriots), the men at the park formed new connections that transcended hometown, region, and even nationality. They may all have looked alike from afar, but there were important differences that became clearer as I came to know them better. By showing how sustained social interaction builds relationships and leads to job referrals and other resource exchanges, this study pushes network analyses beyond static, narrow representations of their form and function that tend to assume more than they explain.

Social Tying

Out of very little, the immigrant men created an eventful life in the park, where they felt things were happening. However, sociability and commitment to a shared experience were hardly a given. Instead, the men worked together to create and sustain their time together. Park life was a form of collective action, a world that could not exist without the men's active collaboration. Sociable occasions were a fluid, ongoing accomplishment built on shared histories and commitments and on a local "interaction order" with its own patterns and dynamics.[33] As with most relationships, disruptions occurred from time to time, but generally these interactions were performed routinely and without challenge. By employing an interactionist approach[34] that privileges the process of tying, my study shows how social interaction was made possible and how these patterned ways of being together created a shared world in which to build relations and bring meaning to their lives.[35]

*

The park worked effectively as a site of interaction and as an incubator for social relations because the participants made their time together fun and compelling. For the men I studied, the shared commitment binding them together was a fascination with playing soccer and socializing in a public park. These collective experiences not only brought the men together and broke down barriers between them, but also helped them develop trust in each other over time. As a result, these men—most of whom met as strangers in the park—were more willing to exchange resources, a key way they made ends meet. This became particularly apparent when they hired or referred one another for painting, construction, or restaurant work—the primary sources of employment for the men at the park.

Take, for example, Valderrama's explanation of how he came to join the group at the park and how he benefited from the relationships he formed there. Originally from Mexico City, Valderrama first came to Mar Vista in 1990. At the time, he lived nearby and had seen men playing soccer in the park as he passed by on his way to work. One day, the then-twenty-one-year-old decided to stop to watch the games. Spotting the newcomer, Chino yelled over to him and asked him if he wanted to play. Missing the sport he grew up playing in Mexico and the camaraderie that came with it, Valderrama eagerly joined the game. Like Polo, he was looking for a life beyond his work. His prompt nicknaming as Valderrama by the others, for his resemblance to the Colombian soccer star Carlos Valderrama with his wild hair, marked his entry into this world. He has consistently played soccer in the park ever since—although now in his early fifties, he spends more time watching than playing. He also became a regular participant in the socializing that accompanies the games. In addition, over the years, the carpenter and general handyman has worked for or hired several of the men he met at the park.

These relationships, while originating in play, were more than *just* play. Pathways gradually were paved toward more personal kinds of relationships and exchanges. For example, drinking beer together set up the interaction through which conviviality and eventually friendship and trust could follow. Sharing "un doce" (a twelve-pack of beer) framed and defined the situation in a way that made sense to the men, masking concerns and emotions that might threaten or delay interaction. These interactional rituals that developed around playing soccer and socializing in the park provided the social glue for spending time together.[36]

But time in the park was about more than building relationships. It became a place to construct rich, meaningful lives and work through fundamental social and psychological concerns about who they were in a new country. By showing themselves in relatively naked ways as they competed on the soccer field and drank beer together afterward, the men created an identity for themselves independent of who they were in other parts of their lives or where they came from. With old ways of being no longer at hand, here they could be heroes in the eyes of their peers. The passion and occasional clashes reminded everyone that this world they created was worth fighting over.

The challenge the men often faced was whether they would live up to—or back down from—the demands and expectations of their buddies at the park. At times, the pleasures and pressures of group life caused the men to neglect more pressing matters related to family or work. The men's search for comfort and connection at the park forced them to come to terms with what was possible in their new home, especially in their relations with the police and with White, higher-income park neighbors, some of whom objected to their presence. The creation of a fun and familiar environment did not simply reproduce preexisting ties and leisure practices; it also reflected the opportunities and constraints of a new interactive context. The men discovered that it was not always easy to play together.

Contrary to the claim of some scholars, the men were not creating urban villages that reproduced the conditions they left behind.[37] Yet although they were living among strangers, they found themselves in an environment filled with Spanish speakers with similar needs, customs, tastes, and resources. This common background drew them to the park, where something unexpected but practical and satisfying happened, given the daily presence of strangers with shared interests. The park provided a space in which to re-create ties and identities lost through immigration in a manner that made sense emotionally but was well suited to their new environment.

The Mar Vista Recreation Center

The Mar Vista Recreation Center was the primary site of interaction and the physical anchor of the social relations examined in this study. The park opened in 1947 in a section of West Los Angeles bearing its name. The conversion of the eighteen-acre lot of private farmland into a public park typified the period of park expansion that accompanied the postwar housing boom in the city.[38] Initially identified as a park, then as a playground, Mar Vista officially became a recreation center in 1976. Over the years, a mix of amenities has been added to the center, including an outdoor pool, a children's playground, basketball courts, an indoor gym, baseball diamonds, tennis courts, barbeque grills and picnic tables, an outdoor hockey rink, and more recently an artificial turf soccer field. Grass, plantings, and trees fill in the space, giving the park a bucolic feel amid the concrete.

The neighborhood around the park has remained primarily residential and White, but has shifted from middle to increasingly upper income, although not as exclusive as neighboring Beverly Hills or Santa Monica. In 2010, 82 percent of the 1,461 residents living in the four census blocks bordering the park identified as White and reported a median family income of $135,108. That same year, in the eighteen city blocks directly north of the park—a neighborhood known as Westdale and home to the most vocal critics of the new soccer field—only 3 percent of the residents identified as Latino. Back in 1947, a racial covenant was established in this housing tract banning "any person not of the White or Caucasian race."[39] Although long since illegal, this redlining practice has had long-lasting effects on the racial and ethnic composition of the area.[40]

Despite similar covenants established in nearby subdivisions, beginning in the early 1990s, other areas within one or two miles of the park have seen increases in foreign-born Latino residents, most of whom rent homes in apartment complexes scattered through the city's historically White and affluent Westside. Latino immigrants are also drawn to the area by employment opportunities—primarily low-wage work in construction, restaurants, gardening, cleaning, and childcare. This development is a part of the general growth in Latin American immigration occurring throughout Southern California since the 1970s.[41]

However, the Latinization of Los Angeles has been uneven, as experienced in the areas bordering the park. The changing patterns of use at Mar Vista Park reflect these shifting demographics. In addition to regular use by its largely White local residential population, the recreation center attracts a broad diversity of users from more distant areas, drawn by the facilities described above, as well as by the park's cleanliness, relative safety, and airy feel. The unequal distribution of park space and differing rates of violence in Los Angeles also pulls in patrons from less resourced and more dangerous areas.[42] According to local residents and park officials, the installation of an artificial turf soccer field in 2005 drew even more newcomers to the park.

My study focuses on a small sample drawn from this latest wave of Latino immigrants and explores how the men's activities and relationships at the park were shaped by the local setting. Like other public spaces, parks provide access but also visibility, which for these strangers from outside the neighborhood created both opportunities and problems. As they came to understand, their interactions did not exist in a vacuum, but in a space that was neither neutral nor static. This was not a street corner, church, bar, work site, or private residence, but a public park located in an area where the men were racial and class outsiders. Possibilities for interaction and community were negotiated based on local conditions—part of what sociologist Eric Klinenberg refers to as the "social infrastructure" shaping our interactions.[43] My book tells the story of how this group of immigrant soccer players were viewed by city officials, park neighbors, and newcomers to their games and of how the players responded. It shows the importance and complexities of open, accessible, and free public space for maintenance of a group.

Los Jugadores del Parque

The men regularly cried "jugador del parque" (park player) whenever someone did something that stood out, especially during a soccer game. In some cases, men shouted the iconic chant to celebrate a good play on the field; but more often, the label was used to playfully mock and belittle. An egregious miss was often greeted with taunts of "jugador del parque," accompanied by other choice insults, as we saw in the opening vignette when Polo bungled what should have been an easy goal. While the label was usually applied to individuals, occasionally whole groups of men were branded "jugadores del parque." Men yelled out the term as they drove past games in progress on the field or as they walked by groups of men socializing at the picnic tables. Presence, as much as behavior, could trigger its use.

While used primarily as an insult, the park rallying cry bound the men together as people with a shared history and culture. The label also differentiated park life from other settings in the men's lives, such as work and home, as well as from the soccer leagues in which some of the men also played. Like Polo, those deemed unsuitable for league play were identified as mere "park players" by their critics. Who was or wasn't a park player was an endless source of debate and intrigue. The seriousness or lightheartedness of the taunt also depended on the situation and cast of characters, sometimes triggering conflict, but more typically generating laughs and camaraderie. Like a wink, the recurring punch line could be interpreted in multiple ways depending on the situation. Indeed, shouting out "jugador del parque" was one of many ways the men creatively transformed the park into a fun and compelling place.

The cherished park expression also joined together a fluid and diverse group of participants. While levels of involvement and commitment varied, approximately 120 men and a few women occupied the world I studied in the park over an eleven-year period. Some played in the midday games, others came to socialize, but most participated in both scenes when their schedules and physical conditions permitted. Playing soccer and hanging out with friends were two sides of the same coin for most of the participants, one activity begetting the other. But, as in my case, the most common entry point into the park was through the soccer games, and only over time did players join the social gatherings that followed.

Numbers also fluctuated as the soccer games and the socializing around them attracted newcomers, while personal developments pulled some participants away from the park. However, many had histories in the park that stretched back several decades, such as Hugo, who first came to the park in 1965, several months after arriving in Los Angeles from his native

Chile. Most of the people who appear in this book had been coming to the park since the 1990s. My yearly short-term visits from 2014 to 2019 made me more aware than before of this continuity and change as I encountered many familiar faces and invariably a few new ones in the park.

This evolving scene was distinguished by several unifying characteristics. My research site was a predominately male space. A few women participated in the soccer games and, on occasion, female companions—usually girlfriends rather than wives or daughters—accompanied the men as they played soccer or socialized in the park. The only regular female participant was Kathy, a White woman in her mid-fifties who lived and worked in the area. She regularly played in the midday soccer games during her lunch break from a nearby elementary school and often helped them out. When a few of the men were facing hard times, she even let them sleep in her home or garage, which earned her the nickname Katy Hilton after the hotel chain—a term of endearment that gently poked fun at the guys who depended on her. She also advocated on the men's behalf at community meetings, especially at the height of debates about the new soccer field. Kathy's religious faith, ability to speak Spanish, and life circumstances (divorced, with a grown daughter) all contributed to her deep commitment to the men. But apart from Kathy and the occasional appearance of a few other women, the interactions and relationships I observed were overwhelmingly male.

For most of the participants, part of the park's charm was that it was a clearly masculine space where they could comfortably "be themselves" in the company of like-minded men. Although this scenario played out in different ways, the park provided most of them with a culturally familiar context in which to perform idealized versions of masculinity and male friendship.[44] Spending hours in the park playing soccer and socializing with other men was normal and safe in ways that typically were not for women.[45] And while their gender created problems, it did not marginalize them in this neighborhood in the same ways as did their race, class, and immigration status. Being a man did not preclude them from hanging out in the park; if anything, socializing in this public setting felt easier and more appropriate than in other places.

The men I came to know in the park were predominately foreign born, the majority from Mexico or Central America. Many had immigrated to the United States in the 1980s and 1990s, including a sizable contingent from El Salvador who were fleeing social and political unrest.[46] For example, Motor came to Los Angeles with his mother and siblings in 1982 when he was fourteen to join his father, who had been living in the city for several years. As Motor recalled, his mother was concerned that he would be drawn into the escalating civil war in his native country. Others, like Polo, had emigrated for economic reasons in their late teens or early twenties during an era when it was easier to travel from Mexico to the United States. Men from Honduras and Guatemala had arrived more recently, pushed out by problems at home and attracted by the prospects of a better life in Los Angeles. Most entered low-wage sectors of the job market, filling a growing need for their labor in restaurants, construction, and gardening.[47] And so for these men, time at the park was a break from—and reward for—their arduous and low-paying work. For the more precariously employed, it was a meaningful place to pass the time between jobs.[48] While I didn't have a full sense of their financial situations, most of the men seemed solidly working class, neither destitute nor secure, although many struggled during the economic downturn that began in 2008. Issues concerning money most often came up during daily beer and food runs, although there was usually someone able to cover for those who couldn't contribute financially.

Whereas roughly two-thirds of the men I studied were immigrants from Mexico and Central America, a third of my interlocutors diverged from this general profile. Various other nationalities were represented at the park, including a small group from Peru, together with individuals from other countries in South America and from places across the globe, as diverse as Jamaica, Cameroon, Morocco, Japan, Lebanon, and Italy. The park (and especially the soccer games) also attracted a number of US-born Whites, Blacks, and second-generation Latinos, including several sons of men who had played soccer and socialized in the park for decades.

There was also a diversity of occupations and incomes among the men I studied. The majority were low-wage laborers, but some worked higher-paying jobs. For example, David worked as a mechanic for a major airline, Moncho was a movie set designer, and Ali owned a body shop and smog-check station. A few others were employed as nurses, teachers, and clerks. The fortunes of independent contractors also varied, with most experiencing periods of success alternating with setbacks. And while most men lived in cramped rental apartments, a few owned single-family homes and condominiums in more distant and affordable parts of Los Angeles. By contrast, a handful of men connected to the scene were regularly penniless and unemployed; a few even slept in the park or in their cars.

Participants in the soccer games were not limited to any particular age group. The majority were men in their twenties, thirties, and forties, but the games also attracted a number of teenagers, as well as a few players in their fifties and sixties, and even one man in his seventies. The socializing that accompanied the games was also characterized by a range of ages (mainly men in their thirties to sixties), but included fewer youngsters. This mix of nationalities and ages was a constant source of amusement and occasional conflict on and off the field. For example, newcomers were habitually asked where they were from, and many participants were given nicknames based on their nationality, appearance, or age—Viejito (Old-timer) being one of the most common and crowd-pleasing.⁴⁹

Family status was also mixed. Most men, especially the older ones, were married with children, but a few were separated, and others, like Polo and Motor, had never married or had children. Several men (including me) became husbands and fathers during my fieldwork. While some men brought their children (mainly sons) to the park with them, most came without family members. Time spent at the park was not only a time-out from work, but also from familial and domestic duties—a fact that some-times caused tension and resentment at home, as I explain later in the book. This mostly male scene contrasted with the many Latino families who played together in this park and in other city parks.⁵⁰

Some of the men were in the United States unlawfully, having either crossed the border without inspection or overstayed their visas. Many shared heartrending stories of crossing the border without permission, of their struggles living "shadowed lives," and of the emotional pain from being separated from family members—sometimes for decades—for fear of being unable to return to the United States.⁵¹ This should come as no surprise, given that many working-class Latino immigrants in Los Angeles are undocumented.⁵² However, because of the risks of deportation faced by these men and their families, especially in the current political climate, I have chosen to limit discussion of their legal status and, in particular, to avoid identifying those who were in the country unlawfully.⁵³

Ethnography in the Park and Beyond

An incident early in my fieldwork set the tone for the trajectory of my research. As I pondered a beer that had been offered to me, Polo quipped: "If you're not a borracho [drunk], look for another park to study." The comment was said in jest, but Polo's not-so-subtle suggestion underscored a larger point. If I wanted to research park life, I had to engage in what was happening there. I couldn't be a squirrel in a tree; I needed to become an active participant in the group's activities at the park. For five and a half years—from January 2008 to July 2013—I took Polo's advice to heart by immersing myself in the lives and routines of the park. After moving across the country in 2013, I kept in touch with the players and park develop-ments over the following six years through phone calls, social media, and annual one- to two-week visits. Below, I offer a short discussion of what my immersion looked like and how it shaped my data and analysis.

*

Like many newcomers to the Mar Vista Recreation Center, I approached the soccer field as a prospective player. As I explain in the following chapter, joining the soccer games proved to be a dynamic and fluid process. My abilities as a soccer player[54] and Spanish speaker[55] facilitated my entry, although it took several months of consistent participation to feel more or less accepted. It was around that time that I introduced myself as a UCLA graduate student interested in studying the games and participants.

The men had varying reactions to my research: some were excited, others indifferent, and a few were initially hostile and suspicious of my intentions. Most, however, seemed to welcome my interest. My presence as a player and researcher seemed to validate their belief that the games and gatherings afterward were special. As the years passed and my relations deepened, my project became more a source of amusement than concern, such as when men playfully urged me to "put *that* in your book" or joked about how long it was taking me to finish. My "book" became a means to shared experience rather than a threat to it. While I never hid the fact that I was conducting research, most soon forgot or made light of it, remarking half-jokingly—along with other people in my life—that it seemed like a weak excuse to play soccer and drink beer all day.

While my research aims were sometimes viewed as odd or suspect by my teammates, they generally accepted my participation in park life. Despite our differences, I could usually blend in on the soccer field or when socializing with them, beer in hand. Part of the appeal of the park was that it facilitated the coming together of diverse individuals, creating the sort of "cosmopolitan canopy" envisioned by sociologist Elijah Anderson.[56] My ability to fit in at the park contrasted with the challenges I faced observing the men at home, at work, and in their neighborhoods—sites that were generally more off-limits to my ethnographic gaze. But even at the park, my identity could set me apart from the men, such as in the differential treatment I received in community meetings or in my dealings with the police.

Fieldwork at the park consisted of long-term participant observation.[57] As Polo understood, I was the primary instrument of data collection. Sometimes this simply meant accepting a beer, but more generally it involved being present and open to sociable interaction. The men came to the park in the hope of socializing with others, and it was only natural for me to reciprocate in the quid pro quo of park life. As in most ethnographic studies, I became a part of the social setting and interactions I was analyzing. While my time in the park varied depending on other responsibilities, I was never away from the park for more than three weeks at a time during my primary phase of fieldwork, which kept me connected and abreast of park developments.

Over the five years of my intensive fieldwork in Los Angeles, the vast majority of my time as a researcher was spent at the park, not only because that was where I could find the men, but also because they tended to keep their time there separate from the rest of their lives. In that sense, my study focuses on this one central aspect of the men's experience—and a heavily gendered one at that. However, my deepening involvement did allow me to push the boundaries of the study beyond the park in order to gain insight into other aspects of the men's lives.

Roughly two years into my fieldwork, I began to shadow fourteen of the men at work. I focused on small-scale home-improvement jobs that I was able to observe and participate in directly. By contrast, restaurant work—another key source of employment at the park—was more difficult for me to access. In most cases, I worked alongside the men, usually performing menial tasks as I asked them questions about their work and life history.[58] The monotony of their work proved conducive for candid conversations. At other times, I simply observed the men, especially when they were interacting with employers or prospective clients. As a White non-Latino, my presence could be startling to homeowners, so I made a point of informing them that I was a graduate student studying the men. At no point did a client ask me to leave, and several spoke to me about their hiring practices, concerns, and motivations. They seemed to be reassured that I was not a real worker, as I did not fit the profile of those they typically hired.

These hands-on experiences helped me contextualize what I was observing at the park. Most importantly, I learned how park ties translated into work opportunities and how similar networking practices played out with other workers and their clients—all of which confirmed that the park was only one piece of a larger web of interactions and relations. The warm welcome the men generally received as workers in people's homes in West Los Angeles provided a stark contrast to the fear and hostility their presence sometimes seemed to provoke at the park.

In addition to observing the men at work, I accompanied them on their daily rounds, including trips to buy materials, to meet clients, or to pay traffic tickets. These "go-alongs" were opportunities to learn how the men navigated the city and to ask them questions free from the distractions and temptations of the park.[59] For once, I welcomed L.A.'s notoriously slow traffic. I was also invited to family gatherings away from the park, including birthdays, baptisms, and house parties. I joined the men on outings to other social settings as well, mainly bars and restaurants, but also to the beach and shopping centers.[60]

Although my study privileges interactions and conversations in their natural settings, I also conducted formal interviews with forty-eight participants. These interviews, which included several repeats, lasted one to three hours and generally took place in more private sections of the park, but sometimes in restaurants or in people's homes. These semi-structured interviews were aimed at gathering biographical information about the men, their views on park life, and their experiences living and working in Los Angeles. While never as rich as my field notes and at times contradicting what I observed firsthand, the interviews were helpful in uncovering meanings and experiences not readily perceptible in the swirl of group interactions.[61] The interviews also signaled the seriousness of my research, which was harder to communicate when playing soccer or socializing in the park.

I almost always tape-recorded the interviews, but I rarely recorded conversations at the park, as I found this practice intrusive and distracting. Instead of blending into the background, the recording device seemed to attract too much notice and commentary. I did, however, take hundreds of photographs that were not only helpful for data analysis and presentations, but that served as something to share and discuss with the men.[62] Rather than connecting photographs to specific passages, I have included a series of pictures showing scenes from the park and beyond, grouped together in a gallery.[63]

Like the interviews, most of the verbal exchanges at the park were in Spanish, which I have usually translated into English when quoting them. However, in cases where the English alone would not have captured the humor or cultural nuances of the exchange, I have included the original Spanish words or phrases, followed by English translation in parentheses.[64] The challenges I faced as a non-native Spanish speaker in accurately transcribing all that was said at the park—especially the more colloquial jokes and expressions of this diverse population of men—explains why my book does not include more quotations from extended dialogue. Especially confusing to me were albures (double entendres) and idiosyncratic cultural references—a creative, ever-changing aspect of park life my book does not fully capture.[65]

With the men's approval, I decided to identify the research subjects by first name—most often using a nickname by which they were known at the park. With appropriate safeguards in place, I felt confident that this decision would not create any harm for the men that did not already exist.[66] At the same time, this compelled me to be more accurate and thoughtful in presenting my findings.[67] I was also motivated by the fact that this was a story the men wanted me to tell, and identifying the park and the men (although never by last name) was one way to honor this sentiment. As much as the guys joked about my study, I believe it gave them pride and a heightened sense of dignity, as other ethnographers have found in their studies.[68]

I have not, however, included the names of local residents, park staff, city officials, or employers who participated in my study.[69] To secure their participation and avoid worsening the already fractious relations in the neighborhood, I promised confidentiality to the twenty-nine people I interviewed from those groups.[70] I also masked their names when citing written materials. In any case, their names were less relevant than those of the men to the story I wanted to tell. On the other hand, identifying the park and neighborhood was crucial for making sense of what I uncovered. At any rate, in the age of the internet, the specifics of the case would have made it difficult to conceal the name of the park without substantially altering key information or removing it altogether. Moreover, anonymizing the site in a way that *might* evade disclosure would strip the book of vital context and insights. Indeed, it is the particularities of the field controversy that make it so illuminating concerning contemporary conflicts over public space in West Los Angeles. Site disclosure also benefits future scholars by enabling "ethnographic revisits" and other forms of comparative research.[71] In fact, for these very reasons, I had already named the park in a previous publication.[72] Although my concluding chapter does raise issues of generalizability, what I recount is very much a story about West Los Angeles.

*

Just as my research interests evolved over time, so did my relations with the men. This was due, in part, to a series of turning points during my fieldwork, including my first fight and first alcohol citation in the park, as well as personal milestones like getting married, turning thirty, and having children. My social standing among the men was also solidified by my commitment to a park-based soccer team that participated in park tournaments and in the Liga Centroamericana de Fútbol, an area soccer league. My willingness to help them by translating forms, offering rides, representing them at community meetings, or simply lending my cell phone also seemed to help my integration into the group. I was as much a resource for the men as they were for me. Although I was subject to some unusual requests, my willingness to help was not unusual, since the men were constantly trading favors. How I became a part of this community was less about me and more about the demands and rewards of park life.

My relations with the men were nevertheless complicated and evolving. I was constantly making decisions about whom or what to observe and to include, and some of these decisions were out of my control. Some men didn't like me, just as some settings were unavailable to me. A different researcher would have generated different interactions and insights. But rather than feeling trapped by my unique position, I embraced its capacity to generate fresh analyses.[73] Well aware of the limitations that came with being an outsider and non-native Spanish speaker, I questioned the taken-for-grantedness of our shared interests and scrutinized the privileges conferred by my race, class, and citizenship. While I will never know what the men really thought about me and my research, I trust my study reflects my engagement with this social world. A more distant and detached approach would no doubt have led to different results. As for the costs and benefits of my intense involvement and editorial decisions, readers will ultimately have to assess those for themselves.

Overview

The following chapters paint a multifaceted portrait of how group life at the Mar Vista Recreation Center was organized and made meaningful in ways that shaped the men's relationships and opportunities. Chapter 1 examines the organization of the midday soccer games at the park. Recounting how newcomers came to appreciate the crucial role of regulars in organizing and sustaining the games, it shows how managing problems on and off the field galvanized group life, just as celebrating a shared past strengthened communal bonds.

Chapter 2 describes action on the soccer field and examines how playing, watching, and commenting on the soccer games gave the men a shared context in which to meet and spend time together. In chapter 3, I look at the park as a place to socialize in a context of limited options and, more specifically, at beer drinking as a catalyst for socializing. By drinking with the men in the park and in other settings, I gained a deeper understanding of why they were willing to put themselves at risk to drink together there. In contrast to more conventional and lawful settings, the park paradoxically emerged as the most respectable, convenient, and affordable place to share a twelve-pack of beer.

Chapter 4 focuses on the fights that periodically broke out at the park and that contrasted with violence in other more anonymous places, such as bars or on street corners. While ties generally developed in nonviolent ways, fights were among a broader context of activities at the park that helped the men develop trusting and committed relationships. The chapter also explores how the men organized and controlled park fights and how they made sense of what had transpired in the retelling of these confrontations.

In chapter 5, I go beyond the park to look at the experiences of fourteen of the men who worked in private homes. For the most part, this involved small-scale, "off the books" construction, painting, and gardening jobs that I could observe firsthand. The chapter shows how informal arrangements and social relations—including those that developed at the park—organized the labor of immigrants in this burgeoning, often precarious sector of the economy. The significance of the park for the men's work proved all the more striking given the hostility they sometimes faced there from local residents who, nevertheless, often depended on immigrant labor.

Addressing the broader implications of my study, the conclusion compares the men's experiences with the ways that other groups socialize and network. This brings into focus similarities, but also the unique challenges the Mar Vista soccer players faced in making a life for themselves in a new place. In drawing these contrasts, I offer my book as a response to those who may view these men and their behavior as deviant and divorced from a broader context of interactions and relations. For as I learned, few of the people who debated whether to fence the soccer field appreciated the potential consequences of restricting access to the men I came to know as los jugadores del parque. Against this backdrop, *Fútbol in the Park* argues for the importance of in-depth, multilayered accounts of the people, practices, and processes we study and outlines policy implications regarding the use of public parks.

1 ＊ Field Insiders, Neighborhood Outsiders

Since the 1970s, men have been playing informal soccer matches at the Mar Vista Recreation Center. Immigrants from Latin America have predominated over the decades of play in the West Los Angeles park.[1] The pickup games (cáscaras), played Monday through Friday around lunchtime, were rooted in this history and included many veterans of previous eras. The games were informal in that no formal organization administered them, nor was the playing space officially reserved. Participants worked together to establish the rules and order of the game on the public field.

For years, the game was played in an open area at the west end of the park. The space was not officially designated for soccer. Instead, the men played in the outfield of two rarely used baseball diamonds that framed the far corners of the recreation center. The men used portable steel-drum garbage cans for goals, and field dimensions varied depending on the number of participants, which ranged from five to nearly twenty players per team. The matches lasted roughly two hours, with men rotating in and out of the continuous play. The games I participated in drew their origins from a version initiated in the early 1990s by a group of mechanics (los mecánicos) on their lunch break from a nearby auto-body shop.

Many old-timers fondly recalled the rowdy competition and rough playing surface of those games. As Barba explained to me, "It used to be una locura [madness]. We would play like fifteen against fifteen. Some guys didn't even have soccer shoes on; they would just jump in and play." Overhearing our conversation, Zapata—whose dark hair from that bygone era had since turned white—reminded Barba of all the fun they had on rainy days when, to dupe their opponents, they deliberately kicked the ball into pools of mud. The men laughed when I asked them if they used jerseys to distinguish the teams, explaining that they didn't need to, as "everyone knew everyone." Keeping time and score were also deemed unnecessary.

In June 2005, the city installed an artificial turf soccer field in this space that radically transformed playing conditions. None of the players were directly involved in the process that brought the regulation-size soccer field to the park, even though their frequent use of the park had created the need for a more sustainable playing surface. The publicly financed project included synthetic grass, field markings, anchored goals, bleachers, and fencing. Although the players were thrilled at these improvements, many worried that they would not be allowed to use the new field once it opened. Some speculated that Windward School, a private high school across the street from the park, was building the complex for their private use. Others assumed it would be restricted to permit-only play, as was the case with the few other artificial turf soccer fields in the city at the time.[2] If anything, they presumed that the field was targeted for neighborhood youths, who had gravitated to soccer over the years. When I pressed David over the men's concerns, he (as usual) mocked my naïveté. Speaking in English, he quipped: "What? You think they built this field for a bunch of wetbacks?"

Despite the men's apprehensions, the new field generally remained open during their usual playing hours. However, the games on the revamped surface required a new playing order precisely because of the field's improved quality and unexpected availability. As Carlos recalled, "Nobody was out here when it was dirt, but now everyone wants to play," adding that "this field was the best and worst thing that could have happened to us." Concerned by an increase in neighborhood scrutiny, Carlos claimed that "before, only Sargento White bothered us," referring to a neighborhood police officer who had regularly broken up the men's drinking parties after their games.

Almost everyone agreed that circumstances had changed with the advent of the new field and that it marked a clear turning point in the park's history. A flow of newcomers followed, many of whom were unaware of or unsympathetic to the regulars' historical claims to the field. These newcomers threatened the order and stability of the soccer games. Not only did they take away valuable playing time from regulars, but they also raised more symbolic concerns over their apparent lack of deference and respect for the old ways of organizing the games. Moreover, the greater presence and visibility of soccer play and players in the park were perceived as deviant and unwelcome by some local residents, sparking protests and attempts to curtail access to and use of the field.

These issues of control were apparent to me during my first visit to the social world of midday pickup soccer at Mar Vista. Like most new recruits, I had heard about the games from other players. I had come to the park for the first time the day before, in January 2008, roughly two and a half years after the new field opened. In the following field note, I describe my initial contact with the pickup game:

I arrived at 11:15 a.m. and observed fifteen guys casually warming up on the field. Most were taking shots on goal, while a few pairs jogged and stretched in unison. Over the next fifteen minutes, about twenty-five more men arrived. Some of them joined the players on the field, while others socialized on the bleachers and along the sidelines. Not everyone looked dressed to play. Most of the men appeared to be working-class Latino, and Spanish was the primary spoken language, which contrasted with the upscale and predominately White neighborhood that surrounded the park.

At around 11:30, someone yelled out: "Ya viene [here comes] Polo." Pregame activities ceased as attention shifted to the man's arrival. Polo was carrying a large bag of jerseys over his shoulder and walked steadily along the sidelines, ignoring pleas for uniforms and playful heckling over his tardiness. Prospective players met him by the midfield bleachers, and I could sense a growing excitement in the men's appeals and movements. Most of the men also seemed to know each other as they slapped hands and traded jokes. By contrast, I felt largely ignored by the group despite my soccer attire.

After shaking hands and speaking to a few of the players, Polo sat down on the top row of the bleachers, opened his bag, and distributed red and green jerseys for two teams. The jerseys were the sleeveless mesh variety used in training sessions, which I grew up referring to as "pinnies," but heard many of the men refer to as "playeras." On the front, I glimpsed a small design with flags from Latin America encircling "Mar Vista Internacional Fútbol Club" and "U.S.A." in block letters. A few men extended their hands and pleaded their case for a uniform, but most maintained eye contact and confidently waited their turn. A couple of rebuffed participants expressed mild anger and frustration but to little consequence. One snubbed young Latino muttered in English: "Fucking Polo, always on his bullshit." An older Latino man responded in Spanish: "Ahora estás aprendiendo, mijo." (Now you're learning, my son.)

More guys showed up during this process; some were given jerseys, despite those who had arrived earlier. One late arrival even demanded "mi playera" from Polo, which he received along with lighthearted insults about his Barcelona soccer team apparel and apparent weight gain. As the teams were taking shape, someone challenged their composition, implying they were imbalanced. Polo glared in his direction, yelling, "Cállate, hombre" (shut up, man), then urging him to "go play with los güeros [the White guys] if you don't like it." Polo pressed on, reminding his now-silent critic that he didn't want any more problems on "la cancha" (the field). His firm tone suggested that this was not the first time the two men had clashed. He then shifted his attention to the broader audience: "¡Escuchen! [Listen!] Here you need to respect the rules, and a la verga [fuck] those that don't want to, no te queremos para nada [we don't want you at all]." Apparently satisfied at the silence, Polo distributed the remaining jerseys for the first game, leaving more than a dozen men empty-handed, myself included.

*

At this public facility, neither fees nor membership restrictions limited the number or type of users. Players did not arrive as members of preexisting teams that had signed up for the right to use the field, and demands for inclusion by potential players exceeded the number that teams could accommodate. As entry was open to all and no system formally controlled use of the space, the result might have been chaos and debilitating conflict. People could play soccer one day, but have no expectation of playing the next day or following week. But that is *not* what happened. For despite complaints by neighbors and the sometimes topsy-turvy organization of the games, soccer playing at Mar Vista continued on a sustained basis, day after day, following patterns and hierarchies that I came to recognize with the passing of time. As I gradually learned, the organization of play—characterized by unequal access to the field among would-be players and shaped by the organizers' sense that they were "outsiders" in this neighborhood—was neither monopolistic nor egalitarian, but a negotiated product based on local conditions.[3]

While urban sociologists like Elijah Anderson and Lyn Lofland have shown how public space can be effectively privatized, this case reveals how much more elaborate and contentious this process can be.[4] Indeed, how the men secured presumptive rights to use of this space was not initially obvious to me, nor a natural or inevitable outcome. As Carlos suggested in the remark quoted above, the open condition of the coveted facility maximized the problems and possibilities of control. What these men created and sustained on the field reflected the exigencies of the setting and situation, as well as their shared interests and histories of play. Fun was important, but fun arose from a supportive structure.

"Soccer Heaven"

Referred to by many participants as "soccer heaven," the Mar Vista field was heavily used, highly desired, and difficult to reserve during my fieldwork. Public access to the field from 2008 through 2013 was unusual in a region where such options were rare.[5] Mike, a longtime African American participant, captured the excitement that followed its opening: "Dude, it was a brand-new turf field, there's no other turf field that's open in all of L.A., and we have it—it's our field. Come on! Soccer heaven! From playing on dirt to playing on turf, that's like playing in the Rose Bowl." Like Mike, most agreed that the new field attracted a greater number of players, spectators, and attention than had the old dirt field.

Paralleling previous iterations, the weekday games were played from around 11:30 to 1:30 in the early afternoon. But rather than one long un-interrupted match, each game lasted fifteen to twenty minutes, depending on the intensity of the contest and mood of the referee. As in the past, the men did not formally reserve the field, since it was generally available for open play at this time of day. Schools, clubs, and leagues often rented the facility for use later in the afternoon or on weekends by purchasing a field permit from the park office. Permits started at thirty dollars per hour but increased substantially in cost and paperwork for adult and for-profit organizations. The fact that few organizations seemed interested in using the field at midday helped account for its relative openness.

Although attendance varied with the weather and time of year, out of an evolving population of approximately 150 members, there were typi-cally thirty to sixty participants—players and spectators—on any given weekday. Late arrivals sometimes delayed kickoff past 11:30, but there were almost always enough players to field a full-sided eleven versus eleven match. The expectation of encountering sufficient players drew men to the field, many of whom rearranged their schedules and drove through L.A. traffic in the hope of playing or watching the games. For example, Puma worked out an arrangement with his employers at a Japa-nese restaurant in Beverly Hills to come in at 2:00 p.m.—a few hours later than his coworkers—so that he could play in the midday games. If anything, participation was discouraged by an excess of players and the long waits that ensued. But for those willing to wait, the quick succession of six or seven contests per day ensured that everyone eventually had a chance to play.

My decade of fieldwork has yielded valuable insight into the fluid and shifting status of regulars and newcomers at the park. Much of my analysis is framed by my own bumpy progression from a bemused and marginal newcomer to an informed and established regular. As I came to appreci-ate, the continual addition of new participants and the unpredictability that resulted were part of the game's charm. The changing composition of the games was most evident to me during my annual short-term follow-up visits in 2014 through 2019, during which I saw men who were strangers to me occupying a prominent place in field activity, while noticing that some past players no longer participated. I also found that I had to re-establish myself as a player with teammates, opponents, and gatekeepers who did not know me.

The majority of players and spectators attributed their initial arrival to prior connections or word of mouth. Many newcomers showed up with someone else, usually a participant with some degree of history at the park. For example, the next generation of players who originally came to the park as children with older family members brought their friends as young adults. Emblematic of this trend were Chepe, Ivan, Luis, and Tulio, who accompanied their fathers as young boys and returned years later with their soccer-playing buddies.

Some men arrived alone after having been told about the field and games by someone in their social circle. Often these men were recent immigrants with limited knowledge of the city's soccer landscape. For example, Walter shared with me that his father-in-law urged him to go play soccer in the park when he sensed his restlessness in the home they shared. Similarly, Chaparro told me that a coworker told him about the cáscaras when he overheard him yearning for a place to play. I, too, had been informed by men who sensed that I would appreciate participating in a regular and quality game, especially when I explained that I was new to the area. In any case, the quality field and games were well publicized and hard to keep secret. Lone arrivals admitted that it took them a while to muster up the courage to approach the vibrant scene on their own, often watching from a distance during their initial visits. By contrast, coming with a regular was considered an easier entry into the games.

A sizable minority of participants came to the field after catching sight of the games in passing, usually from a car window on the busy streets that lined the park. Gabe's account was typical of this group: "I would drive by around this time for work and would always see the guys playing. I wasn't sure if it was a league or something but decided to just show up on my day off to see." Some men initially came to the park for other reasons, such as for a birthday party, only to return in the hope of playing there. As César explained to me, "I knew there was a field here, so I came back one day and was happy to see all these people playing." He then laughed and repeated a common refrain about this unusual playing time: "I was only surprised to see so many people playing—and not working—in the middle of the day."

Most men were thrilled to encounter the open play, even if they later lamented how much time they spent at the park or criticized subsequent arrivals for disturbing "their" game. As Beavis explained to me, "I was really happy because I didn't know where to play soccer and I missed playing." And when I asked him what he would otherwise be doing, he replied: "If not working, at home, bien aburrido [really bored]." Chaparro echoed this sentiment: "What am I going to do in my house all alone? Estar encerrado ahí, nada más [I'd just be cooped up there]."

As with Beavis and Chaparro, many men explained to me that before finding the Mar Vista field, they were unaware of a similar playing space and organized games elsewhere. Fields closer to their homes were either closed, of poor quality, or unsafe. In any case, the pickup games they knew of didn't compare in terms of organization, enthusiasm, and consistency, especially at that time of day. Jay, who lived a good distance away in Hollywood, explained this difference in English: "There's a field over there, but I don't know anybody, and there's not a game like this—organized, jerseys, and stuff. And the field is crap." Overhearing our conversation, his companion added: "I don't think there's another place in all of Los Angeles like this."

Many participants also appreciated the flexibility of the scene, especially in contrast to the commitment required for league play. Moreover, in contrast to requirements in certain other settings, use of the field did not require showing an ID card or proof of residence, which some men were unable or reluctant to do. And when men moved too far away to commute and came back to Mar Vista for a visit, they often bemoaned the lack of a similar setup near their new home. David, an elder statesman of the park, summed up the attraction this way: "We love the field because we can't afford it." Zapata, a fellow old-timer, chimed in, saying, "You can't play soccer by yourself."

Organizing the Games

Throughout the history of pickup soccer at Mar Vista, a handful of men have managed the matches. Polo was the primary organizer during my time in the park. Less than a year before I arrived, Polo had replaced Gary, who was the first to organize games on the new field. Gary, an ex-professional soccer player and coach from Honduras, was a recent transplant to Los Angeles, having been displaced from New Orleans by Hurricane Katrina. Gary recalled finding "absolute chaos" on the new field: "There were too many players, and nobody wanted to wait." Many others confirmed the "desmadre" (mess) that accompanied the opening of the new field. In the hope of bringing some order to the games, Gary brought jerseys and instituted a sign-in policy.

While initially praised for his efforts, Gary soon wore out his welcome, primarily because he didn't favor park veterans—preferring a strict first-come, first-to-play policy. He was also accused of embezzling money he collected to wash the jerseys. More generally, old-timers saw "El Negro Catracho" (the Black Honduran), as he was sometimes called, as an outsider who didn't respect the history of the games and was only in it for himself.

In a fit of rage one afternoon, Polo declared that the worst thing he ever saw at the park was when "we let that hijo de la gran mierda [piece of shit] take over the games."

Polo, by contrast, was viewed by regulars as one of them. Since he had played at the park for over a decade, they felt he would be more likely to honor their privileged status vis-à-vis all the newcomers flocking to the field. Moreover, he was willing and able to be at the park Monday through Friday at midday, a serious commitment few men could match. As one player explained: "He's the leader because he's always here." Polo echoed this explanation for his rise to power: "I think it's because estoy acá diario [I'm here every day]," reminding me that he was single and childless and worked nights. Although many criticized Polo's authoritarian style, participants appreciated his willingness to undertake what most recognized as a difficult yet crucial undertaking. As David put it to me in English, "Someone's got to do it," and the limited resources encouraged the men to give up some control to a more centralized authority. It was clear to everyone that the decentralized and more relaxed way of running the "dirt" games was no longer feasible on the new field, which became painfully evident in the bedlam that ensued whenever Polo failed to show up with the jerseys. By supporting Polo, they supported themselves.

While the forthcoming analysis focuses primarily on Polo's reign, he, too, eventually lost or relinquished control, depending on whom you ask. In 2015 another major shake-up occurred on the field. In the face of mounting criticism, Polo staged a mini-protest by arriving later and later to the games, sometimes not showing up at all. However, his attempt at garnering gratitude backfired. With the support of disgruntled players, Maradona and Don Luis staged the latest coup d'état at the park and took over the games. Like Polo, the two retirees brought their own jerseys and set up shop on the bleachers directly across the field from their predecessor's customary outpost. At this writing in 2020, the pair remain in charge. As for Polo, while still a mainstay of park life, he spends less and less time on the soccer field, joking that his "diputados" (deputies) were filling in for him. Joshing aside, Polo shared with me in private that he was pleased someone "del parque" (from the park) was organizing the game, rather than an outsider like Gary or—even worse—a formal organization.

*

The rest of chapter 1 traces how longtime participants in the games worked out the challenges brought about by the installation of the turf soccer field. Without this daily coordination sustained over years, the men could not have accomplished what they did together at the park. In chapter 2,

I explore how soccer play was made meaningful and compelling by the men, before turning in later chapters to other prominent park activities that also helped bring the men together in rich and memorable ways. But rather than take for granted the stage during which the men were able to build relationships and a sense of self through their soccer play—a tendency found in other studies of this kind—I examine in detail the complex inter-actions and continual give-and-take that made this collective achievement possible.[6] For, as my study shows, having fun in public, and sustaining that experience, was a significant accomplishment, but not a process the men fully controlled.

"I Felt Like an Outsider Right Away"

The sorting out of participants into regulars and newcomers, insiders and outsiders, was neither self-evident nor automatic. Attracted by the first-rate facility and soccer activity, newcomers came to appreciate and take for granted the presence of regulars and their crucial role in organizing and sustaining the games. However, in order to enter the games, newcomers faced competition from the daily flood of players and spectators. The fact that most of the participants appeared to be Latino presented an additional obstacle for non-Latino, non-Spanish speakers. In addition to an average of forty soccer players, there were generally a dozen or so spectators in street clothes scattered around the field, most congregating on the bleachers. In distinguishing between spectators and players, the use of jerseys served as a key sorting mechanism (to be discussed later in greater detail).

While externally visible features—such as soccer gear and jerseys—may have deterred prospective players, as well as those interested in using the soccer field for other purposes, having it "in use" began the work of estab-lishing authority over the public field for that time slot. Before the games commenced, waiting players signaled the start of routine activity, just as the density of players and spectators during the games seemed to justify their recurring presence. In fact, some newcomers like Gabe ascribed their initial hesitancy to join the group to what they perceived as the formal organization of the games. As mentioned earlier, Gabe wasn't sure if the games he noticed on his way to work had been organized by a league.

As in my case, newcomers who were not recruited by regular participants needed to make the first move if they wished to participate. In contrast to other pickup scenes, these games did not require extras or stand-ins to make numbers.[7] In fact, when newcomers asked a player about joining a game, regulars invariably pointed to Polo (or whoever was in charge at the time), providing little helpful information or friendly introductions. Araña's explanation for why newcomers were generally given the cold shoulder reflected the prevailing attitude among the regulars: "We've got too many players here, and they might be loco [crazy] like Tico," referring to a notoriously headstrong participant who had arrived with the new field—a player, he joked, "we can't get rid of now."

With such limited opportunities to participate in the games, newcomers approached the group from a position of marginality and vulnerability. Indeed, many felt confused and uncertain how to proceed. As one player, a self-described gringo like Gabe, recounted: "I didn't know what to do when I first got here, so I just kind of stood there like an idiot." This was in stark contrast to the extended ritual of handshakes, accompanied by playful nicknames and insults, with which regular participants greeted each other in this atmosphere of "competitive sociability."[8]

The following field note illustrates the significance of greeting distinctions in constructing insider and outsider status:

> A recent newcomer to the games steps onto the bleachers to no outward acknowledgment from the half-dozen regulars already seated. But in fact, the young Latino's arrival is accompanied by an awkward silence in the conversations. Several minutes later, the group enthusiastically welcomes Caballo, a longtime participant from Honduras. Trading barbs and shaking hands with the other regulars, he appears to deliberately ignore the newcomer. After someone asks Caballo where he had been for the previous month, Abel jokes that he had been in hiding ever since Honduras lost a crucial World Cup qualifying match. Caballo laughs and blames the referee, but explains that he had been busy driving his son around Southern California with his new soccer team, which prompts a lengthy conversation about the teenager's progress and the state of youth soccer in the country.

I again experienced both sides of this greeting ritual when I returned to the park in May 2017 after a year away:

> When I neared the bleachers, I was startled not to recognize any of the five men seated. They looked at me with indifference as I approached. I nodded and smiled. Only one man returned the gesture. I then asked in Spanish if they were playing that day. The same man responded in English: "Maybe." To my relief, a familiar face soon arrived. Valderrama's eyes lit up when he saw me. I stood up and he gave me a big hug, lifting me off the ground. He then turned to the intrigued others: "Do you all know David? He's one of the más chingones de aquí [best from here]," his use of slang matching the Mexican national team jersey he was wearing. The men smiled, looking back in my direction with some surprise. One of the older guys joked in Spanish: "Órale [All right], Valderrama, we'll see how tu güero [your

White guy] plays." He then explained that Don Luis should be arriving soon with the jerseys, which precipitated a series of jokes about Polo's demise.

It was through these ritual exchanges that newcomers came to further recognize the presence of regulars and history at this particular field—to realize that this was not an unorganized collection of individuals who just happened to be playing soccer together. These differences in greeting provided the first signals of a broader, segmented environment characterized by familiarity among regulars and coolness toward newcomers. As one newcomer, a twenty-four-year-old Mexican American, recalled, "I felt like an outsider right away; people barely said hello." A White male, also in his mid-twenties, echoed this initial impression: "It was a little tough. I think these guys like familiarity, so I felt a little ignored. I definitely didn't get a jersey like I do now."

The prevalence of inside jokes and local sayings reinforced the feelings of difference and strangeness among newcomers. For example, a White newcomer asked me why the guys yelled "jugador de [player from] Santa Monica" whenever he fumbled a play on the field, especially as he did not live in the neighboring city. Although his biography was unknown, this was an oblique reference to his skin color and the perceived Whiteness of Santa Monica. In another case, a Cameroonian newcomer expressed confusion when someone urged him to "buy Polo's video" after he failed to score an easy goal. Having only played a few times at the park, he was unaware of the local intrigue surrounding alleged videotapes documenting Polo's younger soccer-playing days and unable to understand humorous references to his imaginary career in pornography.

For many newcomers, feelings of estrangement were compounded by the dominance of Spanish at the field, a language some were unable (or unwilling) to speak or understand. While often a vehicle for humor and friendly interaction, "linguistic collusion" could also represent a source of difference and suspicion for all those involved.[9] Polo and others even chastised those who didn't speak Spanish when they failed to understand their directives, reversing the usual balance of power in the city. Indeed, access to Spanish was another way that use of the field was sorted out, although Spanish-speaking newcomers faced similar barriers of coldness and indifference. In fact, since most newcomers generally resembled the regulars, newcomer status typically overshadowed perceived commonalities, such as Latino, Spanish speaking, immigrant, or working class.

Occasional commemorations and announcements on the field expressed a recognizable group history to newcomers as well. On multiple occasions, Polo and others assembled the men before the games to announce the death of a past participant or someone related to a current player, sometimes collecting money for funeral costs. Men also requested assistance for players in distress, such as money to cover hospital bills, lawyer fees, or job loss. To deliver the news, spokespersons would gather the men around the bleachers or in the middle of the field as they delivered the news, sometimes bringing a collection box with a photo of the person that was placed on the bleachers for the duration of the games. On one occasion, the men held a brief moment of silence to mark the passing of a player's girlfriend.

There were also more festive examples of these public proclamations when coaches and players of park-based teams brought trophies to the field to publicize their championship victories. In a similar vein, Polo always convened a pregame meeting to unveil new jerseys purchased with funds raised by the participants. Polo was particularly pleased with one set he designed that included the downtown Los Angeles skyline on top of a soccer ball with the year 1965 printed underneath to commemorate the year when Hugo—the longest-surviving player—reportedly came to the park from his native Chile. Newcomers often appeared uncertain of what to do in these moments, but felt pressured to gather with the men as the news was shared. By witnessing these events and learning this history, they also learned that something enduring was happening in that space.

The constant circulation of park memories along the sidelines similarly communicated to newcomers that the games had a long history and one that predated the new field. Participation in storytelling revealed who was part of that history and served as an additional proof of belonging and claim to respect. For example, when a new player questioned why someone received a jersey before him, Mike joked: "He played when it was nothing but dirt, he's earned it," adding: "You only came when it was nice!" Indeed, old-timers like Carlos liked to point out that "nobody was out here when it was dirt" to distinguish themselves from those who arrived after installation of the new field.

As sociologist Randall Collins has argued, the more invisible or informal social gatherings are, "the more effort needs to be put into making them emotionally intense, if they are to be experienced as having much effect upon feelings of social position."[10] At the field, this challenge was recurrent and serious in that us/them distinctions were not necessarily self-evident or acceptable and the group had no formal, externally supported identity or claims to the open facility. Moreover, a collective history could not be taken for granted or assumed, as impromptu and short-lived sporting contests are common in city parks. In contrast to league play, it was the perceived informality and flexibility of this pickup game that propelled newcomers to approach the field in the hope of playing soccer with strangers.

In the face of competing interests and uncertain authority, maintaining distinct boundaries between insiders and outsiders was therefore both essential and less formally manageable. The daily negotiation of social distinctions conveyed to newcomers the presence of a collective unit and presumptive rights of control over the midday soccer games in this public park.

"Man, These Guys Take This Seriously"

A second way that regulars attempted to control use of the public field was through unequal player preferences. Stratified power relations on the field were most directly expressed to newcomers by the preferential playing queue established through the public distribution of jerseys.[11] An additional and often unexpected barrier confronted by newcomers, this process signaled a local system of organization, that served as both a material and symbolic resource to create and sustain the status structure. Since there were usually well over ten players hoping to be included on each team, decisions and debates about the playing queue were frequent and became key "staging areas" to impose social order and hierarchies on the field.[12] Indeed, the right to use the public field took its most pressing form as potential players stood around waiting to play.

At this field, participation was contingent upon receiving a jersey—a material object—and inquiring newcomers were told that they needed to "get a jersey" to play. The instruction was clear, providing regulars with a ready response to newcomers and a way to identify themselves as sanctioned participants. But for the newcomer, just how to get a jersey was far from self-evident. Unlike formal leagues or meetup groups, there was no office or website to standardize registration and scheduling. And the regulars' unhelpful replies simply reinforced newcomers' confusion about access to the field, a distinction materially represented by those with and without jerseys.

Because newcomers were deliberately ignored when they arrived, it required active work on their part to decipher the system and to make themselves known as potential players—an especially intimidating challenge for non-Spanish speakers. Moreover, the jerseys, whether worn or hanging from the fence or bleachers, served to establish claims on the public facility before the games even began on a given day. Operating as a "language of space"[13] like a draped coat on a "reserved" library seat, the jerseys served to indicate expectations to newcomers, who understood that they must either fit in or mount a battle to get access to a team through the jerseys.[14] As one newcomer explained to me in English, "I knew I couldn't go on the field without a jersey, but it wasn't really clear how to get one." And on the rare occasion that someone tried to join the games without a jersey, they were quickly identified and told without equivocation "you need una playera to play." Invariably, Polo or the referee stopped the game until the rule-breaker exited the field, and any resistance was usually overcome by the collective pressure of players anxious to resume play.

While only so many people could play at a time, the partiality of the playing queue also signaled a power differential and in-group dynamic.[15] The games did not operate on a strictly first-come, first-served basis; regulars were often given preference over newcomers, which is precisely why Gary was toppled and replaced by Polo. While most players eventually got to play, deliberate rituals of selection helped to confirm the power and autonomy of regulars, as well as the subordination and dependence of newcomers. As shown in the opening vignette, the jerseys were dispensed or withheld to distinguish—both materially and symbolically—between insiders and outsiders. In fact, regulars often reprimanded newcomers for taking or passing out jerseys without consent, as seen in the following field note:

> A newcomer attempts to gain entry into the games by seizing a lone jersey hanging from the fence. Polo confronts the young Latino male and asks: "Where did you get that jersey?" When he replies that he took it from the fence, Polo assertively responds, "You can't just take a jersey!" With a confused look, the newcomer replies, "I thought I could take it," to which another regular retorts in English, "No, you can't just take a jersey here. You have to respect our rules if you want to play here." Polo, in a mix of English and Spanish, demands: "Give me the jersey, güey [dude]." The baffled youngster returned the jersey to Polo, who then promptly tossed it to the much older Gato—a longtime participant who, by appearances and reputation, was a downgrade from the fit youngster. I later talked to the young man about the incident, and he seemed surprised by it all: "I don't know what happened. I saw the jersey and took it. I don't know why he got all in my face like that. I just wanted to play."

Jerseys were also tactically withheld to sanction "disobedience" and to reinforce social hierarchies. For example, after a newcomer got into an altercation on the field, he was blatantly passed over in a following game. However, inequitable distribution of jerseys sometimes occurred for less apparent reasons, such as when newcomers failed to defer to regulars on and off the field. For example, when I asked Roberto to explain why Eli, a skillful White participant, appeared to wait longer than others for a jersey, he replied: "He thinks he's all that, like he's better than us. He should have to wait." Eli explained the slight somewhat differently: "I usually don't get a jersey for the first game because Polo doesn't like me." Thus, players measured their status according to when and how they received a jersey.

For the most part, the games adhered to a structured system of play following standard soccer rules: regulation-size teams (despite the occasional "extra"), use of yellow and red cards, and timed matches. However, there were also a series of field-specific modifications that included no offside, irregular throw-ins, punted goal kicks, and a transition period during which the winning team remained on the field or both teams exited if the game ended in a tie. Like the awarding or denying of jerseys, these field-specific practices had been unnecessary on the dirt field, but made for a more ordered and satisfying game on the popular turf field. For example, running the games without the tricky offside call avoided arguments and delays. Similarly, permitting nonstandard play and idiosyncratic timekeeping increased action on the field, just as the rotation system raised the stakes while providing more opportunities to participate. A referee appointed by Polo enforced these rules, rather than entrusting the players to self-regulate, as in the past.[16] Refereeing also provided an additional role and source of status for typically older men who no longer played, like Chino, whose goals and passing were legendary, but who hadn't played competitively in years. That said, each referee had his own style of arbitrating—some allowing more physical play, others being greater sticklers for the rules. This, along with the "winner stays" model, fed into the excitement and drama of the park games.

Not only did these particular rules and routines reflect considerable local organization, but they also became additional practices to defend when challenged by newcomers. For example, frequent complaints about biased decisions or lack of the offside rule were countered with such comments as "that's how *we* do it here" and "if you don't like it, *you* don't have to play here." As the following field note makes clear, even the smallest suggestion could provoke hostility, signaling that these practices were to be taken "seriously":

> The team's goalie, a newcomer I didn't recognize, started yelling before kickoff that he wanted to change the game ball. He felt that it was lopsided. The referee overheard the request and yelled back at the White guy in Spanish and English: "¿Qué pedo? [What's the problem?] What do you want?" Before the goalie had finished explaining himself, the referee responded, "Who are you? Keep your mouth shut! If you don't like it, then get out of here!" The newcomer reacted with perplexed silence, until mumbling aloud: "Man, these guys take this seriously."

Novice new arrivals faced ridicule and criticism for their field mishaps, and even skilled newcomers sometimes received a period of unfriendly scrutiny. For example, when a newcomer, a White male wearing an Italian soccer jersey, missed a wide-open goal, several spectators screamed, "Go back to Italy!" In contrast, despite scoring a spectacular goal, a talented new player from Morocco—already dubbed Pita Bread—was chastised by a teammate for "not passing the ball." Non-Spanish speakers often didn't understand the more colloquial meanings of the insults that inevitably followed shoddy play at the park, such as "basura" (garbage), "maleta" (lousy), "torta" (oaf), "culero" (asshole), and—most notably—"jugador del parque" (park player), which only furthered feelings of marginality. Usually the name-calling was good-natured, but sometimes Polo interrupted a live game to castigate a player for "offensive" behavior, showing the considerable power he wielded, as we see in the following excerpt from my field notes:

> Ricky Martin, as the men jokingly called him for his good looks and flamboyant style, had recently started playing in the games. In his early twenties, the Mexican national had already made a few enemies for his overly aggressive play. Polo warned him to "take it easy" before the games commenced that day, but the young hotshot refused to tame his style for anyone. In the first game, he mocked an old-timer after he dribbled the ball through his legs. Although Polo seemed unimpressed, spectators whistled in approval of the skillful move—a "cuca" (tunnel) in local lingo. A few minutes later, when Ricky pulled on an opponent's jersey as they battled for the ball, Polo stormed over to Roberto, the acting referee, and ordered him to stop the game. Roberto obliged, and Polo confronted the offending player and demanded the jersey: "Give it to me. I told you, I don't want your pendejadas [bullshit]; it's always the same with you. And now you want to rip the jerseys. ¡Jamás en tu vida! [Never in your life!]" Ricky laughed and searched for support from his teammates, but none was forthcoming. Instead, someone yelled out in English from the bleachers: "Watch out, bro, you can get knocked out for that shit." Another spectator added: "¡Afuera, puto!" (Get out, bitch!) With a cold smirk that suggested "me vale madre" (I don't give a fuck), he took off the jersey and tossed it to Polo.

Outbursts of this kind directed at newcomers for seemingly minor "violations" served to reinforce control over the field by the regulars. By aggressively disciplining seemingly innocuous and trivial actions, insiders signaled to outsiders that they had entered territory where participation was contingent upon appropriate conduct, even submission. Like the preferential playing queue, such displays of punitive or mocking behavior breached newcomers' expectations of "normal" interaction among strangers.[17] For example, men joked that they could never get away with personal insults like those shouted at the park in dealing with a stranger at a grocery store or on the bus. And while race and place of origin shaped the reception that outsiders were given, almost all newcomers, regardless of background, confronted barriers that hindered entry and rapport. Following Erving Goffman's famous dictum, it was more about the moment than the men.[18]

Most newcomers expressed a mixture of confusion, surprise, and discomfort during such interactions with regulars. Some even found the abuse entertaining or "part of the show," as one participant put it. However, as when men break norms when interacting with unfamiliar women in public, there was the sense that newcomers "gotta deal with it" if they wished to participate.[19] In fact, many newcomers understood and experienced these interactions as a rite of passage. For example, after being repeatedly passed over in the playing queue, a White male in his late twenties named Dan explained to me, "I get it, you've got to put your time in." Colombia also appreciated the strong opposition he initially faced: "They were challenging me, definitely, but it's because I play physical and they wanted to test me as the new guy." Whatever their interpretation, most newcomers were excited to encounter the free games and hence willing to put up with this price of admission.

Urban ethnography is replete with similar examples of individuals and groups claiming public space as their own, often at the expense of others. For example, in her foundational study of "home territory" in public settings, Sherri Cavan writes of how members of the "Hangout" defended "their" bar by greeting newcomers with a "parody of deference" that violated the norms and expectations of "polite society," thereby making their visit startling and unpleasant.[20] In Elijah Anderson's study, regular patrons of Jelly's bar and liquor store received strangers with a mixture of silence and suspicion.[21] In other cases, more physical and violent forms of "turf defense" are employed.[22]

At the park, newcomers' expectations of an informal, impartial, and relaxed pickup game were disrupted by an organized and inequitable system and by firm demands for compliance and deference to a preexisting social order. In other contexts, banning newcomers could have provided a way to monopolize use of the facility, whereas a system treating all participants as equal (i.e., first come, first served) would have erased any ambiguity in the playing order. However, given the public nature of this scarce resource and the regulars' desire to maintain their privileged access to the field, a more negotiated order was required. Regulars achieved that objective by presenting their practices as fixed and intrinsic to this particular field—a reified reality that newcomers confronted and accepted, along with the jerseys, as the ticket for entry. Consequently, points of conflict generally centered on more manageable, less threatening debates over the makeup of the teams and organization of the games, rather than over exclusive rights to use the public field.

"Now They'll See That We Do More than Just Drink Beer and Play Soccer Here"

In addition to managing the steady arrival of newcomers, regulars also had to confront local opposition and bureaucratic threats to their use of the field. As detailed in the conclusion, some area residents mobilized to restrict access to the new field. The facility was also occasionally reserved by permit for local schools and youth teams, thereby temporarily displacing the informal pickup game. This broader context became an additional challenge for the regulars. In response to concerns over how they fit into the neighborhood, game leaders attempted to ingratiate themselves with park officials, community organizations, and local residents by presenting themselves as respectable patrons of the field and by monitoring and policing objectionable behavior. In short, they imposed a strong moral order on the players in the hope of avoiding conflict with the community.

On several occasions, select members of the group chose to interact with neighbors and local officials. For example, a half-dozen regulars attended several of the many community meetings concerning the field held in the park gym. As the only Latino men in the audience, they clearly represented the players, although White allies, some of whom also played in the games, usually spoke for them. Occasionally, Latino regulars did speak at public forums, which were conducted almost exclusively in English. For example, at a smaller park meeting, Roberto—a respected veteran of the pickup games and (unlike Polo) proficient in English—publicly voiced his frustration with the increase in permit play: "I've been coming to this park for over twenty years, and it's great that we have such a great field, but it's hard when it's taken away from us. We're just asking for some leniency. We've been playing here a long time."

As with Roberto's appeal to history to make his case, regulars frequently attempted to present themselves as legitimate users of the field when interacting with third parties, although usually in more informal settings.[23] For example, in the hope of bolstering their claims to use of the field—"getting on the books," so to speak—Polo presented the park director with a copy of game rules written in English and Spanish that he had recently distributed on the field. These included such regulations as "Be a good sport and a good neighbor!" and "Please do not litter the park or its surrounding neighborhoods!" The branding of the games as "Mar Vista Park pick-up soccer" ("Fútbol Recreativo" in the Spanish version) on the document—and "Mar Vista Internacional Fútbol Club" on the jerseys—

also spoke to the men's attempts to institutionalize the soccer matches in the eyes of park staff. Along with other paraphernalia associated with the games—banners, photographs, trophies, rules—these soccer jerseys were created and distributed with multiple audiences and multiple aims in mind.

At a subsequent Park Advisory Board meeting, several regulars informed the director of their voluntary purchase of nets for the goals and proposed a formal cleanup of the field to the board members, for which they received a grateful and appreciative response. To make sure the board knew of their efforts, they gave the park office photographs I had taken of the cleanup. In addition, members of the park-based Mar Vista Fútbol Club hand-delivered our championship trophy to park staff, which they displayed for years in the office. Barba's explanation for these multiple efforts was telling: "Now they'll see that we do more than just drink beer and play soccer here." Without an official clubhouse or local bar at their disposal, the park office served in this way as a public place to store their growing collection of trophies.

Players' interactions with third parties were not limited to administrative settings. In a particularly notable example, after the nearby home of a notorious field critic was vandalized, Polo assembled a group of regulars to approach the residence and offer to repaint the defaced walls. Although the offer was declined, Polo felt that "it was good that we did so she knows it wasn't us."

Regulars also interacted with third parties when monitoring and policing park behavior. For example, when a player hurriedly pulled out of the parking lot, causing his car tires to screech, Polo confronted him the following day and publicly asserted: "You can't drive off like that. The neighbors see that and they are going to complain about us." He then proceeded to inform the young man and his friends about area residents who wanted to "echarnos" (kick us out). Polo and others made it a point to let newcomers know about the delicate situation, which wasn't necessarily evident when they played on the open field in the middle of the day, especially since local residents did not bring their grievances directly to the players. For example, to galvanize interest in an upcoming community meeting about the field, Polo stressed that "some of you may not know, but there's people around here who don't want us here."

In addition to warning of possible intervention by hostile neighbors, Polo and others also invoked the threat to the group's continued use of the field posed by police or park officials. For example, when Tico tried to defend his participation in a fight, Polo unsympathetically retorted, "I don't care what happened. We can't have them [pointing to the park office] or the police messing with us. You want to keep playing here, right?" Similarly, the men reprimanded others for littering, openly drinking beer or smoking marijuana, excessive noise, or harassing park visitors—especially women—in and around the field.

On a large banner temporarily affixed to the bleachers, Polo publicly acknowledged perceived neighborhood concerns, as he had done earlier in the printed list of game rules. The banner read, in both Spanish and English: "Help us show a friendly appearance" and "Don't cause problems by offending people and try not to bother the neighbors with a lot of noise and scandal." In addition, players almost always made room for park users walking or jogging around the field; and, on the rare occasion that a non-participant lingered to watch the games, they typically quieted down and concealed any activity they feared might be seen as inappropriate. Daily cleanups and material investments, such as purchasing nets and jerseys, further demonstrated the dedication of the regulars to the field and their concern for appearances. Indeed, since their midday use of the field did not actually require official authorization, these efforts were strategic attempts to publicize and formalize their consideration for a neighborhood with which they had no formal ties.

In addition to vaunting the benefits of the field and managing player conduct, regulars also touted the "social good" their presence provided. For example, Polo made a deliberate point of including an occasional woman or child in the games because "it looks good if they're out here." And he called attention to the fact that a local resident, a middle-aged White man, had inquired about participating in the games. Polo and the other men understood the privileges that came with Whiteness in Los Angeles and felt that it was good that "los güeros" played soccer in the park, even if they found some of them irritating and a bit arrogant. More generally, regulars argued that the organized games made the park safer and more enjoyable. They even took credit for "keeping the gangs out of the park" through their consistent and vigilant presence—a claim hard to verify, despite stories of several violent and mythologized confrontations. In any case, their readiness to assist strangers in need was demonstrated to me many times.

Regulars thus highlighted their productive and long-term use of the field in an attempt to legitimize their precarious claims to it. As one player put it to me when we were discussing possible construction of a fence around the field: "We've been playing here for years, they can't lock us out." The opening words in Polo's banner affirmed this historical claim: "Nuestro club, Mar Vista Club, ha practicado fútbol muchos años y disfrutado de conocer a muchas personas que siempre han sido muy bien recibidas." (Our club, Mar Vista Club, has played soccer for many years and enjoyed meeting many people who have always been very welcome.) While outsiders were unlikely to see the temporary display, it bolstered the men's belief that something good and enduring was happening in that space.

There was nevertheless a dialectical tension in relations between players and residents: neighborhood opposition drove regulars to better organize and institutionalize the games, which by increasing their visibility paradoxically served to intensify local anxiety. For example, while jerseys helped prevent disorder and conflict on the field, they also made the games more visible and potentially threatening to other park users and neighbors. Many of the men also suspected that they had not been noticed when playing on the previous dirt field. A local resident confirmed this suspicion when I asked her about the soccer games that predated the new field: "Before it wasn't uniforms and stuff, it wasn't a big deal." As I explain in the conclusion, the neighbors' objections, while triggered by the new turf field, reflected broader concerns about the changing "nature" of the park and region, which—like the men's skin color—were beyond the players' control.

Despite the rhetoric, many regulars, including Polo, threatened the status of the games by partaking in illegal or offensive behavior at the park, such as littering, drinking beer, smoking marijuana, fighting, and catcalling. When criticized for this conduct, they attempted to normalize it by claiming this behavior was typical, even unavoidable in urban parks. Attempts at concealment and moderation were probably motivated more by fear of receiving costly police citations than by a concern for upsetting the neighbors' moral sensibilities. In fact, many of the players privately expressed incredulity and resentment toward what they perceived as "excessive" objections by intolerant neighbors. In any case, regardless of how the men imagined that other people viewed their behavior, their time together at the park had to be fun.

At the same time, opposition by neighbors reinforced the power of group leaders because participants understood that they needed someone in control or they might be kicked out—an additional pretext exploited by group leaders to bolster their authority. For example, while Polo alluded to external interference when confronting Tico over his latest fight, he seemed more concerned with preserving order on the field than assuaging the feelings of outsiders. Similarly, the players themselves, rather than the neighbors, appeared to be the real targets of banners and statements evoking neighborhood concerns over disorderly conduct.

Despite their occasional appearance at community meetings, for the most part the players were not involved in the formulation of park policy. Men from the midday games appeared at only four of the forty-three field-related park meetings I attended, and none served on the various committees established to deal with field issues. They attributed their nonparticipation to lack of time and interest and, more importantly perhaps, to feelings of discomfort in these settings, which involved primarily upper-class Whites from the neighborhood. Jokes about "la migra" (immigration enforcement) showing up may have also dissuaded those with criminal records or without legal documentation. Some were even discouraged by others from attending because they worried that their behavior or appearance might reflect poorly on the group. Although a source of strength on the field, being Latino and speaking Spanish were perceived as weaknesses away from it. As such, Kathy and I were encouraged by the men to speak on their behalf, whether at public meetings or when dealing with park staff, police officers, or frustrated neighbors. Feelings of marginality and vulnerability kept the men from intervening in community debates about the field, even as they attempted to control behavior on and around the field.

The men avoided taking their attempts to institutionalize their presence in the park too far, such as by applying for field permits or creating a formal league. My sense is that they resisted these efforts, which might have generated too much oversight and attention, not to mention the related costs and paperwork. Indeed, a major appeal of the field was that there was no charge to use it, they weren't required to show identification, and they were largely left alone during their usual playing time. The men learned the risks of attracting too much attention when an aggrieved older White participant complained about the preferential playing order when he accompanied a group of regulars to confront park staff about an increase in permit play. Kathy later reflected on the unexpected intrusion: "I just wanted him to shut up. He has no idea of the history of this field." Polo, for his part, wondered who invited the intruder to join them. Fortunately, park officials expressed little interest in supervising the midday pickup games, but several officials confided to me that they would shut it down if problems arose—a risk the men fully understood.

Despite these challenges and contradictions, the group leaders' strategies to increase their visibility as responsible field patrons—whether by policing player behavior or through their interactions with neighbors and park officials—served to sustain their tenuous claims to the field. A comment by the park director at a community meeting suggested to them that their efforts were acknowledged and worthwhile: "I know there's a group of you who have come here for a long time, and it is not my intention to displace you."

"I Get So Tired of Organizing the Games, but Somebody Has to Do It"

During my time at the park, regulars were remarkably successful in their efforts to maintain control of the public field during the midday games. The daily organization of play described in the previous sections is a testament to their achievement. However, not all newcomers or outsiders accepted their authority or the rules and practices they instituted at the field. In fact, responses varied along a wide continuum from passive compliance to aggressive defiance.

As more and more people came to the new field, the veterans' control over the midday games was increasingly threatened. For example, newcomers challenged exclusive claims to the field by citing its "public character," as exemplified by such rejoinders as "I pay taxes" or "I have equal rights to this field" or "You don't own the park." Others contested the legitimacy of the group's unsanctioned authority at the public facility, singling Polo out with various appellations, such as "Mussolini," a "nobody," and "borracho del parque" (park drunk). Newcomers frequently disputed decisions made during the games that they considered unfair or biased, arguing on moral grounds that the regulars should not play favorites.

It was the preferential playing queue that produced the most controversy and resentment. Indeed, it was through dramatic and at times violent conflicts over this aspect of social control and status that regulars and newcomers most frequently and ardently clashed. Although newcomers generally waited their turn as they made themselves known as worthy players, objections were often raised. And while local rules and routines were publicly defended and enforced by regulars, newcomers and less frequent participants did openly defy them at times. The following episode demonstrates the form that objections could take over thwarted expectations for equitable access to the games:

> As the second match was about to commence, Colombia entered the field without a jersey. Polo yelled at Mario, the acting referee, to get him off the field: "¡Sácalo!" As if anticipating the challenge, Colombia responded immediately in English: "Fuck you, Polo! I'm not moving." Players from both teams moaned and shook their heads, foreseeing another drawn-out delay.
>
> Two of Colombia's teammates walked over and pleaded with him to wait for a later game. Mario Policía said calmly: "Look, man, I had to drop off my daughter to come play here. Please get off the field." Mike followed up in a sterner tone: "There's twenty-two of us waiting for you! Come on!" Colombia seemed indifferent to the appeals, responding, "So what?" to both men, and then explained in a mix of English and Spanish: "I want to show you guys that you have to be fair out here. What about Christian, he just played? ¡Siempre es lo mismo! [It's always the same!]"
>
> While most participants seemed content to wait him out, two players from the other team stormed over and demanded that Colombia get off the field. Tico, as usual, threatened violence, but Colombia remained unmoved. From the sidelines, Gambino commented on the interruption: "We only have fifteen minutes out here, look at all the time we're wasting for him." David,

sitting next to Gambino, yelled out: "We set this shit up a long time ago, we let you play." As if anticipating the old-timer's interjection, Colombia quickly responded: "Nobody was talking to you. I don't care how long you've been out here, I'm out here *now!*" Brazil, who needed to get back to his car dealership, walked over to the crowd gathered around Colombia and tossed him his jersey, but not without insulting him in English: "Fuck you, Colombia."

In this dispute and others, the "publicness" of the park served competing interests and created opposing contexts for negotiation. Reflecting both the legitimacy and illegitimacy of claims and counterclaims to the field, these confrontations struck at the core of the tensions structuring public space.[24] In the minds of the regulars, the park's publicness validated their claims to it and their resistance to external interference. However, for disgruntled participants, the publicness of the field made clear the illegitimacy of exclusive claims to its use. Colombia's challenge to game leaders' claims based on their history in the park showed that such historical entitlements did not always resonate as relevant or valid. Indeed, newcomer dissatisfaction was generally voiced in response to attempts by regulars to exclusive control of the field. As public space "belongs" to everybody yet to nobody, this tension is persistent and not easily resolved; saying that a space "belongs to the people" does not really tell us who uses it or under what conditions.

Game leaders believed that their organizational and material improvements to the field solidified their authority. For many newcomers, these measures made the games more predictable and attractive; they would not have come back had the playing conditions been less appealing. Like the dialectical nature of player-neighbor relations, the game leaders' authority was both strengthened *and* weakened by their organization of good games at the first-rate field. The quality of the experience usually encouraged compliance with their rules, but sustaining the games sometimes required giving into rule-breakers. To repeat Carlos's appraisal of the new field, it was indeed the best and worst thing that could have happened to the men

With the high-quality field and organized game attracting more and more talented players, the ability of regulars to assert influence on the field became increasingly difficult, especially for older participants. Skill and physicality could represent a powerful challenge to the supremacy of regulars, and the "winner stays" structure allowed newcomers and outsiders to independently affect the playing order once they obtained a jersey. Eli, for example, did not seem too bothered by the snubbing he received off the field because, as he explained, "I kick their asses on the field." In any case, the balance between skill and status varied from day to day. Some days, players like Eli were preferred over well-liked, but incompetent teammates; on other days, seniority or popularity prevailed.

Notwithstanding a few mythologized incidents, regulars rarely barred newcomers' participation outright or claimed formal rights to the field. Instead, there was a constant renegotiation regarding appropriate game behavior and status within the pecking order. There generally was collective pressure to avert or resolve extended disputes that took precious time away from the men's limited leisure hours. Chaos was bad for everyone, as Brazil conceded when giving up his place to Colombia in the incident recounted earlier.

For these reasons, expressions of power and deference should not be regarded as zero-sum interactions at the park. For even when faced with intense discomfort and disrespect, newcomers ultimately received an opportunity to play and to exhibit their own forms of influence on and off the field. As Polo liked to remind impatient players: "Vamos a jugar todos." (We're all going to play.) And as much as he and other regulars resented the influx of new players, most relished the diversity and entertainment these newcomers brought to the park, especially the more skillful and compelling characters. For example, when Polo tried to block a rebellious French player of Senegalese descent from taking a jersey, several old-timers urged him to let Patas Locas (Crazy Feet) play, as he was becoming a crowd favorite for his audacious style of play. Most participants also recognized that banning players could become self-defeating since—as Zapata astutely observed—"you can't play soccer by yourself."

It became increasingly clear to me that regulars recognized the limits of their power and the vulnerability of their control over the open facility, an increasingly valued and scarce resource in the region. For example, in discussing the difficulties of incorporating defiant newcomers, Polo confided that the regulars want to "fight them, but I tell them that we can't risk losing the field if the police are called." And while he acquired status and self-worth in running the games, Polo also admitted to me the frustrations that accompanied these efforts: "I get so tired of organizing the games, but somebody has to do it." This was a sentiment reiterated by others. In light of these demands and changing circumstances, I was not surprised to learn that Polo eventually "retired," as he put it, after an eight-year run as "el jefe" (the boss). Yet despite a change in leadership and the endless appearance of new dramas and recruits, the games played on in familiar form up through my last visit to the park in May 2019.

Conflict and Community

This chapter has focused on insiders' attempts to control newcomers' participation in the games and outsiders' perceptions of what was happening on and around the field. As the bumpy transition from the dirt to turf field revealed, nothing was taken for granted or guaranteed. However, the men's efforts to continue the games under changing circumstances also produced feelings of community and camaraderie. These consequences of group activity are explored more fully in later chapters, but merit preliminary consideration here. Briefly stated, the challenge of establishing and maintaining social order was also a source of meaning and affiliation. In constructing newcomers as "outsiders," regulars simultaneously established themselves as "insiders." Cold shoulders, deliberate delays, and local customs differentiated newcomers, but at the same time made clear who belonged and who was favored in that setting. The same set of practices that confused and diminished newcomers bolstered a sense of comfort and status among regulars, who—unlike newcomers—were welcomed and at ease in that vibrant scene. Here they were recognized as people with social standing who shared a common history.

Managing problems on and off the field also galvanized group life and strengthened communal bonds. As in many group settings, conflict and solidarity were closely linked at the park.[25] When confronting external threats, such as defiant newcomers or disapproving park neighbors, the men acted collectively and affirmed their commitments to one another. Similarly, marking some players as "deviant" or threatening reinforced who conformed to group standards and deserved respect.[26] Celebrating a shared past also conveyed a history worth defending. Another source of pride was the fact of having organized soccer games for years in that space from dirt to turf, which also served to differentiate old-timers from those who had arrived with the new field.

These everyday challenges compelled regulars to act in concert. Their deference to imperfect leaders and to homegrown rules and routines conveyed their shared interests and desire to collaborate. Indeed, part of the meaning of the park to the players was that control was contingent on a local culture that they had come to know and defend. What the men created and sustained reflected changes brought about by the new field, as well as a history of play and friendship that predated its installation. In their collective efforts, they set the foundations for building relationships and constructing identities on and off the field—the full implications of which are explored in subsequent chapters.

2 * Men at Play

Ivan receives the ball from his goalie, deep in his own half of the field. The game is tied and in its closing seconds. Adding to the suspense, thirty or so spectators call for the acting referee Chino to end the contest by aggressively shouting, "¡Tiempo!" (Time!) One man blurts out: "Árbitro corrupto" (corrupt referee), earning laughs for his good-natured accusation. As they all know, a game ending in a tie would require both teams to leave the field and make way for two new teams. With the sidelines packed with eager players, a long wait looms for at least one of the teams, possibly both.

The tension mounts as Ivan contemplates his next move. Sensing his indecision, a spectator urges him on: "Enséñales [teach them], Ivan!" His companion on the bleachers raises the stakes: "Su marido Motor está" (your husband Motor is here), identifying in playful terms the coach of the young man's park-based team. Polo, as usual, taunts the latest park galáctico (superstar): "Ivan's garbage, just like Motor, no sabe jugar [he doesn't know how to play]." In mock encouragement, he yells out: "¡Vamos, Cien Tacos!" (Let's go, One Hundred Tacos!), using the nickname given to Ivan by the players due to his hearty appetite.

Despite Polo's putdowns, defenders keep their distance from the skillful twenty-one-year-old, sensing it was better to hold their ground than risk embarrassment so far from their own goal. The ball safely at his feet, Ivan—decked out in his favorite FC Barcelona attire—scans the field for options. As if reading his mind, Caballo makes a sudden move down the sidelines, and Ivan swiftly delivers a booming aerial pass to his forty-two-year-old teammate. Caballo traps the ball in midstride and cuts inside, deftly beating three defenders on his way to the opposing goal. Excitement builds as the powerful Honduran gallops toward the net. A teammate yells out: "¡Métalo, Negro Caballo!" (Put it in, Black Horse!) Several spectators implore the goalie to make a save, keen to keep the game deadlocked. Caballo fakes a shot and the goalie dives to block the phantom strike. As he tumbles out of play, Caballo calmly taps the ball into the empty goal.

Victory in sight, Caballo circles around to celebrate. With his signature gold-tooth smile, he mimics an in-flight airplane, arms extended, swaying side to side. A teammate embraces him, and the grown men jump up and down in each other's arms, before Caballo playfully pushes him away. The spotlight back on him, he points to the applauding men in the bleachers, many of whom are stomping their feet on the metal steps. One man yells: "¡Eso es fútbol!" (That's soccer!), while another adds: "¡Que viva el viejo Catracho!" (Long live the Honduran old-timer!) Motor joins in, using the occasion to goad his rival: "¡Aprenda [learn], Polo!" A fellow spectator demands that Polo "buy un doce [a twelve-pack of beer]" to atone for his negative comments. Polo downplays the goal-scorer's feat by blaming the goalie—that "portero de agua" (leaky goalie)—and denigrating all the participants as mere "jugadores del parque."

As if yielding to this climactic moment, Chino blows his whistle to signal the end of the loosely timed match. Players from the defeated team make their way to the sidelines, where they are greeted with friendly taunts and demands for their jerseys. New opponents enter the field and join Caballo's teammates in congratulating the old-timer for his thrilling goal.

*

During the midday pickup soccer games, I witnessed many such scenes of excitement and euphoria. The exploits and enthusiasm varied, but together made for a lively and stimulating arena. The fun and intrigue migrated off the field to sideline and post-match conversations that inevitably rehashed and debated action on the field from that day or years past. The games and commentary fed off each other, weaving a collective history and foundation for shared experiences. And one need not be a particularly good player, active spectator, or effusive storyteller to participate. Although the world these men created around pickup soccer was not without its challenges, it was an environment in which interaction and creativity flourished.[1]

However, these sociable outcomes were hardly automatic; nor were they inherent in the sport or in any system of material rewards. Instead, the games were built up as meaningful and dramatic by the men. The fun was in the soccer playing itself, yet also in the layering of additional sources of excitement based on the men's relationships, biographies, and presentations of self. For even scoring goals and winning matches meant little without these layers of self-understanding and communal life.

What follows takes the reader back inside this world of play and shows its potential for generating transcendent meanings. The games provided moments that participants understood as emotionally resonant as they moved through their life cycle—from young boys accompanying their fathers to old-timers defending their legacies. In this chapter, I examine how the men made the games feel profoundly meaningful and discuss how these "playful" encounters with seemingly so little at stake generated deep connections and lasting reputations, giving the men a unique context in which to make claims about who they were and how they related to each other.

The Pickup Soccer Games

Once teams were set, players took their positions on the field. Most participants were more or less familiar with each other, but there was often an odd stranger or two. Like Ivan, many wore their favorite soccer apparel underneath the park jerseys. Others played in jeans and work boots. The colorfully dressed players positioned themselves on their own, but there was often disagreement about who should play where. These decisions were complicated by a wide range of playing abilities and passions, even if performance did not always correspond to appearance or reputation. There were plenty of "gordos" (fat guys), "viejitos" (old-timers), and "borrachos" (drunks) who dominated and "gorilas" (meat heads), "culeros" (pompous assholes), and "sanos" (teetotalers) who disappointed. Women and teenagers also exceeded expectations to the delight of onlookers.

With lineups eventually in place, the game commenced. Players dribbled, kicked, and headed the ball around the field. Some players saw the ball more than others, but everyone had a chance to participate over the course of what was typically a fifteen- to twenty-minute game. Like many team sports, soccer allows for a variety of initiatives, whether or not a player is in possession of the fast-moving ball. So even an old, slow, or unskilled player can still feel engaged by moving around the field in support of his teammates, even if he rarely touches the ball. Given its low threshold and high ceiling of skill, soccer can be played with satisfaction by beginners and experts alike. An effortless trap or pass of the ball for one player could be a significant accomplishment for another. This mix of playing abilities and passions provided ample opportunities for challenges and triumphs on the open field, which teammates, opponents, and spectators took pleasure in sharing. And with the games attracting such a diversity of talent and personalities, there was always plenty of room for commentary.

Kathy explained how she was able to find satisfaction in the games, even as a fringe contributor. As she suggests, players can lose themselves in the collective act by "influencing play":

> I may never touch the ball but I make things happen because if I run here, that guy passes the ball or he speeds to go past me, that causes a chain reaction. So even though some people think I'm just running up and down the field wasting my time, I'm not because I'm influencing play and my

mind is working. I just love that part of it, and if I ever do get to touch the ball [*laughs*], that's just an extra bonus.

Like Kathy, many spoke about soccer as the common denominator bringing people together, regardless of their talent or background. For César, the game's broad appeal and accessibility worked "like magic":

> I think of football this way—*como mágico* [as magical]. It doesn't matter where you come from or what job you have. It makes everyone come together to participate in something that makes you *sentir diferente* [feel different]. And at that moment, it's like a constant equalizer. No matter the skill level, lo disfrutan todos en ese momento [everyone enjoys it at that moment].

The games unfolded out of this magic.[2] The outcomes were uncertain, even if some games felt rigged by the selection of players or by referee decisions. As in all forms of competitive play, there was a balance of spontaneity and structure that sustained the men's involvement.[3] Some matches were more hotly contested than others, with an occasional verbal spat or even a fistfight breaking out. The prospect of long waits and heckling from la porra (the crowd) encouraged victory, although few people took winning or losing too seriously. There were not set rosters, and no one was playing for a trophy or a paycheck. In any case, with roughly thirty midday matches per week, opportunities for redemption abounded.

Fun in Soccer[4]

The soccer games at Mar Vista were regularly punctuated by bursts of collective excitement. As described in the opening vignette, these moments generated charged reactions and commentary by players and spectators alike that transformed mere soccer matches into lively social affairs—occasions of "high emotional energy," as sociologist Randall Collins would say [5] In no way mandated by the rules or programmed into the play, these bursts of excitement were rooted in a shared appreciation of the situation. Some moments were treated as having more transcendent meaning than others. As the reader might expect, a spectacular goal, pass, dribble, or tackle generally elicited collective celebration, regardless of the player's history or relationship to others at the park.

The following case involves a player who infrequently attended the games and rarely socialized with others at the park:

> Standing roughly twenty feet away from the opponent's goal, Oleg met the ball in midair with his right foot, smashing it into the roof of the net. Fifteen

or so men seated on the bleachers applauded in approval, one yelling out "golazo" to celebrate the quality goal. Another spectator added in English, "That's how you do it," pointing to his friend Eric, whose team had given up the goal. Polo, who was standing along the sidelines by himself, pivoted toward the men on the bleachers and claimed the skillful newcomer as "mi jugador" (my player). He then turned to Motor and declared: "Don't even think about it. He's too good for your team of maletas [lousy players]!" However, as a White recent college graduate, Oleg was an unlikely recruit for any of the league teams that drew from the park.

In this situation, the men's responses were connected to the quality of the play, given that Oleg was a relative stranger and atypical participant. Nor was the men's fun contingent on Oleg's reactions to the game or his understanding of its social context. Indeed, most of the dramatic meaning was generated by others, as Oleg didn't invite the applause and actually seemed ambivalent toward it. Even without personal knowledge of Oleg or connection to him, there was the shooting, passing, dribbling, and scoring to galvanize interest. Excitement wasn't necessarily contingent on being skillful either, as newcomers also drew attention with their miskicks, stumbles, and defeats.

While the men were excited by the action on the field, their responses were above all about their relationships and history of play at the park. They made all kinds of statements about themselves and others when discussing play by participants they barely knew. Talented newcomers like Oleg provided fresh challenges and plotlines to drum up tension on the field. Like a prop in a theatrical production, he enlivened the games by providing a spectacle for the men to observe and comment on, such as when Polo used Oleg's goal as an opportunity to mock the team coached by Motor and to claim the newcomer as his own.

But if they could generate excitement with a stranger, they could do it much more with one another, given their overlapping ties and mutually known biographies. With more to draw on, the responses tended to be deeper, more personalized and creative, and characterized by greater interaction between players and spectators. As with Caballo in the opening excerpt and with Polo in the excerpt below, veteran players tended to be much more exuberant and effusive in promoting their achievements and in playing to the crowd:

> Polo received the ball thirty yards from the goal. An opposing player inched back, almost begging him to shoot. Having seen him miss spectacularly before, players and spectators egged him on. "¡Pégale!" (Hit it!) cried one man from the bleachers; another pressed him to "teach us." As expected,

Polo ripped a shot on goal. To everyone's amazement, the ball sped past the goalie into the upper corner of the net. Polo immediately ran toward the packed bleachers, pushing teammates and opponents out of his way, screaming, "¡Golazo, hijos de putas!" (Goal, you sons of bitches!), before unleashing his signature line for his many detractors, expressed in English for dramatic effect: "Buy my video!" He stopped several feet from the bleachers and stood triumphantly before the spectators. Polo concluded his celebration by raising his shorts and pounding his naked thighs with his fist, declaring "como [Cristiano] Ronaldo" in reference to the famous and well-built soccer player. Someone joked that he's a "puto como Ronaldo" (homosexual like Ronaldo). Another told him to "go make sandwiches"—a dig at his high-end restaurant work. But most of the men gave Polo his due praise for the unexpected golazo, the talk of the park for several days following.

Unlike Oleg, Polo was much more of a participant in construction of the dramatic moment. The celebration following his goal had an "I told you so" quality, which was impossible for Oleg since he didn't have a history to have "told them so" in the past. Polo's goal was all the more remarkable because of his history of bungled shots and his embracing of a more self-aggrandizing celebration. In cheering or mocking Polo's achievement, spectators drew on their relationship with him and knowledge of his character in ways they couldn't with Oleg. Cheers were not only for the play—as with Oleg—but for the player himself, and they all understood their response to Polo's goal in light of their shared history at the park. Indeed, this was not the first time, nor presumably the last, that Polo would provoke such excitement.

Stopping Play to Revel

Excitement was not simply over scoring goals; the game provided a wide range of opportunities to excel and to attract attention, such as when players made strong tackles or clever passes or adroitly dribbled past defenders. And in contrast to the natural break when goals were scored, the men built in stoppage of play to revel in dramatic moments:

> The goalie kicked the ball high in the air in Chaparro's direction. In his late twenties, Chaparro was one of the weaker players to regularly participate in the games. His small stature and lighthearted personality hindered his play, but made him popular with the crowd. As the ball rapidly descended, several men in the bleachers urged him to trap the ball, rather than let it bounce: "Vamos [let's go], Chaparro, it's yours." Another man joked, "Con la panza [with your belly]." Chaparro controlled the ball in midair, a difficult feat for any player. Then, like a hunter posing with his prey, he put his foot on

top of the ball, placed his hands on his hips, and stuck out his chest to the delight of onlookers. Someone shouted out: "Eso [that's it], Chihuahua," a playful jab at his diminutive physique. Another spectator compared him to a celebrated professional soccer player: "Puro Messi" (just like [Lionel] Messi) and called out for more: "¡Más, más!" Rather than attack the ball, the closest defender held his ground, waiting for a beaming Chaparro to make the next move.

In this case and countless others, the men toyed with the rules of the game, creating their own momentary stoppage to acknowledge an achievement, even if it meant forsaking a tactical advantage or opportunity. Unlike in the games they watched on television, there was no opportunity in these pickup games to play back the tape. By building suspense and pausing for Chaparro to revel in the moment, the men also called attention to the broader implications of the play. The feat was remarkable because nobody expected it, given their experience watching Chaparro play. Shouts of "Chihuahua" and "Messi" spoke to their good-natured relationship with the park personality. As with Polo, the responses were as much about the player as the play, and a less charismatic, cherished, or competent player would not have elicited such a strong reaction. Chaparro, for his part, embraced the moment, fully anticipating that his opponent would give him time to revel in his moment of triumph.

As with Chaparro, applause and commentary intensified when an inferior player outclassed a superior opponent. This difference was usually attributed to a combination of skill, physical condition, and age. The greater the perceived gap, the greater the excitement when expectations were upended. Connections between the opponents—whether friendly, hostile, or a source of amusement—also heightened the stakes. For example, when rivals or buddies confronted each other on the field, new layers of tension emerged well beyond tactics or the score line. Game action was almost always evaluated and enhanced through the prism of the men's histories and relationships at the park. With the game attracting a wide range of players and relationships, mismatches and dramas abounded on the field. The following example involves such a case and highlights generational differences as a source of suspense:

At fifty-four years old, Oscar walks with a slight limp from years of restaurant work and playing soccer. As he himself would admit, the extra pounds he's packed around his midsection slowed his movements on the field. He often jokingly described himself to me as "gordo" (fat) and "viejo" (old). The Honduran old-timer was well liked at the park and renowned for his signature yell ("yaaaahhhh") when he did something notable on or off the field, which earned him the nickname "El Viejo Loco" (the crazy old man). It was therefore not surprising that the men erupted in applause when he won the ball from the younger and more talented Tulio. Oscar stuck out his foot at just the right time to win the ball from his unsuspecting opponent, who tumbled out of play. With the ball at his feet, the victorious Oscar belted out his signature yell. Many responded in kind. Tulio laughed as he shook his head in embarrassment and appeared to let Oscar dribble freely away from him.

"Parte del Show"

Excitement, however, did not necessarily depend on "good" plays. In fact, bad or humorous actions were just as likely to elicit collective recognition and commentary. The more egregious or entertaining the blunder, the more extended the abuse and amusement. The better known the player, the more personalized the response. Players with longer and more celebrated histories at the park provided more fodder to exploit when responding to their blunders. For example, Tulio's gaffe became as much a focus of attention as Oscar's triumph, especially as Tulio was recognized as one of the star players on Motor's park-based league team. One man mocked him as "jugador de Motor" (Motor's player), another spectator urged him, "Toma leche" (Drink milk)—the usual taunt whenever a player was over-powered. But like Chaparro's opponent, he too appreciated Oscar's triumph and let the fifty-four-year-old revel in the attention. In some instances, a bad or embarrassing move could result in angry confrontations, but such occasions were more often greeted with good humor and camaraderie. As we saw with Tulio's gracious response when Oscar outmaneuvered him, the men accepted missteps and mistakes—and the accompanying "trash talk"—as part of the fun and bonding experience. Indeed, most matches were punctuated with boisterous responses to player blunders, as we see in the following excerpt:

> Titi receives the ball a few feet from the opponent's defenseless goal. To the astonishment of those watching, he shoots the ball over the empty net. An avalanche of whistles and insults pour in from players and spectators: "Viejito" (old-timer), "basura" (garbage), "estúpido" (stupid), "maleta" (lousy), "torta" (oaf), and "jugador del parque" (park player). One man launches a more up-to-date taunt, yelling out "Ramos," referring to the Real Madrid star Sergio Ramos, who had also missed an easy goal the previous weekend. Chango adds a more personalized attack on the house painter: "¡Va pintar toilets!" (Go paint toilets!) Barba piled on the abuse: "That's why Motor no te quiere [doesn't want you]," in reference to the fact that

Titi no longer was playing for the park-based league team. For more laughs, Maradona draws from Titi's biography: "¡Váyase a cuidar a sus niños!" (Go take care of your children!) To similar crowd approval, Ali—of Lebanese descent—calls him a "cerote" (turd), using a Salvadoran slur in his non-native language. Titi, a Salvadoran father of three, pulls his shirt over his face and pretends to walk off the field in shame as play resumes.

In addition to Polo, Oscar, and Titi, there was a handful of crowd favorites who regularly animated the games through their personality and playing style. Some impressed through their bravado and stunning misses; others inspired with their signature moves and backstories. For example, America delighted onlookers with his lightning-bolt goal celebration, like his hero Cuauhtémoc Blanco. Huguito fueled interest by dramatically dancing over the ball when taking on defenders. As with Polo's erratic shots on goal, Ali frustrated and amused by never passing the ball. By contrast, Brazil's pinpoint passes invariably sparked speculation about a possible past career as a professional player. Gary, for his part, often yelled "Olé" whenever he made or observed a nice play, while Tico was notorious for his intensity and for demanding that Motor sign him up for his team whenever he scored. Spectators took special joy in jeering missed chances by a half-dozen park whipping boys, just as they championed goals by beloved underdogs. For example, nothing seemed to please the men more than seeing Kathy or Mi Chavo score an unexpected goal or watching Belize or Payaso botch an easy play. Hits and misses were not all equal at the park.

Most of these players embraced and even provoked attention, understanding it in the context of their relationships and park history. Aware of how their play was being observed and interpreted, players self-consciously constructed a game persona that others recognized and would remember. For example, Polo relished the role of villain, knowing that his taunts would not be taken seriously, just as Huguito knew that his teammates would tolerate his senseless dancing over the ball. Similarly, old-timers like Oscar recognized that any applause they garnered was due more to their long-standing association with the park than to the quality of their play. Players generally laughed off the exaggerated abuse and personalized attacks that followed their blunders. Few took offense to heckling by their peers and acknowledged it as "parte del [part of the] show."[6] Local lingo and nicknames also lightened the mood.

Playing with Difference

Demographic diversity was another source of meaning and entertainment during the games. Newcomers quickly came to appreciate the heterogeneity of what many initially assumed was a homogenous playing population—or "just a bunch of Mexicans"—as several new players candidly joked with me. But for those in the know, key axes of difference included race, nationality, occupation, religion, as well as marital, family, and legal status. The following field note highlights the multiple layers of diversity at play on and off the field:

> Off from work for the day, Taco makes an unexpected appearance at the midday games. His friends in the bleachers are excited to see him and express their enthusiasm through heckling and horseplay. The teasing is all the more fun because Taco's five-year-old son has joined him and is being looked after by the men as he plays. After his father shoots harmlessly on goal, someone jokes that "Tacito" (Little Taco) should take his place on the field. After another miscue, he suggests instead that Taco make way for Kathy, who is walking toward the field. Another spectator piles on: "That's why Peru never makes it to the World Cup." Following up on this reference to Taco's country of birth, someone yells out: "¡Vamos, come gato!" (Let's go, cat-eater!), alluding to a myth about Peruvian food that drew laughs from the men. Barba, who is from Mexico, exclaimed: "¡Qué huevón pe!" (What an idiot!), using a Peruvian-tinged pejorative for comic effect. Another man quipped: "Go prepare ceviche with Christian," referring to Taco's compatriot and to a favorite Peruvian dish. When the outflanked Taco tried to take the ball from Senegal, Caballo cheered him on: "Don't be scared of the black lion." After Senegal moved effortlessly past Taco, the West African turned toward the men and in his accented and imperfect Spanish yelled out: "¡Cállate, pendejos!" (Shut up, fools!) Senegal's use of the vulgar Spanish slur delighted the men, who whistled in appreciation, one Latino man playfully firing back in English: "Go back to Africa!"

There seemed to be endless opportunities to mine these differences as a source of excitement and humor.[7] Occasionally, these remarks led to hurt feelings and even hostility, but more typically they enlivened the atmosphere and served as an additional way that the men added to the fun and profundity of the games.

Age, family, gender, race, and nationality could all spontaneously come into play during the games. For example, the categories "father," "Peruvian," and "African" took on new meaning in the incident involving Taco and Senegal recounted above. Jokes about sexuality, age, religion, and legal status similarly sparked interest and intimacy. Instead of trying to transcend their differences, the men reinforced them as a way to bond through their soccer play.[8] They made fun of what could potentially divide and create distance between them, such as when spectators referred to Ali as a "camel," Caballo as "Negro" (Black), and Polo as a "puto" (homosexual). As with other kinds of taunts, the men generally didn't take these "insults" too seriously, understanding them in the context of their relationships and as part of park fun. They also made clear that they weren't intimidated by "la paja" (the shit talking), as when Payaso explained to me: "No les hago caso, los mando a la verga." (I don't pay attention to them, I tell them to fuck off.) In fact, these slights were seen as proof of belonging. Indeed, newcomers explained to me that it wasn't until people began making fun of them that they felt fully welcome.[9] Silence and disregard were considered far more insulting.

The men also understood the situational or contextual meaning of comments made at the soccer field that might seem racist, homophobic, or threatening to outsiders. For example, as he watched an animated game from the sidelines, Barba remarked: "Man, it would be wild if people yelled this shit out at Ralph's," referring to the local supermarket. Donovan— nicknamed after the White soccer player Landon Donovan he somewhat resembled—nodded his head in agreement and responded: "I couldn't get away with half of what I've said here anywhere else." With a laugh, Barba (from the Pacific coast of Mexico) replied: "You'd get your ass kicked." But at the park, the men could talk more openly about their differences. While there was always a risk that someone might take offense at ethnic or homophobic taunts, however playful, tying moments to people's back- grounds was part of the fun and conviviality.[10]

While jerseys, nicknames, and skin color sometimes conveyed identity, the men had to know each other in order to play around with each other's biographies in a meaningful way.[11] For example, Taco earned his nickname not due to his nationality but because of his decades-old employment at Taco Bell. Similarly, Peru de Oaxaca earned his nickname because the Mexican native used to socialize and play soccer with a group of Peruvians. Ali was occasionally called a "camel" because he was of Middle Eastern descent, which was not obvious from his appearance and fluency in Spanish. Like- wise, the men understood that Ivan and Motor ("los maridos") were not really married, but were linked as star player and coach. As mentioned in the previous chapter, the men recognized that most White players ("los jugadores de Santa Monica") were not actually from neighboring Santa Monica, but associated them with that town as a playful proxy for White- ness, just as Latinos grasped the irony when Black players were jokingly told to "go back to Africa." The terms negro (Black), güero (light-skinned), Chino (Asian), joto (homosexual), and mojado (undocumented) were often used in ways that conveyed more about the men's relationships and park histories than anything fixed or essential about the individuals themselves.

The steady stream of newcomers added new ingredients to the mix, and new associations emerged as they became better known. Questions about "where are you from?" (¿de dónde eres?) invariably followed new arrivals. Not only did this help to make sense of these newcomers, but it also added to a growing stock of material on which to draw to spice up the matches. The arrival of players from different countries offered others the opportunity to try out fresh myths and stereotypes, as when Polo nicknamed an obstinate Italian player Mussolini or when Nestor playfully asked a dreadlocked Jamaican participant for marijuana when he entered the field. Newcomers brought new cultural and linguistic practices to the park, such as when a group of Iraqi and Moroccan players taught the regulars a series of Arabic insults, which they then yelled out during the games. In my case, it was only after several months of playing that word circulated that my father was French and my partner Costa Rican—two sources of information eventually used to craft creative responses to my play. The birth of my son several years later became an additional source of fun, such as when Moncho told me to go change my son's diapers when I missed an easy shot on goal. Like me, most participants acquired a backstory of some kind tied to a combination of personal biography and general demographics that invigorated responses to their play.

*

As these examples suggest, the games were taken seriously, but were also made fun and compelling. By acknowledging players, whether in admiration or mockery, the men filled the games with meaning and pleasure. Soccer provided the basic dramatic tension, but the men enlivened the games by adding many more layers of drama. Polo's goal, Chaparro's trap, and Titi's miss meant all the more because of the charged responses that went well beyond the specifics of the play or rules of the game. Far from automatic, the fun grew as the men brought onto the field their prior or off-field relationships and shared histories.[12] In the opening excerpt, the men weren't simply cheering Caballo's goal, but also celebrating his dogged perseverance and exuberant reaction. Caballo's self-aggrandizement was far from egocentric, but a way to forge a bond with the audience. His joy was as much theirs as his.

Newcomers contributed to the excitement, but were frequently confused by the hubbub that accompanied the action. Unfamiliar with the history of play constructed layer by layer over time, they often had trouble understanding reactions to the game, such as the exaggerated applause for Oscar's mundane tackle, the over-the-top criticisms of Titi's forgivable miss, and the racialized rhetoric accompanying Taco and Senegal's halfhearted skirmish over the ball. But newcomers were gradually assimilated into the local scene. With the passage of time, they learned how participants drew on their relationships and a shared history at the park to transform what might otherwise be dispassionate sporting events into something deeply playful and personal. While they might initially have come to play one version of soccer, they, too, learned to revel in the social context surrounding these games and, over time, contributed their own storylines and performances.

Moments of Greatness

Moments of celebration and mockery did more than make the games fun to play and watch. They also offered the men bursts of recognition they rarely received in other settings. In contrast to their lives at work or at home, the games were full of festive responses to the men's successes and failures. Moreover, the mix of players and quick succession of games provided ample opportunities for the men to shine in front of their peers. All participants received this attention over time, regardless of their playing ability.

A conversation I had with Motor one day revealed how the matches lifted the men out of the daily grind of their everyday lives. As we sat on the bleachers, he spoke about frustrations with one of his clients. He had been installing a wooden fence, taxing work exacerbated by the home-owner's constant meddling. Motor explained that he would return later that day, but had come to the park for a much-needed "descanso" (break). He didn't plan on playing, but as was often the case, he soon found himself on the field. Midway through the match, Motor scored a stunning goal with his work boots. His face lit up with excitement as he zigzagged in celebration back to midfield. The crowd reciprocated with roars of approval. With a big smile, Motor sauntered to the sidelines and tossed his jersey to a waiting player, signaling that his work was done. He briefly rejoined his friends on the bleachers, who shared in his joy, and then left for the job site.

There was something grand about Motor smiling and waving his arms, like a professional player saluting his adoring fans. Arriving after a morning of dull and frustrating work, Motor quickly found himself celebrating joyfully on the field.[13] Nor was he the only one who had arrived stressed and worn-out. For Motor and many other participants, the games provided a temporary reprieve from their everyday lives, leaving them feeling connected and emotionally recharged. Ali affirmed the game's appeal in these terms as we spoke in his empty auto-emissions test shop: "When you play good, you feel so good about yourself. You feel like you did something, and you need that, especially when you're not doing so good outside." Several men said they even thought about their game exploits as they lay in bed at night, which even kept some of them up at night, as Polo explained:

No sé, me emociona. [I don't know, it excites me.] Kicking the ball is what makes me feel the most; it gives me, I don't know, me hace feliz [it makes me happy]. And I know that un futbolista [a soccer player] likes it when he has a ball and makes a good play; he becomes happy. Sometimes I don't sleep when I score, or I think about like when you celebrate, estoy riéndome en la cama [I'm laughing in bed]. Or when we win something, a championship, or when I score a goal here, un golazo; ¡puta! [an amazing goal; wow!]

While weddings, birthdays, and other ritual celebrations provide similar recognition and transcendence, they are less frequent and more obvious in their intent. Flashes of greatness and experiences of community happened all the time during the games and emerged more organically and unpredictably. Although stimulated by the soccer play and structure of the game, most of the dramatic meaning was layered on by the men. The soccer matches gave them a chance to shape that world. As Polo joked one day, "I don't need to go to Disneyland after scoring a goal."

The men's awareness of potential recognition was made clear as they repeatedly promised to make each other "famous" on the field. In fact, they gave significance to their play by comparing themselves to the professionals they admired on television, such as when a spectator yelled out, "¡Puro Messi!" after Chaparro had excelled on the field or when Polo demanded the ball from his teammate, so he could score "como Rooney," his latest idol, Wayne Rooney. In the same way that they superimposed the park games onto what they watched on television, they also brought the professionals into the park games to further immortalize their achievements. By contrast, game play seemed not to matter unless others responded. For example, when I congratulated Locksmith on his goal, he replied: "Who cares? Nobody saw it." But in most cases, others were ready to transform the men's action on the field into something remarkable. As I came to appreciate, this scene was less about exercise or winning and much more about basking in the collective fun and glory.

Familiar Sensations

For many of the men, these were familiar sensations. Most grew up playing soccer, learning at an early age to revel in the excitement and camaraderie. These experiences regularly came up in my interviews with the men in which they recalled intricate details of their childhood play. For example, Peru de Oaxaca shared fond memories of playing soccer on a hill as a young boy in rural Mexico:

We played cáscaras [pickup soccer games] all the time when I was a kid. We always went al cerrito [to the small hill], where we played every afternoon. I remember there were people who took us. All the chamacos [kids] went like that. Siempre estábamos tirando tiros a la portería. [We were always taking shots on goal.]

Mario, who was in his mid-fifties and decades removed from his native Honduras when he spoke to me, remembered the sacrifices he made as a child to play the game he so loved:

For me, soccer is part of my life. I have played since I was seven years old. I played there on a team in Honduras, yo jugaba [I played]. We had no shoes, and my mother punished me when I arrived with my pants all dirty; there they punish very hard. But they never killed my love for the game because es parte de mí el soccer [soccer is part of me]. Creo que voy a morir pensando que todavía puedo jugar. [I think I'm going to die thinking I can still play.]

Playing soccer as adults was a way to carry on these experiences. As Carlos put it, the park "was the place where I could be myself. I felt like I was back home in my friend's backyard playing soccer, like I did when I was growing up in El Salvador." For Caballo, "soccer was something que traes en la sangre [that you carry in your blood]." Themes of place and home and claims about soccer being "in the blood" regularly came up as the men described what they were re-creating in the park. As many explained, soccer was one thing they had not given up in their journeys to Los Angeles. Like "back home," playing soccer captivated and connected the men, adding meaning and richness to their lives. As Walter explained, "No hay mejor manera de disfrutar la vida como cuando tú juegas fútbol." (There is no better way to enjoy life as when you play soccer.)

Soccer Talk

Many of the men came to the Mar Vista Recreation Center not only to play and watch soccer, but also to socialize with friends. The park soccer games and players were a recurrent focus of discussion that helped sustain their socializing. This was not all the men talked about, but they did spend an inordinate amount of their time there evaluating local talent, discussing player histories, and recalling soccer memories. Much as the meaning of play was enhanced by sideline chatter and celebrations, playing soccer together also enriched the life of the group off the field.

As we have seen, spectators reveled in the game action as much as the players; they were not simply passive bystanders waiting for an opportunity to play. In fact, excitement intensified in the collective back-and-forth between players and spectators. But like television commentators, spectators often responded to the games on their own terms, well out of earshot of the players:

> A young player contorts his body at just the right time and angle to score a tricky goal. Watching from the sidelines, Valderrama spins around and pumps his fist in celebration. He turns to Don Luis and asks if he had seen the "golazo." Before Don Luis can answer, Valderrama explains, "That's how you have to do it," adding "mira" (look) as he reconstructs the complex maneuver with his own body. He then boasts that he'd scored a lot of goals using a similar technique. Don Luis smiles at the dubious claim, before pointing out other factors involved in such a difficult shot.

In this interaction, as in many others, action on the field served as a pretext for spectators to engage with one another and to work out their own sense of self in the process. In analyzing the youngster's goal, the old-timers bonded and said something about themselves as soccer players. They had an "eye for talent," even if their bodies no longer—or never had—achieved such feats. Sideline commentary could also reveal other facets of the speaker's character. For example, Valderrama praised the young man for attempting such an audacious shot, joking: "Ese chiquito tiene huevos." (That boy has balls.) And by association, he suggested that he had shown the same audacity in his time, which gave Don Luis an opening to question his friend's boasting.

Valderrama, Don Luis, and the others incessantly judged soccer players at the park and then debated each other's opinions. They did this as they watched the games, but also when socializing afterward. Some debates were more contentious and drawn-out than others, but it was rare to chat with the men and not hear them talk about the teams, players, and their performance. And as with action on the field, everyone eventually had his turn in the spotlight.

In their evaluations, the men expressed what they thought made a good soccer player. Their judgments were not merely about quality of play, but also about other considerations, such as style of play and teamwork. Some favored skill and finesse on the field, whereas others preferred selflessness and grit. Many criticized bad attitudes and wasted talent. A few men called attention to players' improvement and championed underdogs. All these various judgments tended to reflect how they saw themselves as players. Martín, for example, appreciated players with technical ability: "I like players who know the game and keep it simple. That's how I try to play, not like these brutos [brutes]." Locksmith, a self-styled tough guy, celebrated those with "ganas" (desire) and criticized those who played like "maricas" (pansies). The men contextualized performance at the park in light of the competition, generally privileging participation in league and tournament play, which is why the label "jugador del parque" was considered such a put-down.

In the course of these discussions, the potential of individual players was also a favorite subject of debate:

> Ever since he first started playing in the midday games, Oscar had gener-ated a great deal of interest among the regulars. Only nineteen years old, he impressed with his athleticism, but the men disagreed about his potential. Polo was adamant about Oscar's promise, saying that, with his help, this son of Mexican immigrants could be one of the best players at the park. He encouraged Motor to sign Oscar up for his league team before another team beat him to it. Others disagreed, mocking Oscar as "hijo de Polo" (Polo's son) and questioning whether he would show up on Sundays for league play. An older man compared Oscar to the other young "jugadores de Nintendo" (video game players)—a double-edged denunciation of their propensity to play video games and to attempt flashy plays on the field.

During a typical post-match gathering, Oscar had joined a long list of controversial players at the park as a focus for debate. These discussions persisted because the games continued to attract new talent, including many youngsters full of potential. Rarely a week went by without the men's attention being drawn to a new subject, whether a recent arrival or a regular whose playing had blossomed or faded before their eyes. Everyone seemed to have their personal favorites, talking them up against their inevitable detractors. Nicknames gradually arose that reflected these alliances, such as the joking reference to Ivan as "Motor's husband" and to Oscar as "Polo's son."

But it was the actual sons of players that drew the most curiosity and scrutiny. As mentioned earlier, many fathers brought their sons to the park, and some of them eventually joined the games as full participants. The men celebrated this history and enjoyed evaluating the prospects of those "nacido en el parque" (born in the park), as they liked to put it. Adding to the intrigue, their performance as players was often judged in relation to that of their father, as was their character. For example, Chepe's success, which included a Division I college soccer scholarship, was attributed to his father, Chino, both for bringing him to the park and for the skills he passed down to him. Similar enthusiasm followed Caballo's son's progression from the park to a college soccer career in Louisiana. When these young men returned to the park, old-timers were eager to remind them that they knew them as boys, sometimes even taking credit for their development. A son's perceived failures were also connected to their father's, such as when a spectator mocked Luis for playing "like your father" when he missed an easy shot on goal. Similarly, when a young boy looked upset, someone joked that he was going to be a "llorón" (crybaby) like his father.

How talk about sons was, above all, talk about fathers became clearer to me after my own son was born. Nicknamed Zizou by the men (after the French soccer star Zinedine Zidane), he became another focus in ongoing discussions about the "nueva generación" (new generation). Whatever promise or pitfalls they envisioned for him became a reflection of how they saw me as a soccer player and new father. The men clearly valued the presence of fathers and sons at the park, viewing it as a sign of group cohesion and longevity of the games played there.

League and tournament play were another source of conversation and dramatic tension at the park. Questions about who should and should not be included on these select teams provided additional fodder for debate—in contrast to participation in the daily pickup games, where roster decisions were less an issue:

> As the Fourth of July tournament neared, a half-dozen men gathered to discuss players for a team Tico was trying to organize. As Motor and Alex had already secured the top talent, Tico's options were limited. Somewhat unconventional choices were suggested. I joined the fray, recommending Peru de Oaxaca. The men dismissed the forty-four-year-old as a candidate and berated me for even making the suggestion. According to several of the men, he could no longer compete at the tournament level. Tico joked that he didn't want a "sub-cien" (under-100) team. To the amusement of those listening, the men mentioned several other players they considered unsuitable, including several of the people gathered around the picnic table.

Old-Timer Tales

As much as the men enjoyed debating the present and speculating about the future, it was the shadow of the past that most invigorated the men's soccer talk. These discussions focused on old-timers still playing, as well as those long retired, a few of whom were no longer around or even alive. However, the memory of their accomplishments lived on at the park.[14] Legacies flourished in the plethora of soccer-related nicknames, most of which were only used at the park. Some were tied to their appearance or quality of play, such as Motor, Caballo (Horse), Garfield (for his catlike reflexes), Pasmado (Clueless), Crazy Legs, Payaso (Clown), Zurdo (Lefty), Cabezón (Big-Headed), Ropero (Armoire), Burro Panzón (Potbellied Donkey), Chango (Monkey), Bomboncito (Big Butt), Pecho de Hule (Rubber Chest), and Vaca Loca (Crazy Cow). Others were named after famous soccer players they played like or resembled, including Maradona, Valderrama, Chilavert, Coloccini, Donovan, Totti, Benzema, and Mago (short for Mágico González). Nationality-based labels were also common, such as Brazil, Tico (Costa Rican), Catracho (Honduran), Chino (Asian), Senegal, Inglaterra (England), and Gringo (North American). In all, I counted over thirty soccer nicknames, even if in many cases, monikers belied a player's performance. Indeed, it had been years since Motor had zoomed around the field or Maradona had dazzled like his namesake, Diego Maradona.

Older players also refreshed their soccer histories by wearing old jerseys or by sharing team photos, news clippings, and player ID cards at the park. And when I visited the men at home, I discovered that many had mementos of this kind prominently displayed, along with trophies and medals. However, it was through the men's incessant storytelling that the past endured most consistently:

> Asprilla joins a group of men drinking beer by the picnic tables. Surprised to see him, Moncho yells out: "¡Mi negra! [My Black woman!] Where have you been?" Asprilla laughs and responds, "Tú sabes" (You know), alluding to the demands of family and work. Asprilla hugs Moncho and salutes the other men. After tossing him a cold beer, Moncho reintroduces me to Asprilla, adding: "You need to talk to him. He used to be one of the best out here, before he gained all this weight," playfully patting his former teammate's protruding belly. Moncho pressed on: "See what happens when you stop playing?" I later learned that Carlos was nicknamed after the Colombian star of the 1990s Faustino Asprilla because of their shared prowess at goal scoring. Asprilla's presence sparked the sharing of old stories, including a famous goal he scored from midfield during a holiday tournament and a comical fight with Darwin on the field. Asprilla asked about old friends not around that day, which inspired further reminiscences and laughs.

In this exchange and many others, the men revived their playing pasts and defined themselves as having a place in that world. These stories sometimes came as a surprise to those who, like me, were unfamiliar with this history. But contemporaries were ready to confirm these memories and to contextualize current play in light of a formidable past, such as when Moncho recalled Asprilla's prowess as he patted his friend's belly. For example, when a group of youngsters mocked Abel for missing an easy goal, Barba let them know that in his prime, Abel was one of the most prolific goal scorers around. As there was no way to evaluate Abel's past play in the present, his qualities lived on in the tales the men told about him. As with Asprilla, I often heard fantastic stories about a dozen or more "estrellas del parque" (park stars) who no longer played, several of whom I never met in person.

Soccer memories and legacies could also lead to controversy when the past was revisited, but not always in ways that the men wanted. As the men socialized, older players' claims were regularly challenged, whether out of disbelief or through conflicting accounts. How these discussions unfolded is illustrated in the following extended conversation between two old-timers debating their playing histories. I happened to be interviewing the fifty-year-old Filemón in the park when Zurdo sat down to join us. Zurdo caught sight of the tape recorder, which he presumably recognized from my interview with him a few months earlier. Intrigued, he listened quietly, but couldn't resist interjecting as Filemón vaunted his soccer-playing prowess in Oaxaca and Los Angeles:

> *Filemón*: Yo tengo la técnica. Yo le sé pegar a la pelota. [I have the technique. I know how to hit the ball.]
>
> *Zurdo*: Pero ya no quieres jugar. Te retiraste antes de que la mara te viera. [But you don't want to play anymore. You retired before the gang saw you.]
>
> *Filemón*: Pero tengo mucha gente en México que sabe que yo era canijo. Pero estoy cansado de esta mierda, que me putean en la cancha. [But there are many people in Mexico who know I was very good. But I'm tired of this shit, that they berate me on the field.]
>
> *Zurdo*: Pero te conozco desde hace diez años y todavía no jugabas. Y tengo cincuenta años y todavía estoy jugando. ¡Pregúntale a cualquiera! [But I've known you for ten years and you still hadn't played. And I'm fifty years old and I'm still playing. Ask anyone!]
>
> *Filemón*: Pero yo corro. Todo el tiempo me mantengo corriendo. [But I run. I continue to keep myself in shape by running.]
>
> *Zurdo*: ¡Pero no juegas! [But you don't play!]
>
> *Filemón*: No juego, pero me mantengo físicamente corriendo, papá. Tengo cincuenta años, y viejos de mi edad están acabados, hechos mierda. No, papá, me mantengo en forma todos los días. [I no longer play, but I stay in shape physically by running, buddy. I'm fifty years old, and old guys my age are finished, turned to shit. No, buddy, I keep in shape every day.]
>
> *Zurdo*: ¿Y todavía pisa a Polo? [And you still fuck Polo?]
>
> *Filemón*: ¡Ya lo pisé! [I already fucked him!]

As if prosecuting a case, the men questioned player histories and credentials, which led to animated discussions of days gone by. In response, defendants offered evidence and solicited support from others, as Zurdo had when he exclaimed: "Ask anyone!" Others brought photos or, as in Filemón's case, relied on their powers of persuasion. As we see in the following exchange, comparisons to the present also intensified debate in which old-timers typically argued that their performance as players in the past was far superior to the current state of play:

> Araña asks Robert why he hadn't played that day. Robert, twenty-three years old and a stalwart on Motor's celebrated league team, responds that he was tired. Araña, in his late forties, shakes his head in disbelief: "When I was your age, I would play all day." Barba supports the claim: "We used to play two games on Sunday," adding, "Players were a lot tougher back then. Referees let you play." Araña then interjects: "You're wasting your talents; all you guys do is drink beer and hang out." Robert, who had initially ignored Araña's criticisms, snaps back in English: "Look at you!" Like Robert, Araña hadn't played either. With a beer in his hand and smiling at his own hypocrisy, Araña responds: "I'm old, but I played." He then adds: "This guy used to pay Zapata and me to play in tournaments. Once we went to Arizona. Ask him!" Christian, a frequent target of old-timer criticism, exclaims: "I'm sick of these stories, these fantasies! You're bad now and were probably bad back then. You're going to tell me that Pasmado and the rest of this bola de viejitos [bunch of old-timers] were good too?"

Park players were not the only source of intrigue. The men also drew contrasts to the professionals to enrich their soccer talk. They did this during the midday games, but also when socializing afterward. Like the steady stream of newcomers to the park, the wide array of players and year-round schedule provided an endless supply of characters and storylines from which to draw. Sometimes these discussions focused solely on the professionals, but the men were quick to connect them to the park players. They did this at the park, but also on the rare occasions they watched games together on television:[15]

> Big Nelson and I were the last to arrive at Araña's single-family home on the eastern edge of Santa Monica. The Champions League match had just begun, and seven men from the park watched intensely between sips of beer. Polo backed Manchester United, led by Chicharito [Javier Hernández], one of his favorite players. To tease Polo, the rest of us rooted for Schalke, Manchester's German opponents. The match provoked spirited commentary and, on numerous occasions, the men brought park players into their analysis. For example, when Chicharito missed a clear chance on goal, several men yelled out: "Como Polo!" When a Schalke player was easily pushed over

and feigned injury, Polo fired back: "Looks like Ivan!" And every time Ryan
Giggs powered down the field, Polo urged his companions to learn from
Manchester's legendary winger. Several times during the game, he jumped
to his feet to mimic the veteran's movements. To Polo's delight, Manchester
United won the match. True to form, he gloated and challenged Motor and
several other players in attendance: "Why can't you play like that?"

*

Soccer gave the men a steady supply of things to talk about—a common
discursive space that sustained hours of lively conversation and debate in
the park. The arrival of newcomers, blossoming of regulars, and decline
of old-timers opened up new sources of drama and analysis, with sons,
league play, and professional players providing additional topics of discussion. Claims about the past were especially controversial as memories and
park histories differed. In many cases, there was no way to know for sure
whether or not these claims were valid. Old-timers enjoyed critiquing the
present in relation to the past, claiming that the soccer used to be better,
tougher, and more serious. Youngsters fired back, mocking the older players as washed-up and delusional.

However, building consensus was not really the point. It was the arguing,
along with all the teasing and verbal one-upmanship, that provided a basis
for interaction. As Ali explained: "If there are no mistakes and everything
is perfect, then what's there to talk about?" Some men even adopted un-
popular positions simply to prolong debate. And, as Christian suspected,
many old-timers offered "fantasies" instead of truthful representations of
the past in order to spice up the exchanges. Like many male gatherings,
"talking shit" (hablando mierda) was part of the fun.[16]

Whatever its form, soccer talk provided a way for the men to participate
in park life. This was especially important for those who no longer played
in the games, at least at a competitive level. But unlike players who could
let their play speak for itself, older participants felt the need to resurrect
and defend an image that had become distorted or diminished with the
passage of time. Restoring that image required active work to transcend
current circumstances through persuasive references to the past. Sometimes
peers served as corroborators; but more often they took the role of skeptics
and critics. Yet even when they disagreed, the men generally managed to
bond. Indeed, a willingness to argue or to tease was a sign of friendship
and mutual trust.

As seriously as the men took their soccer talk, the stakes paled in comparison to how they viewed themselves and each other as workers and
as family men. While the men did broach these subjects at times, these

discussions rarely became as animated as their soccer talk and were more likely to cause conflict and hurt feelings. Conversations about soccer tended to dominate because it was a topic that all the men could participate in comfortably, whereas other aspects of their lives proved more contentious or alienating. The stakes were high, but not uncomfortably high, which Filemón and Zurdo revealed by defusing their potentially heated debate over a shared joke about having sex with Polo. As we have seen, jokes of this kind often came up in the men's conversations. It was never clear to me to what extent such sexual banter may have reflected homoerotic or homophobic sentiments. As with other displays of male bravado at the park, I took it mainly as just another form of talking shit and having fun. But in this specific case, the joke about Filemón's sexual prowess was a flippant way for him to confirm his vigor, while at the same time easing an otherwise tense exchange.[17]

In short, talking about soccer made it fun to be together. In fact, I sometimes suspected that the men played in order to talk about it later and that they anticipated being talked about, particularly when they excelled or floundered on the field. Soccer talk also provided a comfortable platform for players to defend a certain image of themselves to others—an indirect, but convenient means of self-presentation. While ostensibly about soccer, these discussions inevitably led to analyses of character and relationships. For example, it didn't take much digging to see that Polo's praise of Oscar's soccer abilities reflected their budding father-son relationship, just as the stories shared by Moncho and Asprilla helped to renew their friendship. Similarly, when Locksmith championed players who competed "sin llorar" (without whining), others understood that he was saying something about his stoic vision of soccer and manhood, whereas Martín's emphasis on grace and skill reflected a different self-image.

Puros Viejitos

The men constantly talked about "being young" and "getting old" at the park. They did this when discussing school, work, and family, as well as when joking about their sex lives and drinking habits. But it was in relation to playing soccer that concerns over aging took their most palpable form. For some, playing soccer was a way to feel potent, signaling to themselves and others that they were in their physical prime. They experienced this on the field when overpowering challengers and in the adulation they received afterward. Even without eye-catching plays, active participation in the games indicated that they were no longer "extras"—that is, boys.

Older men were quick to attribute the success of younger players to their youth. For example, when a player gloated about winning three games in a row, an old-timer responded: "Porque eres joven." (Because you're young.) As we saw in Araña and Robert's exchange mentioned earlier, veterans criticized youngsters they felt were wasting their talents, inevitably drawing attention to their own youthful achievements and regrets. While the soccer field was not the only arena in which age was scrutinized, the nature of the scene—with its mix of ages and bodies in battle—lent a special poignancy to the old-timers' anxieties over growing older.

For players at the end of their soccer careers, the games were opportunities to feel young *and* old—young in the sense that they were still playing (even well at times), but old in that they could no longer compete as they used to, especially when pitted against the ever-younger talent streaming into the park. The physicality of the games made them especially conscious of their advancing age. Soccer forced them to feel their age, many reaching a point where they had to call it quits or at least cut back considerably on their play.

These mixed experiences inspired pride and frustration. For example, when Martín beat me to a ball, he joked: "Not bad for a forty-nine-year-old!" In another case, an older player challenged some young hecklers by quipping: "We'll see what you're doing at my age." Old-timers savored their triumphs on the field in similar age-specific ways, such as when Gary exclaimed, "I still got it," after scoring a crafty goal or when Polo declared that he was "giving classes to los niños." But for most, simply playing—even as an "extra"—was gratifying, especially in comparison to their peers who had long since retired.

At the same time, many of the older players felt frustrated that they could no longer play like they used to. At times, they even excused their performance in light of their age, such as when Roberto declared, after losing the ball: "¿Estoy viejo, qué quieres?" (I'm old, what do you expect?) Unlike their younger counterparts, old-timers were quick to publicize their age on the field as a way to account for their shortcomings. In our interview, Carlos voiced his concerns about "getting older":

> I think that's the most difficult part—getting older. Not the fact that you get up and have pains all over your muscles, but the fact that you can't keep up with these youngsters. Like now, I'm much heavier than I used to be, so I don't run as fast. It's been difficult to see some of these kids fly by you. But you know, I still enjoy the game.

Later in our conversation, Carlos expressed regret that I had not seen him play when he could "keep up." Stories and flattering nicknames helped, but he knew that such testimonies to his past prowess weren't the same as seeing him play in the flesh. Mario echoed these sentiments: "I can't play like I used to, but you should have seen me hace años [years ago]." While not the only setting in which old-timers felt their age, the physical games and spirited commentary amplified the dilemma of "getting old." The men both honored and ridiculed old age—an attitude reflected in the shifting meaning of viejito. In some cases, the taunt was a mark of respect; in other cases, an expression of mockery.

Telling stories thus became a way to cope with the anxiety of aging. Soccer had a "referential afterlife" at the park that kept the men's histories alive and well.[18] In fact, I knew many men as soccer players only through these tales. Men could be great in the games, but also in the narratives woven around them. By claiming that the past was far superior to the present, old-timers attempted to regain control over how they were remembered. Coaching and championing the next generation also became a way to impart and solidify a legacy.[19] For example, although Motor still had his moments on the field, his identity as a soccer player mainly lived on in story form. As old-timers reminisced about Motor's boundless energy in his youth, the origin of his nickname became clear to others, who compared his stamina on the field to that of some of the more energetic younger players. As a coach, he invoked his past to motivate his players and silence his critics. His association with current park stars like Chepe and Ivan also bolstered his authority. Thanks to these stories and relationships, Motor was regarded as someone with a soccer history worthy of respect, despite his potbelly and increasingly rare appearances on the field.

For Motor and others, part of the game's appeal was in gaining a place in the collective memory of this community. By playing and reminiscing, they sought to construct a self that would be remembered. They came to play *and* to talk soccer. For many, these discussions recovered a past that was harder for them to memorialize in other settings. Unable to live on through written accounts, they were able to do so through oral history. The occupations of working-class men such as those at the park offer scant institutional memory. Indeed, many of them are living and working without documentation, which makes them doubly removed from formal organizations. Hope for the next generation also spoke to the "immigrant bargain" many had struck when leaving their homelands.[20] By aligning themselves with players "born in the park," they gave greater meaning to their own hardships and sacrifices. Over time, the park soccer games became a way to achieve some sense of immortality in their lives. As such, old-timers made sure that newcomers knew about this history, challenging those who tried to ignore or gloss it over. Through soccer and their relationships at the park, they acquired a history.

What They Do When They Play

I often asked the men what they liked about playing and watching soccer in the park. They found the question difficult to answer. Words escaped them or failed to capture how they felt about the midday games. Most responded with some version of "it's fun" (es divertido) and spoke of their time at the park as a welcome break (descanso) from the rest of their lives, a place where they could unwind and forget about their troubles. As César put it, "Le quita el estrés." (It's stress relieving.) For Beavis, playing soccer was "un medio de olvidar todo lo que está a mi alrededor" (a means of forgetting everything that's around me). And for Pachanga, it was an experience that left him feeling "más despejado en mi cabeza" (more clear-headed and mentally relaxed). But whenever I pressed this line of questioning, most men cut it short by replying, "Ya sabes" (you know what I mean), and by reminding me that soccer was a passion we all shared. The truth seemed obvious to them and lay in the doing, not in questions or answers.

I gradually gained an appreciation for what the men meant by "ya sabes" and why they seemed to find my interview-based approach so puzzling. For them, soccer in the park mattered because it was grounded in action and a collective history. Playing together provided a constant stock of characters, drama, and shared moments to discuss and debate, discussions that framed the significance of stepping onto the field together. For the men, there was a sense that this was fun far beyond the simple pleasure of physical exercise and the excitement of scoring goals. As Locksmith explained, merely putting a ball in a net meant nothing if the action was separated from the men's histories, identities, and relationships. Instead, the soccer games in the park and the stories the men constructed around them served as a framework for building a life together. César eloquently captured the game's more basic role in connecting the men: "No matter what you do in life or work, at that moment we share the same thought: disfrutar el fútbol y ganarle al contrario [to enjoy soccer and beat the other team]."

For Pachanga, there was something natural and seamless about this process:

Tulio and Motor saw me playing and when we finished, they called me. "¡Ven, güey!" [Come here, dude!] "Where are you from, compa [pal]?"

"Chilango, I'm Mexican, from Mexico City."

"You play well, we are Salvadorans, nearly all of us. Do you want to play with us on Sundays?"

"The truth is that I don't have a car."

"We'll go and pick you up."

That's when I learned about this place, y aquí estoy [and here I am].

Pachanga grew up playing soccer but had yet to find a game in Los Angeles that accommodated his schedule and interests, so he was thrilled to find the matches at Mar Vista. In showing off his skills and passion, he also found a community of like-minded men who were keen to include him on their team and in the social life that accompanied it. Years later, Pachanga is still a fixture of park life, even though he readily admits that by his late forties, he no longer plays as well as he used to. But over time, Pachanga's relationships with the men and his connection to the park had transcended the game. For him and the others, the park games offered not only a sense of belonging, but also new meanings and possibilities as they moved through their life cycle as individuals. By enriching the games, they enriched themselves.

Soccer's importance to the men became clearer when the turf field was temporarily closed to install the fence. Rather than interrupt the games, players reconvened on the east end of the park. Yet only the most committed members of the group participated, whereas more peripheral members opted to wait for the field's reopening. But even though numbers fell and the quality of play declined, the games were characterized by the same excitement and intimacy. Moments of greatness abounded on the bumpy field and in the stories surrounding the games, with the matches and commentary continuing to enrich the other. Whether played on turf or dirt, soccer was about being together and taking pleasure in the social relations and memories generated by the activity.

Yet the park soccer games were not experienced the same way by everyone, nor was it always a carefree scene. Problems emerged and tensions persisted. As noted in the previous chapter, it took work to sustain the pickup games, which were under constant threat from newcomers, local residents, and park officials. Playing soccer created other difficulties as well, such as injuries or neglect of family and work obligations. Seeking reprieve from life's demands did not necessarily resolve them. Moreover, while heckling and critiquing was part of the fun, some found it tiresome and unpleasant. Hierarchies based on talent and toughness could lead some players to feel excluded and demeaned. And as much as stories kept old-timers' histories alive, aging could be a disheartening process heightened by the physicality of the game and the jagged edge of soccer talk. For these reasons, some men stayed away or participated only under certain conditions.

Associated with the soccer games were two other prominent park

activities—beer drinking and fighting—that could lead to greater problems and stigmatization. Yet, as with the soccer games, there was more to
those activities than could be understood from a distance. As we shall see
in the following chapters, fighting and drinking provided further opportunities for group life in ways similarly grounded in the men's interactions,
relationships, and histories, but also reaching beyond the park to other
parts of their lives.

3 * Para Convivir: Drinking Beer in the Park

It was early afternoon at the Mar Vista Recreation Center. As was usual at this time of day, a small group of men were sitting together around the cement picnic tables by the soccer field. The six of us were quietly recounting the midday matches when Zapata walked over and, feigning confusion, sharply asked: "Where are the chelas [beers]? ¡Tan seco aquí! [So dry here!]" He then quickly pulled out money from his pocket: "Here are my dos pesitos [two dollars]!" The men laughed, Polo mocking Zapata for his paltry contribution. Nevertheless, funds were slowly gathered for beers and given to Roberto, the treasurer of many such gatherings.

Roused from their post-game lethargy, Polo and Locksmith each provided three dollars, and the men praised Raul for his ten-dollar contribution. Locksmith joked, "I like your new job," alluding to Raul's steady plumbing gig. Pasmado as usual was sitting quietly during collection time. Several dollars short for an eighteen-pack of Modelo, Polo pressured him to contribute. When Pasmado, an intermittently employed house painter from Chihuahua, Mexico, pleaded poverty, a frustrated Polo berated him for never having money, adding the proverbial park insult: "¡Busca trabajo!" (Look for work!) Announcing the arrival of Taco, Roberto told Polo "to relax," as their problems appeared to be solved. Taco typically arrived around this time after his shift as an orderly at a nearby hospital. Luckily for the group, Taco was usually looking for a beer after work and normally contributed a few dollars to the cause. In any case, the men enjoyed the Peruvian's quirky ways and easygoing company. By contrast, the group ignored other potential sources of revenue scattered around the park, at least at this early stage of the collection process. Roberto waved the handful of bills in Taco's direction and, as expected, the steadily employed park regular made up the difference. Mi Chavo, who had joined the growing circle of thirsty men, was sent to buy the beer, biking the well-traveled six blocks to the Rite Aid convenience store, a trek that usually earned him a beer or two. Mi Chavo welcomed the opportunity to contribute since he was short on money and currently sleeping in the park.

When Mi Chavo returned, he placed the cold beers inside a steel garbage can, which was where the men typically stored their stash. Under Polo's control, the beers were distributed, including to some who had not contributed financially, like Mi Chavo. Two men who earlier that day had told me they did not wish to drink—one because he was "crudo" (hungover), the other because he hoped to finish a small construction job—accepted Polo's offer anyway. Barba declined, reminding the men that his afternoon shift at a nearby supermarket was approaching, and Martín, a well-known abstainer, was as usual passed over as beers were handed out.

After taking a long drink from his beer, Polo grudgingly tossed Pasmado a can he had hidden under his jacket, although not without again defaming his character, advising him to "go paint something" if he wished to continue drinking with the men. Pasmado discreetly winked at me, presumably in light of our earlier conversations about drinking "for free" at the park. David, who had recently joined the circle and had also not put in any money, shouted over to Polo: "Give me a beer, mi amor [sweetheart]." The guys whistled in appreciation as Polo pointed to the familiar hiding spot. Unlike less dependable contributors, the steadily employed airline mechanic was a reliable sponsor of the men's drinking. And like Taco, the Salvadoran added a touch of prestige to the gathering. Polo eventually looked over in my direction as I sat empty-handed and playfully reminded me: "If you're not a borracho [drunk], look for another park to study."

Drinks in hand, the men's talk intensified in tempo and tenor. It was difficult to be heard above the growing chatter as the men drank around the picnic tables. A range of topics were discussed and familiar stories retold, most centering on park life. That particular afternoon, what elicited the greatest interest and speculation was the recent absence from the park of Filemón, Polo's so-called lover.

The men generally concealed their beers as they socialized by hiding the can under a shirt or in a bag or by transferring the beer into a plastic bottle. As soon as the beer arrived, Enrique quietly removed himself from the group. The previous week he had been issued a drinking ticket by a police officer, even though he had not been drinking in the park at the time. With his pool-cleaning route reduced to a half-dozen homes, the old-timer could not afford another $185 misdemeanor citation. Yet, as was often the case, several nondrinkers, including Barba and Martín, remained with the group.

As the men moved from debating park players to discussing Manchester United's Chicharito, Motor—who was sitting alone on a picnic table roughly a hundred feet away—yelled out: "¡La jura, la chota!" The guys scrambled to hide the beer, and some darted away from the group. Sure enough, a police car appeared from behind a building and entered the park. There was dead silence as the men feigned innocence and pretended to ignore the passing cruiser. Several of the drinkers were hiding beer cans under their shirts or between their legs. A few also had marijuana on them (and potentially other illegal substances), and it was well known that Morgan was on probation. Many of the men did not possess valid identification, and there was no way to know how the police would respond or what they would uncover if they interrogated them. These questions would for the time being go unanswered as the police drove slowly through the park without stopping. With a collective sigh of relief, the men returned to their beers.

*

I observed many such drinking sessions at the park. The men I spent time with regularly assembled in the park to socialize and unwind after they played soccer or watched park or league games. Men on break or done with a day's work also joined in, and these lively gatherings could last for hours as men cycled in and out. Beer drinking played a pivotal role in generating and galvanizing these sociable interactions.

The men's drinking in this public park was not without problems or contradictions. It not only put the men at risk from the police, but also threatened their family and work relationships. Yet most men did not drink in the park to get drunk, and many socialized without drinking at all. By drinking beer with the men at the park and elsewhere, I sought to gain a deeper understanding of why the men put themselves at risk to be together and the practical problems they were trying to solve by drinking in the park. This chapter is a response to these questions. I found that the men drank to invigorate group life, which—for better or worse—provided friendship and feelings of self-worth. Out of seemingly very little, drinking together constructed an eventful, revealing life in the park, making it feel as if things were "happening." Moreover, the park—in contrast to more conventional and lawful settings—emerged as the most respectable, engrossing, and convenient place for the men to drink.[1]

I focused my attention on beer drinking because of its prominence and because I could participate firsthand as a fellow drinker, whereas my knowledge of other intoxicants, primarily marijuana, was more secondhand. As with soccer, sharing a beer with the men was initially a way to become part of the group and explain my presence. Joining in the prohibited consumption of beer was a way for newcomers like me to put the men at ease. But like many scholars who "stumble" upon the subject, it soon became a research focus in itself.[2] The prominence of beer drinking was difficult to ignore or avoid, as Polo was keen to remind me in the opening vignette. Like the men, I drank to participate in group life and—with important differences—my regular park drinking presented its share of pleasures and problems within and beyond the dynamic setting.

Park Drinking in a World of Limited Options

The previous chapters on soccer play focused primarily on what happened at the park. For context and perspective, this chapter looks beyond the park to other drinking sites in the men's lives—namely, bars and private residences. As I gradually discovered, these sites proved unsatisfying, impractical, even dangerous for many of the men when compared with socializing and drinking beer in the park.

While legal consumption in cantinas (bars catering to working-class Latinos) could present a similar social appeal, collecting funds for store-bought beer made drinking in the park far more affordable, even though it was prohibited and could lead to hefty fines.[3] And, as suggested in the opening vignette, token participation could result in drinking well beyond one's own financial contribution. Moreover, unlike in a commercial establishment, one could socialize with the group at the park without consuming or drink there without spending money if funds were short. Other gatekeeping measures (such as ID cards, dress codes, and door fees) were also absent from the park. As I explain later, the potential for becoming embroiled in conflict with strangers also made bars far more precarious and threatening places. In particular, the presence of women in bars changed the dynamics of drinking. Drunken behavior, such as making a scene or falling asleep, was generally less tolerated in bars and could be the cause of serious trouble, including getting assaulted, robbed, or arrested. The park—although not without threats and problems—offered relative safety and flexibility, primarily because the men had more control over the setting and generally looked out for one another.

On my occasional visits to bars with the men, I developed a sense of how cantinas differed from the park. The following field note taken over the course of one day illustrates how similar behaviors were more viable and manageable in the park than in commercial establishments:

> As usual when he was drinking, Mario both entertained and annoyed his drinking partners. He was certainly living up to his park nickname Tamagás, one of Central America's most venomous snakes. This afternoon he was criticizing a handful of men from the park who, in his opinion, worked like "burros" for little pay and with scant future prospects. Chango, one of Mario's targets, implored him to "give it a rest" and in a mocking tone asked him: "When are you going back to Honduras?" As his compatriot had no doubt anticipated, Mario jumped at the implication that his long-standing

talk of return to his native country was "pura hablada" (empty talk). Mario responded by criticizing Chango's infatuation with "making money" and told him that if he didn't like his opinion, he could go elsewhere. Chango happily accepted Mario's suggestion and joined a different group of men playing dominoes nearby.

Emboldened by Chango's exit, Mario shifted his attention to Polo, whom he claimed was mismanaging the midday soccer games. When Polo retorted that the old-timer was past his prime and urged him to "retire" from the game, Mario snatched one of Polo's soccer shoes from the picnic table and kicked it high in the air. After the shoe dropped to the ground, Mario ceremoniously declared: "Look, I still got it!" And in a sarcastic manner, he asked: "Can I keep playing?" When Motor told him to pick up the shoe before Polo gave him "una puteada" (a beating), Mario turned his wrath on the park coach, contending that he knew even less than Polo. Motor laughed off the insult and muttered: "Pinche viejo Catracho [fucking Honduran old-timer] thinks he can play on my team. ¡Estás loco! [You're crazy!]" Mario reminded Motor that he had been one of his first league players when nobody believed in his coaching and that he had played for a winning team in a park tournament only a few years earlier. However, he did concede that his time was probably past as he stroked his graying hair and let out his signature crackle.

Mario eventually picked up Polo's shoe and theatrically wiped off the dirt before tossing it back to him. Polo inspected the shoe and advised Mario to "call Kathy," who helped Mario and several other men from the park when they were down on their luck. Mario laughed off the familiar suggestion, but soon left the group to sit by Pikachu and his brother on the grass. Mario took several hits of marijuana offered by Pikachu and promptly fell asleep by the two brothers from Oaxaca. Motor, who was now playing dominoes with Chango, reflected on the predictable development: "Por fin, lo noqueó" (finally, it knocked him out), the "it" presumably in reference to the beer, weed, and excitement.

Mario's behavior when drinking followed a rhythm the men knew all too well. When intoxicated, he regularly challenged the men and jumped at any perceived slight. Deeply knowledgeable of others, his insults were skillfully personalized and stinging. But his companions rarely took real offense and knew that they could generally "wait him out" before the drink and commotion "knocked him out." Most also viewed Mario's drunken spells as a performance that masked a core of decency they had come to know over the years. In any case, his theatrics were an entertaining "part of the show," as one reluctant admirer put it. Mario, for his part, anticipated that the men would read his behavior in the manner he intended—as provocative yet playful—so long as he stayed within limits. And only rarely did this backfire and lead to hurt feelings or physical confrontations. The ease with which Mario fell asleep in the park among the group of men also revealed his comfort and familiarity with the drinking scene.

Other drinking sites in the men's lives did not prove as accommodating or as protective. Later that evening, I observed firsthand how differently Mario's antics played out away from the park:

Around nightfall, I accompanied a revived Mario and three other men to a nearby bar-restaurant to watch a televised boxing match. As they drank in the park, the men had debated whether or not to go, but several agreed when Vino Tinto offered to drive and to pick up the tab. In any case, they wanted to see the Pacquiao-Márquez rematch.

As soon as we entered the Latino-run business, Mario succeeded in annoying a bartender and several patrons who were waiting to watch the fight. After admonishing the bartender for having only one small working television, Mario made unwanted conversation with a patron sitting on a bar stool, almost knocking over the man's beer in the process. Tío whispered in my ear: "Watch out, we're going to have some problems." He later likened Mario's entrance to that of a hurricane.

Vino Tinto bought Mario a beer and urged him to settle down, but as in the park, he refused to take orders. As Tío predicted, problems quickly surfaced between Mario and the patron he had collided with earlier, who grew increasingly impatient with him for yelling and blocking his view of the television. He initially addressed Tío, hoping he would control his "compa" (pal), but this seemed only to provoke Mario, who turned toward him and said, "He's not my father. Speak to me if you have a problem." The customer, who appeared twenty years younger than fifty-three-year-old Mario, replied that he didn't want to "beat up an old man," but would do so if he continued to bother him. Mario tried to make light of the situation by saying that he came to watch a fight, not fight himself, but nonetheless told the younger man to "go to church" if he didn't like how he was behaving. Mario turned back toward us and cracked another joke at the man's expense: "That's why I got divorced, so I don't have anyone telling me what to do."

Visibly incensed, the man stepped down from his stool and moved toward Mario, but two bartenders intervened before he could make good on his threat. One of the bartenders told Mario to leave and pleaded with us to remove him. Mario at first resisted calls to go. But as his companions moved toward the door, he relented when it was clear he would have to fend for himself.

As I learned on this occasion and others, drinking in commercial establishments posed threats and challenges that were more easily avoided or managed at the park. Not surprisingly, the stranger at the bar had interpreted Mario's antics not as playful and harmless, but instead as annoying and threatening and requiring an aggressive response. Mario was fortunate that problems had not escalated, thanks largely to his level-headed allies. When I asked Tío why he left, he confirmed my suspicion that he had preferred to remove himself from the difficult situation Mario had created: "No se meta [You shouldn't get involved] with those guys. But he doesn't learn, it's always the same with him. Why should I fight over his pendejadas [bullshit]?"

I regularly witnessed "drunken" behavior at the park that would likely have been problematic in bars, such as yelling, fighting, stumbling around, falling asleep, and so on. As I learned firsthand and through their stories, the men were physically expelled from bars by unruly bouncers, robbed or assaulted by unknown assailants, and sometimes arrested by police officers for such conduct. Yet in the park, while "drunken comportment" was rare and only occasionally a source of problems, it was typically interpreted and controlled in ways that avoided more serious repercussions.[4] Using tactics unavailable or less feasible in commercial establishments, the men censured, but also assisted men who overstepped the bounds of acceptable park behavior when they were drinking, as the following field note shows:

The men were surprised to see Filemón drinking, as it had been over a year since he had stopped. As he fell in and out of sleep from the heavy drinking in the hot sun, it soon became evident that he was out of practice. At first the men cracked jokes at his expense, warning him, for example, that Polo "te va a chingar" (will screw with you) if he fell asleep. The men's tone shifted when the rotund man nearly toppled off the picnic table where he was precariously perched. When he failed to respond to their verbal pleas to "wake up," Motor shook him awake. Filemón opened his eyes and muttered "yes, yes" as he rubbed his face and looked around, a wry smile concealing a hint of embarrassment. After regaining his bearings, he playfully insulted the men for voicing their concerns and repeated several times, "I'm fine, I'm fine." Stepping away from the table and stumbling toward the bathroom, he warned the men: "I'm coming back, culeros [assholes]."

The men whistled and jeered as Filemón lumbered across the grass toward the portable toilet. They roared with laughter when an errant Frisbee came close to hitting him. Yet when Filemón went to reach for the fallen Frisbee in order to throw it back to a trio of young White men playing catch, Motor hurried over to intervene. As Filemón struggled to pick up the Frisbee, Motor grabbed him by the waist and pushed him away from the approaching Frisbee players. He then veered away from the toilet toward Filemón's car in the parking lot. As the interlocked men walked, someone shouted, "Vivan los novios" (Long live the couple), although all seemed to understand and embrace Motor's intentions. Polo muttered: "Good idea, Motor. Put him to sleep!"

*

Drinking as a group in the men's homes was equally rare because it tended to be problematic. Many men told me that they were uncomfortable inviting their friends from the park to their homes to spend time around their families or roommates, especially given crowded living conditions and lack of outdoor space. Uncomplicated features of park drinking (such as using the bathroom, making noise, and wearing dirty work or sweaty soccer attire) also proved tricky in the men's homes. For those in relationships, many spoke of the home as the moral domain of their wife or girlfriend, who were invariably upset by their drinking.[5] Guests also expressed discomfort with drinking in people's homes, preferring the park, where everyone felt "más cómodo" (more comfortable). Pachanga explained the challenges of socializing in the cramped apartment he shared with his three roommates:

> Most people come here to distraerse de la casa [to get away from home]— people like me who live with two families. One family is an elderly couple, the other a single lady. I arrive and they are in the living room watching television, and I say [to myself], "¿Qué hago aquí?" [What am I doing here?]

Whom to invite into one's home and whom to exclude could also be a delicate matter. This was less an issue in the open and spacious park where the men could gloss over some of the challenges of commitment and friendship that arose with more restricted social gatherings. In any case, part of the appeal of the park was time away from family members and domestic responsibilities. Many of the men also attempted to conceal their drinking from family members or at least minimize it. For example, Peru de Oaxaca confided to me: "I don't want my daughters to get worried seeing me drunk. It's better I do it here at the park, where they think I'm just playing soccer." However, he admitted that his wife knew better. And even though drinking at the park could be a source of tension (as I explain later), the men's partners seemed to prefer for the men to drink at Mar Vista than in bars, where the threats were greater—especially from violence or infidelity. When I talked to the women about the park, they also explained that they appreciated knowing where to find their partners, even though most of them detested park drinking. Some of these tensions and challenges played out when David uncharacteristically invited a few men to his home to watch a soccer match:

When we arrived at David's home, his wife didn't seem particularly pleased to see us. Holding two eighteen-packs of beer, David explained that he was home to watch a game. She exhaled deeply but greeted us with a half-smile and retreated to the back patio. We settled in the living room, where David's two young children periodically joined us. Barba soon appeared with two uninvited men from the park and said that he thought several more guys were headed over. I could sense that David was irritated. He even joked about not sending out invitations and questioned why they hadn't at least brought beer. Five more men eventually arrived, all of whom David reluctantly welcomed into his home. By midway through the first half, eleven men from the park were watching the game in the small living room.

David was visibly upset by this incident. As he confided to me afterward, he was angry that people showed up uninvited and acted disrespectfully in his home. He complained that the men failed to clean up after themselves and expected him to offer them beer and food. He also resented the men's loud and vulgar conversations because he knew his neighbors would be unhappy with the noise. More importantly, the men's presence created problems with his wife and children, who didn't like the "borrachos del parque" (park drunks) in their home.

Several men shared similar tales of men drinking in their homes and disturbing their domestic arrangements. Two notable tales involved one man who took a shower without asking and another who urinated on a couch when he fell asleep. However, people who heard these stories were rarely sympathetic, since it was generally considered unwise to invite the park into one's home and family life.

*

As these incidents suggest, the men drank in the park because of limited options elsewhere. In fact, many of the men told me that they *only* drank in the park. As one man claimed, "I don't go out at night and drink; this is the only time I can get away and have some fun." And while some men did frequent cantinas—more for the music, privacy, and female company not found at the park—most of them preferred the park as a drinking site. Moreover, as many of the men lived scattered throughout the region but worked nearby, the park provided a central meeting place to socialize and play soccer. A key appeal of the park was the expectation of encountering friendly drinking partners, including abstainers, who were even less likely to visit bars. The park thus emerged as the most respectable, forgiving, and economical place to meet and drink together—a fact that may seem counterintuitive to those who wonder why the men did not drink legally at home or in bars. Yet structural inequalities and the men's limited drinking options only partly explain their marked preference for drinking in the park. As suggested in the opening vignette, the social appeal of drinking beer with others pushed them to regularly consume in *this* park.

Drinking as Social Activity

Drinking was central to social life at the park and far more than a strategic way to consume alcohol. Beer drinking, like playing soccer, served as something engrossing to do with others. The men spent hours upon hours in the park, whether on a day off from work or during a long stretch of unemployment. With few suitable alternatives, they came to the park in the hope of being taken in by the scene. When this failed to happen, the men could become frustrated and disappointed. Returning to the opening vignette, one man left before Zapata arrived with his "dos pesitos" for beer because, as he put it, "the park is dead." Regardless of the circumstances that took them to the park, the men recognized that "doing something" and "being together" required work and could not be taken for granted. While the men occupied themselves through a range of activities at the park besides soccer—such as reading the newspaper, fixing cars, or playing cards—drinking beer was a favorite and prominent leisure activity there.

The men appeared to prefer drinking over other activities because of its social effects.[6] Drinking beer tended to generate and sustain the sociable interactions that the men were seeking. And alcohol need not be consumed in large amounts to change the atmosphere. In fact, few men became noticeably intoxicated, and most drinking sessions involved a mix of drinkers and abstainers. Like a self-fulfilling prophecy, alcohol tended to enhance sociability regardless of the amount consumed. As we have seen in the opening scene, when beer arrived there was the sense that something was "happening"—that the men were part of an occasion that justified being together. In contrast, the absence of beer often signaled obstacles to sociability, such as lack of money, the presence of police, or an incompatible gathering of people.

For those searching for affiliation and interaction, drinking helped kickstart this project. Akin to Jack London's memorable claim that he was "no longer a stranger in any town the moment [he] entered the saloon," shared beers provided an almost unquestioned rationale for being together.[7] People need to feel that something is "going on," and drinking afforded that feeling of eventfulness out of seemingly very little. Consider, for example, the following scene from the park:

As Chicharito passed a half-dozen men sitting around the picnic tables, Polo shouted out: "Where are you going, Chicharito? Come, have a beer."[8] Several of Polo's companions laughed at the sarcastic park nickname as the young man was not a very good soccer player. Chicharito replied that he was headed home but welcomed the detour as he had the day off from work. Polo told Motor to give him a beer, joking that he had recruited a new "galáctico" (superstar) for his team. Chicharito blushed, knowing he wasn't good enough for Motor's team, but accepted the beer and sat down with the others. Polo explained to the newcomer that the guys gathered after the games to drink beer and that he was welcome to join them. To this, Roberto interjected: "Si traes feria" (if you bring money), but quickly added: "Don't worry, there's no peligro [danger] here. Just La Pola," feminizing Polo's name for comic effect.

As the men drank and conversed, Chicharito learned more about park life. He was told about the game's history and the pleasures and perils of park life—a discussion that, as always, generated amusement and controversy. The men also learned about Chicharito: where he was from, where he worked, his family situation, and so on. The beer eventually ran out and discussions about gathering funds for the next beer run ensued. Although Roberto did not directly ask him for money, Chicharito took out a twenty-dollar bill from his wallet and handed it to Roberto, which was far more than anyone else contributed. Polo smiled widely and remarked to the group: "See, I only invite los buenos [the good ones]."

In this way, beer served to welcome a newcomer into the group and created a situation for the men to be together and share information, massaging or concealing concerns or emotions that could threaten or delay interaction. For his part, Chicharito signaled a willingness to socialize with the men by accepting the offer, which he reaffirmed by providing ample funds to purchase additional beer to keep the interaction going. Months later, Chicharito confided to me that before he found the park, he had not made many friends in Los Angeles besides a few work acquaintances. A craving for companionship pushed him to play in the games and later to accept Polo's offer to drink with the men. Like many others, Chicharito was not searching for friends to drink with, but found that drinking helped form new friendships.[9]

Beer drinking worked as a social catalyst because it provided a reliable narrative to structure and sustain sociable interactions. In general, inviting someone for a beer or yelling out "here are my dos pesitos" was enough to initiate a drinking session, which led to a series of scripts and dramas that could sustain the men's socializing for hours. As described in the opening vignette, this included recurring controversies concerning the collection of funds and distribution of beer, as well as the more mundane tasks of opening, concealing, drinking, and disposing of the cans. These activities were collective projects with built-in opportunities for sociability and collaboration repeated day after day at the park. Most importantly, sharing a beer established the expectation of time spent together, which men rarely violated by taking a beer and drinking it elsewhere.

Like the timed soccer matches that often came first, drinking also established a set time to be together, which meant that the men need not hang around awkwardly, waiting for some script of conduct to emerge. However, drinking proved more inclusive than soccer; it was something everyone could participate in, even if many abstained. Drinking also tended to work on a slower narrative arc than the soccer matches, allowing the men to be together for longer. Despite police patrols, the men tended to drink slowly, preferring to revel in the social interaction brought about by drinking.

Beer drinking also allowed the men to be together without appearing to look for camaraderie—a less intrusive means of interaction through which friendship could follow. Zapata, for example, offered money for beer to frame his arrival, even if his intentions were geared more toward socializing with the men than necessarily consuming alcohol. Similarly, Polo used beer to welcome Chicharito instead of an invitation simply to chat. And by offering Roberto the first beer from the communal haul, he paid tribute to their long-standing friendship. Even abstainers demonstrated an appreciation for the social function of beer drinking by occasionally chipping in funds or bringing a twelve-pack to the park.

The implicit understanding of the role of drinking in the park was made clear in the general disdain for consuming "alone," a practice the men viewed as deviant and antisocial.[10] Few men enjoyed drinking by themselves, which in part explains why they came to the park and pressured others to participate, even if this meant awarding "free" beer for continued companionship. Drinking privately was certainly more cost effective and predictable, but inebriation was not the primary motivation for consuming beer in the park. "Toma solos" (solo drinkers) violated the social significance of drinking with others in the park by suggesting that the consumption of alcohol was an end in itself. Only the few genuine borrachos del parque were left alone when drinking from a private stash, since it was understood that they were physically dependent on alcohol and usually low on funds. Indeed, it was by drinking alone that "toma solos" distinguished themselves as real "drunks." Despite the playful use of "borracho" and various alcohol-related park nicknames (Vino Tinto, Chupón, Pachanga, Michelada, Portero de Budweiser), most men drank to participate in group life. Refusing an invitation to drink did not so much indicate a weakness for alcohol as it did a reluctance to socialize with the others.

For moderate drinkers like Beavis, drinking was a way to participate in the "ambiente" (scene):

Yo no tomo. [I don't drink.] I drink a beer sometimes, but not because I want to, but instead to share in the scene they create. They do not pressure me to drink. Pero para sentirme parte del mismo ambiente de ellos, agarro una cerveza o dos. [But to feel part of the group, I grab a beer or two.]

The men's choice of beer spoke to the communal and ritualized nature of park drinking. During my fieldwork, the men generally drank Modelo, a relatively expensive Mexican lager. They told me that they preferred Modelo because of its taste and effect, but having a settled "park beer" also reduced disagreements over what to purchase. Those arriving with cold Modelos to the park revealed their understanding and connection to local customs. And beer, while still intoxicating, slowed down the process of inebriation, in contrast to stronger, even cheaper substances. As with childhood soccer, many men connected their drinking practices to memories of their fathers and uncles drinking in similar ways in Latin America and Los Angeles.[11]

The men almost always bought cases of twelve-ounce bottles or cans of beer to be shared with others at the park, which also reflected the social appeal of beer drinking. This contrasted with the practice of purchasing "caguamas" (one-liter bottles of beer) that are more typically consumed individually. Yet when I followed several men to informal day-laborer spots, I regularly observed them drinking caguamas with other men. They explained that, in that context, they drank individually from larger bottles because they rarely lingered or socialized for long periods of time. And because the men were typically less familiar with others on "la esquina" (the corner), sharing beers with relative strangers was a risky proposition.[12] While more economical and sociable, sharing with strangers opened up tricky questions about payment, distribution, and consumption, as well as personal responsibility if the authorities were to arrive in the midst of an ever-changing group of people. This was borne out by a conversation I had with Coloccini following his failed attempt to find employment on the periphery of an organized day-laborer center in West Los Angeles. When I asked him why he purchased a forty-ounce bottle of Miller High Life rather than pooling money for a twelve-pack of beer, he bluntly replied: "I don't drink with people I don't know," and a caguama, as opposed to un doce (a twelve-pack), was not something that was shared. In contrast to beer consumption in the park, while drinking on "the corner," security and alcohol intake took precedence over building social relationships.

While the men did not always encounter their favorite drinking partners at the park, there was usually someone there willing to share a beer or pool money to buy a twelve-pack. My fieldwork revealed a similar relationship among marijuana smokers. Individuals with limited leisure time due to work schedules or family commitments were especially likely to trade beer for conversation, and any loosely identified group member would generally suffice. The days of the week were in fact distinguishable by who typically arrived with drinking plans, which also reflected work and family obligations that otherwise kept the men away from the park or abstaining if they were there. Taco, for example, generally had a window after work before picking up his son from school to drink a beer or two at the park. And Mondays were often heavier drinking occasions because many restaurant workers had the day off. Independent contractors also took "vacation days" between jobs, as they liked to joke, although not always by choice.

As a result of these diverse schedules, there was usually a contingent of men at the park hoping to socialize. Jokes about men not leaving the park because of the abundance of beer and good times reflected this steady cycle of arrivals. And while men like Pasmado were occasionally ridiculed for not contributing financially and goaded to "look for work," they played a crucial role in park drinking. Their consistent park presence meant that others need not drink alone.[13] Pinocho (Pinocchio, nicknamed for his big nose) explained the social attraction of drinking with others in these terms:

Al borracho no le gusta tomar solo. Al borracho no le importa gastar, comprar; lo que él quiere es emborracharse él y emborrachar al otro que esté con él, haciéndole compañía porque si no, va a estar solo. O sea, tiene que estar otro igual que lo pueda entender y al mismo nivel de alcohol. El borracho toma acompañado.

(The drunkard doesn't like to drink alone. He doesn't mind spending or buying; what he wants is to get drunk and to get the others who are with him drunk, keeping him company because otherwise he will be alone. That is, there needs to be someone like him who is equally drunk and can understand him. The drunk drinks in the company of others.)

The desire to socialize with others was especially pronounced when the men had reason to celebrate, such as a birthday, a lucrative day at work, or a nice goal during a soccer game. The men's lives provided a variety of reasons to celebrate—even to mark the end of a difficult day.

Twenty or so dollars for beer represented a reasonable price for company and recognition. In contrast, there was tremendous disappointment when plans to rejoice or lament, backed up with a few cases of beer, failed to materialize. Failed "borracheras" (drunken parties) could even be taken as social slights, indicating that others did not value one's accomplishments or friendship. A few park veterans also criticized the new generation for their more restricted park gatherings, especially the youngsters on Motor's league team, most of whom were born in Los Angeles. With more opportunities to socialize away from the park, they felt less committed to the old-timers' more open-ended drinking practices. For the most part, however, there were usually men willing and able to celebrate one's achievements and milestones, especially if surplus beer was provided. Indeed, a major appeal of gatherings at the park was that others would be present and feel obligated to participate.

I felt the galvanizing power of "celebrations" firsthand when I returned to the park a year after moving away from Los Angeles:

> The instant Polo saw me walking toward the field, he began organizing a post-game party to commemorate my return. Polo pressured everyone he saw to put in money "for David." Most men contributed a few dollars as they warmly welcomed me back, although some questioned Polo's motives and asked how much he had put in. Polo joked that he was jealous of all my "novios" (boyfriends) at the park and commented that when he himself had grounds to celebrate, "nadie trae nada" (no one brings anything). Several men responded that this was because he was always at the park.

My homecoming, along with many other park happenings, sparked a celebration. Polo used my return to generate funds and enthusiasm for a festive social gathering. Others, for their part, responded to Polo's requests as an opportunity to communicate their affection and connection to me, although the prospects of a party presumably also motivated their contributions. As Polo predicted, money was raised, people participated, and a celebration was produced. With scores of affiliated men, it was rare for a week or two to go by without some sort of similar beer-infused party at the park.

These patterned drinking sessions regularly transformed individual and group events—such as birthdays, promotions, or league championships—into moments of park lore and communal memory recounted for years to come, often while drinking. A memorable experience of my own was when the men threw a festive baby shower for my wife and me the day before our son was born, which became a tellable story for the group every time I brought him to the park. As in the celebration prompted by my homecoming or in the more everyday scene depicted in the opening vignette, drinking played an important role in sustaining interactions at the park, whether between longtime friends or new acquaintances.

Drinking Friendships

Beer drinking at the park was about much more than simply having fun and passing the time. Drinking offered the men opportunities to express their "real self."[14] Letting down one's guard could reveal things about the self that were usually hidden, creating special knowledge known only to the group. Men frequently confided to me that they could not control themselves when they drank—"me pierdo" (I lose myself)—and suggested that I was seeing "la verdad" (the truth) when I drank with them. Men also described how others disclosed their true feelings when under the influence—or "at the same level," as Pinocho put it. For example, Roberto told me that he took no offense to Polo's criticisms of his refereeing during the midday games because "he'll tell me he loves me when he's drinking." The men's affection for one another was more pronounced when they were drinking and was often expressed through playful shoves and insults, such as when Filemón referred to the men as "assholes" in the exchange discussed earlier. The men hardly needed to be intoxicated to send messages to each other encoded in the kidding around they did when drinking. In the opening excerpt, David referred to Polo as "mi amor" (my love) when requesting his first beer, just as Martín, a longtime abstainer, freely participated in the "drunken" banter.

Traits of character emerged when the men drank together because these occasions were understood as generating "fateful moments."[15] "Drinking" was a taken-for-granted euphemism at the park that framed and created "news," in ways that drinking water or coffee did not. Consumption of alcohol together transformed the park into a place "where the action is."[16] In fact, to make sense of strange behavior, the men often asked others if they were drunk. ("¿Estás pedo?") For example, when Motor unexpectedly snapped at Barba, he searched for clarification before responding in kind: "¿Qué onda, güey? ¿Estás pedo o qué?" (What's up dude? Are you drunk or what?) Likewise, men needed to know if people were "tomando" (drinking) to fully understand the stories they recounted. Many members of the group were known for drinking behaviors that augmented or even contrasted sharply from their sober personas.

Some men explained to me that they avoided certain people when they were drinking because of potential problems. And people who didn't drink ("no toman") explained their current sobriety as a consequence of past problems with alcohol. To substantiate these claims, they shared dramatic tales of their intoxicated exploits, suggesting that they needed to keep at bay the deeper, "realer," and typically less responsible renditions of self that drinking could inadvertently unleash.[17] Whether any of this was actually true was beside the point as the men believed that alcohol chipped away at the "gloss" that usually hides one's true character.[18] Drinking was understood to dissolve the social self, bringing out what was underneath and presumably always there.

The men used this folk theory about drinking to meet the challenges of forging friendships. For example, Ali, who was particularly interested in my research project, suggested early on in English that if "you really want to be part of the crowd, show up drunk one day, really fucking drunk, and they'll say, '*This* is David.'" He also suggested I supply beer during my interviews if I wanted "real answers," implying that a willingness to get drunk in the company of the men showed both self-confidence and trust in the group in the most revealing of situations. "Dry" occasions, by contrast, did not provide the same opportunities for the men to expose to others what was most essential about themselves.

Beer Exchanges

Drinking as a group in the park not only revealed character, but also brought the men together in other ways. As the men regularly shared beers, how they contributed and reciprocated served to reveal personality and group standing. Offering beer without demanding immediate payment created ambiguity and uncertainty through which the men learned about each other. For example, when Darwin repeatedly disclosed that he had contributed fifty dollars to help pay for food and beer one Sunday afternoon, an exasperated Motor responded: "You should have put in a hundred dollars for all the times you ate and drank for free!" By calling attention so explicitly to his contribution, Darwin diminished its meaning, implying that this was indeed a rare occurrence. Besides Darwin, there were several other men known for rarely putting in money for beer, just as there were a handful of generous sponsors.

Beer served as a kind of common currency to establish reputation and credit within the group. Many of the men, for example, told me they did not recommend one individual for painting jobs because he "can't even put in two dollars for beer," as one person explained. Spending money on beer at the park was a sign of achievement and assuaged the anxieties of others about getting paid or recommending someone for jobs. If someone was given beer on "credit," it indicated to others that he was "good for it," as in the opening scene when Polo gave David (a steadily employed airlines mechanic) a "free" Modelo.

Along with its financial implications, offering free beers also sent messages about social standing. Chicharito, for example, was offered a beer to signal that he was welcomed into a more intimate sphere of park life, whereas Pasmado received a beer in a more delayed, less respectful manner to signal a less favorable position in the local hierarchy. Beer exchanges honored some men more than others depending on the prestige they gave the drinking occasion; and, as previously discussed, they ritualistically encoded social ties by giving symbolic expression to the men's relationships. "Si tienes muchos amigos y te llevas bien con todos," Pinocho quipped, "te emborrachas fácil sin dinero." (If you have many friends and you get along with them all, you can get drunk easily without money.)

Beer served as social currency in more mundane ways as well. In particular, gifted beers and the moral economy they generated played a crucial role in mobilizing drink exchanges. At the park, as in most settings, there was a moral obligation to reciprocate.[19] Gift-giving inevitably resulted in gift-getting. Repayments for treated beers, however, were rarely direct or quid pro quo—such as when buying rounds at a bar—but less structured and more informal. For example, men who drank beer provided by Chicharito's sizable contribution repaid his generosity in subsequent drinking sessions that did not necessarily include the newcomer, and they certainly did not reimburse him twenty dollars—a transaction that would have appeared absurd, even insulting. Moreover, most of the working-class men anticipated that, at some point, they would be on the other side of the exchange, and so they expected to be provided for in a later moment of need. In any case, the balance of debt was impossible to really know, especially since the men had traded rounds with a revolving cast of characters for years. As Marcel Mauss famously pointed out, gifts serve to connect people when reciprocation is imprecise and thus never-ending. In this way, the endless cycle of beer exchanges at the park bound the men together in an ever-evolving culture of open-ended reciprocation.[20] Consider the following interaction:

> When his turn came to contribute, Pachanga requested five dollars in return for a ten-dollar bill he held firmly in his hand. Several onlookers groaned and Roberto, in his customary treasurer role, pressured him to contribute the full ten dollars: "Come on Pachanga, we're all going to drink, dame diez [give me ten]." As Pachanga considered the appeal, Roberto upped the ante: "You always drink when you don't bring anything, ya sabes [you know]." Visibly perturbed by the accusation, Pachanga shifted attention to others: "I always put in. Why don't you ask the others?" Sensing that he was the target of Pachanga's pointed question, Valderrama interjected: "Don't start with me, I always put in, ask anybody. I just put in five dollars!" Pachanga responded in disbelief: "Five dollars? ¡No mames! [No way!] When?" Seemingly worried about the fire he was unintentionally stoking, Roberto told

Valderrama to ignore him as he hastily looked for five dollars among the crumpled bills he had collected. Pachanga shrugged off the gesture and left without collecting change, but warned Roberto and the others: "Don't ask me for anything more." But with a smile and true to his "party" nickname, he added: "Make sure the beers are cold!"[21]

The men regularly drew on a history of shared drinks to stake claims on "free" beer or to push others to contribute. These statements had implications for reputation and character, but they also motivated participation. Regardless of their day-to-day financial contributions, the men felt a moral right to participate equally as drinking partners.[22] Among this group, unequal financial exchanges did not create strong hierarchical barriers. The imprecision of debt and credit was crucial, as was the men's belief that the balance generally evened out over time. Moreover, some men spent far more than their drinking partners to keep the interaction going, just as others were recognized for their nonmonetary contributions through friendly conversation and sympathetic ears. Thus, when Roberto pressured Pachanga to give, he reminded him that his time on the receiving end had passed, but would undoubtedly return. In response, Pachanga told him not to ask for anything more, highlighting the fact that he had already given more than he initially intended, while displaying his trust that he would be treated again someday. Denying these obligations and expectations—or overdoing them as in Darwin's case—meant flouting the collective and open-ended nature of park drinking that proved so fulfilling and entertaining to its participants.

Drinking and Jobs

The men's drinking provided fun, solidarity, and friendships, but also created valuable opportunities for networking, professional and otherwise. Take, for example, what transpired later on in the gathering recounted at the beginning of this chapter:

> When Polo cracked open his third beer, Roberto urged him to slow down as his evening restaurant shift was approaching. Polo brushed off the advice, reminding Roberto that he always drank before work. He added that he would discreetly chew some fresh ginger if the manager approached. I asked him why he did this, and he explained that it masked the smell of alcohol. David added: "And it wakes the son of a bitch up!"
> Chaparro asked Polo where he was now working. After Polo gave the name of a popular Santa Monica restaurant, Chaparro asked if he knew of any job openings. Polo replied that they were always looking for "lavaplatos" (dishwashers). Chaparro expressed interest and stressed that he needed

"something." Always eager to ruffle Polo's feathers, David joked that he would be of little help, adding he was lucky to have the job himself. Titi piled on: "All he does is heat up soup in the microwave!" Polo dismissed the comments, telling Titi to "go paint toilets," in mocking reference to his profession. He countered that even though he was only a line chef, the head chef had asked him to suggest new menu items. To Polo's credit, the following week Chaparro was hired as a lunchtime dishwasher.

While his employment needs were presumably ever present in his thoughts, Chaparro's networking moment emerged spontaneously in the course of the social gathering. Shared drinks created a sociable situation in which Chaparro could learn about a possible position and leverage a job referral. His interest in the job, however, did not come across as forced or inappropriate, but emerged in the natural flow of the conversation. Social, not professional, interests motivated his participation. Moreover, as a familiar drinking companion, Chaparro had earned the right to interject freely in park talk. Polo, for his part, responded well to his request, especially as a way to burnish his reputation and counter the ribbing from others.

While drinking was framed as a "time-out" from the world of work, the subject of work frequently came up in conversations as the men drank.[23] This was not unusual or surprising, especially as job opportunities could prove so elusive for this group. While the men did not require alcohol to discuss work, shop talk was more likely to be heard and discussed while drinking together, as Chaparro was fortunate to discover.[24]

Establishing trust (confianza) was a pressing concern for the men; for at its most fundamental, networking involved giving tips to people whose actions affected their own reputations.[25] In middle- and upper-class communities, people often develop reputations through academic or professional networks and achievements. For these men, interactions around beer—such as who contributed, who repaid their debts, and how they handled their liquor—became local methods to measure and project creditworthiness. As stated earlier, the men's fascination with drinking beer together stemmed from bringing out the truth of who they "really are"—the implications of which are further explored in chapter 5, which deals with the men's work experiences. However, this process was not without complications, since it led to a series of problems that both threatened and galvanized their collective consumption.

Drinking Problems

Given how central drinking was to park life and to the men's relationships, the number of serious problems it produced was jarring. Most notably, alcohol consumption in this park was illegal. And while the law against public drinking applied equally to everyone, the men were subject to disproportionate surveillance because of who they were and where they were drinking. Although hard to verify, this heightened surveillance seemed to result from two interrelated factors: On the one hand, the historical frequency of their drinking in this park made it a well-known "problem" for the police and other park users; on the other, the men's marked and stigmatized presence in West Los Angeles rendered their drinking especially visible and problematic.[26]

Whatever the cause, the men were subject to periodic police patrols, including those that specifically targeted their drinking. In fact, it was rare to spend an entire day at the park without a police car driving slowly through the grounds. The presumption of drinking apparently provided justification for the police to interrogate the men at any time, a practice I observed many times when no one was even drinking. Over the course of my research, forty-four men claimed to have received at least one drinking ticket at this park, some several more, and one individual told me he collected nine citations over a twenty-five-year period. The men even joked that full membership in the group was not achieved until one received a drinking ticket, a change in status I can attest to after earning one myself.

While memories of arrests and group surveillance added a degree of excitement to the drinking, it also created stress and discomfort. As one man put it after a string of police interrogations, "There's no peace in the park." The men knew the consequences of getting caught by the police, who could strike at any moment and entrap even the most law-abiding and vigilant. Detainment led to police harassment and a $185 misdemeanor citation.[27] Due to the cost or to unfamiliarity with the legal system, some of the men did not pay the fine, which led to greater problems, including late fees and a possible warrant for their arrest. Consequently, the men generally encouraged others to pay, whether or not they had grounds to contest the charge. For example, nine men went ahead and paid what they claimed to be unwarranted drinking tickets.

Suspected alcohol consumption, which could ensnare anyone whether or not they were drinking, could lead to more serious legal problems. Some of the men had a range of prior offenses, paid and unpaid, that could increase the charges well beyond the cost of a drinking citation. One man, for example, was sent back to jail for six months for violating his parole by drinking in the park. Sometimes outstanding charges came as a surprise to the men, as in the case of another man, who—after receiving a ticket for drinking in the park—was stunned to find that he owed $500 in unpaid traffic tickets, which earned him a night in jail. It is therefore hardly surprising that the men feared something known or unknown might "pop up" if their name was run through the system, which only intensified the fear of being detained.[28]

In the course of an investigation, additional offenses could be discovered and charged. For example, several men were temporarily jailed for possession of small amounts of marijuana or cocaine after being apprehended for drinking beer.[29] I also witnessed three men without proper identification brought into the police station for fingerprinting. All were visibly intoxicated at the time of arrest and were released the following morning after they had sobered up.[30]

The fact that many of the men were in the United States without legal authorization certainly complicated the proceedings. However, most were able to establish their identity without being brought in for further questioning, whether or not they had some form of identification, such as a driver's license or matrícula consular.[31] In most cases, simply providing a name and address was enough to satisfy officers on the scene. Men who shared some form of valid identification with the police were more likely to receive a drinking citation than those who did not, presumably because the paperwork was easier to process. It seemed at the time that the police were unwilling or unable to process the undocumented individuals they encountered committing relatively minor offenses.[32] Tellingly, in 2013 the city of Los Angeles downgraded public drinking to a civil rather than criminal infraction.[33] The men claimed that this shift in policy led to a decline in the policing of their park drinking.

Nevertheless, the threat of deportation was always present, especially if a more serious crime was committed or suspected or if the men were dealing with a particularly obstinate police officer. However, few of the undocumented men were actually taken to the station for formal identification. And while I know of no one who was deported after being detained at the park, the men did consider it a real possibility, especially if they were somehow implicated in a more serious crime or if the political climate was to change in Los Angeles, as it did following Trump's election. Although the men claimed that the situation did not really change at Mar Vista following Trump's election, there was a more general, citywide fear of intensified policing of undocumented immigrants.

In one of the more upsetting and widely discussed events at the park—an event corroborated by over a dozen witnesses—Caballo was physically restrained by two police officers, who apparently felt he was "disobeying orders." My understanding is that Caballo was not drinking when the police arrived, but they nevertheless ordered him to leave the park. And when the prideful Honduran failed to exit the picnic area in the direction ordered by the officers, they arrested him after allegedly tackling him to the ground. While the charges were eventually dropped, a bruised Caballo spent three nights in jail, missing work and leaving his family worried and upset. Although Caballo has the legal right to live and work in the United States, if the charges had stuck (charges that eventually included assaulting a police officer), as a noncitizen he might well have been deported.

In another frightening incident, I was questioned along with six other men by two police officers for suspected drinking:

Seemingly out of nowhere, two police officers appeared on foot as we drank beer, sitting on the bleachers by the soccer field. Catching us by surprise, one of the officers told us in English not to move. And when he saw a few of us try to conceal the cans, he added: "Come on, guys, we know you're drinking. Let me see some IDs." Everyone seemed resigned to receiving a ticket—or hopefully some leniency—except for Valderrama. He asked in English: "Why don't you guys go look for real criminals. We're not bothering anybody." One of the officers cut him off: "Quiet, I don't want to hear another thing coming from your mouth. And clean up those cans, there's kids and families out here."

When Valderrama persisted, making the case that he and the others actually looked after the park, the officer grabbed him by his collar and ordered him to face the fence in front of the bleachers, with his legs and arms spread apart. Unbeknownst to the police officers, Valderrama had concealed an open beer in his pants. When the can started to slip, Valderrama reached down in hopes of better securing it. The instant he moved, one of the officers grabbed his wrist, twisted it behind his back, and slammed his chest and face against the chain-link fence. The other officer quickly pulled out his Taser gun, aiming it at Valderrama and then at the six of us sitting on the bleachers, yelling: "Don't move!"

Valderrama cried in pain, shouting in English: "My shoulder, my shoulder!" Filemón and I pleaded with the officers to stop, explaining that he was reaching for his beer, which had since spilled all over his jeans. The officers told us to stay back and ordered Valderrama not to "resist" as they placed him in handcuffs. When they eventually realized Valderrama did not have a weapon or more serious contraband, the officer relented. He then turned Valderrama around and delivered a stern lecture: "I told you not to move!" And referring to the other police officer, he added: "You're lucky [the other police officer] didn't shoot you."

These were the only two incidents involving serious physical mistreatment by police that I heard about or witnessed at the park. Yet the men certainly knew of instances of police brutality elsewhere. Consequently, most men respectfully deferred to the police and did their best to control or shield those who might be perceived as stepping "out of line."

Of greater concern than physical violence at the hands of the police was the threat of unwarranted tickets brought about by suspected park drinking. As in Caballo's case, drinking citations were sometimes issued to those who were not drinking, at least at the time of arrest. Since the police usually arrived after the beers were stashed away, there was rarely direct evidence of who was or was not drinking. Police officers generally assumed that those in proximity of the suspected drinking scene were guilty and issued tickets accordingly, even to men who had not been drinking.

The fact that I was ignored by the police or able to talk myself out of a disproportionately greater number of drinking tickets than my darker-skinned companions with limited English revealed how the police constructed guilt and innocence at the park. In fact, the one ticket I received in all my years drinking in the park (during the incident described above) was never officially recorded, which meant there was no fine to pay. I believe the arresting officer was worried I would contest the citation and his manhandling of Valderrama, potentially creating problems for him and his partner, whereas the six Latino men I was cited with, who presumably posed less of a threat, were summarily fined. The officer may also have believed my (false) claim that I was not drinking because of the presumed incongruity between my background and the men's, which may explain why I avoided receiving other tickets during my eleven-year history at the park. Well aware of the privileges that came with my race and class, the men often urged me to intercede on their behalf with the police.

Drinking in Public

Drinking in the park also opened the men up to public scrutiny, which had subtler consequences. Latino men drinking beer in this park was a stigmatized practice, which fed into local fears about park life and broader demographic changes. As I explain in the conclusion, some local homeowners expressed concern over the changing nature of the park and made repeated references to men drinking beer in and around the soccer field. The men's drinking, along with other objections, were used to bolster allegations that the park was descending into disorder and that it had become unsightly and perhaps unsafe. Photographs of empty beer bottles in the park were especially common in reports that circulated about field-related problems.

While most of the men did their best to conceal their consumption and to ease anxieties, their marked visibility in the park made this difficult. The men were visible both because they were recognizably working-class Latino men and in the general sense that they were out in the open. As such, they embodied the stigmatized outsider disparaged in community meetings and in broader immigration debates. Regular police interrogations—which sometimes involved handcuffing the men and searching their bodies and belongings—also signaled to other park users that the men were up to no good, regardless of their guilt or innocence. Although alcohol consumption marked a conventional "passage from work to play" in the men's lives, it did not necessarily conform to onlookers' expectations about appropriate drinking times and locations, such as restaurant workers drinking midday on Monday, the first day of the conventional work week.[34] Indeed, other parkgoers and local residents wondered why the men needed to drink in the park at all.

Intolerance of the men's drinking due to class and cultural differences was an important factor fueling local opposition to Latino men using the park soccer field. Most men were generally aware of these local attitudes and did their best to conceal and control their drinking, even if they personally found such concerns unwarranted and overblown. And while they did not glamorize their drinking, few of the men found it strange or deviant to drink beer together in the park. As previously mentioned, most of the Latino men described public drinking as a culturally familiar practice rooted in past experiences. Like some local residents, police officers tried to shame the men by asking them why they were drinking in the park around children and ordered them to drink elsewhere. But as several people asked me when I brought it up: "Where else are we going to drink?" This question was not merely rhetorical, given the contrast between the men's situation and that of the local residents whose homes offered an abundance of private indoor and outdoor space generally not available to the men.

"I Lose Myself When I Drink"

Conflicts with police and local residents were not the only negative consequences of alcohol consumption in the park. Drinking, especially in large quantities, was more likely to create problems within the group itself. For example, the men were more prone to argue and disagree when drinking. While a source of fun and excitement, this could also lead to trouble, including hurt feelings and the violent altercations detailed in the next chapter. Time and the cover of alcohol usually mended relationships, but not always. In addition to lasting resentment, a bloodied face or bruised hand could also result in shame, injury, and frightened family members.

Park drinking, whether self-funded or facilitated by others, could lead to additional health problems. Jokes about "beer bellies" and talk of "sacando las chelas" (sweating out the beer) when playing soccer reflected some of these concerns. There were three or four men who were regularly intoxicated at the park. In fact, many problem drinkers confided to me that they needed to cut ties with the park in order to control their drinking. For example, when I asked Tío why he was moving to Maryland, he explained in a mix of English and Spanish: "Un montón de party aquí" (A lot of party here), adding in Spanish, "I can't control myself." When heavy drinkers like Tío stopped coming to the park, drinking was how other men usually explained their departures. However, most doubted that they would ever leave, dependent as they were on the ready supply of alcohol and drugs at the park. This is what Chango seemed to imply when questioning Mario's plans to return to Honduras. The reappearance of men—and their claims of boredom while away—also contributed to the image of the park as a place that was uniquely social and eventful.

The vast majority of the men seemed able to handle their drinking, but still could fall prey to its harmful effects. An abundance of beer could push men to drink more than they planned. As several men put it to me, "Me pierdo [I lose myself] when I drink." Yet when beer was offered, the social and relational implications made these offers difficult to resist. On many occasions, I observed arrests, fights, accidents, job losses, problems with family members, and drained resources that were all due to excessive drinking. Moreover, when I asked men to account for a recent setback, they often pointed to heavy drinking in the park as the cause of their troubles. For some, drinking pushed them to use harder drugs, such as crack and cocaine, which tended to compound problems.

The ill effects of alcohol sometimes extended beyond the park. For example, I knew of five individuals who received costly DUI tickets when leaving the park under the influence. One man spent eight years in jail for a lethal car accident after driving from the park over the legal limit. Two men flipped their cars blocks from the park and were both lucky to walk away with only expensive tickets and suspended licenses. Another favorite tale at the park involved Coloccini's two-week search to locate his truck that he had parked near the field in anticipation of an afternoon of drinking. Jokes aside, Coloccini lost work and faced an angry wife over this drunken mishap, not to mention several parking tickets. Others shared blurry stories of leaving the park drunk, either on foot or by car, and getting mugged, assaulted, or arrested on the way.

I also observed many men drinking in the park when they admitted they could or should be working or looking for work. According to the men, being crudo (hungover) or pedo (drunk) was also the cause of neglected work obligations and opportunities, especially for independent contractors. Several restaurant workers also shared with me that they lost their jobs because of alcohol-related absences or showing up to work drunk. While the men frequently expressed love for the park, they detested its unhealthy pull that purportedly kept them from accomplishing other goals, usually work related. Discomfited by the persistent park insults of "busca trabajo" (look for work) and "borracho del parque" (park drunk), the men recognized that spending hours drinking in the park was not the most productive way to spend their time. As they liked to joke, the park "no paga" (doesn't pay). And excessive drinking could be the cause of censure and exclusion from job referrals, which showed the fine line the men navigated to maintain respectability while drinking.

Not surprisingly, park drinking sometimes created problems with family members. Most of the men claimed that their spouses loathed the park and tried to keep them away from it. Families experienced the park through the men's absence or when they stumbled home, wasting paychecks, getting arrested or beaten up. To the amusement of others, some wives and girlfriends came to collect their partners at the park, whether by discreetly parking their car at a distance or by publicly confronting them. Although such direct contact in the park was rare, I often observed the men negotiating with their partner by cell phone for additional time, and they frequently spoke to me of the challenges of balancing park life with family commitments.

Zurdo, for example, explained to me that his wife became so upset with his park drinking and his absences, especially on Sundays, that she threatened to leave him. As a compromise and in an attempt to save their marriage, they agreed that he would come to the park every other Sunday. For Zurdo, who had played soccer and socialized at the park for decades, this was a significant sacrifice and sign of commitment to his wife and family. When I asked him why he did not bring his wife and daughters to the park, he replied: "They hate the park!" This was a sentiment apparently shared by many of the other men's family members. At the same time, I sensed that neither Zurdo nor other men particularly wanted their female family members with them at the park.

While each man's relationship with his spouse or girlfriend was different, most admitted that their relationships were strained by drinking at the park. For example, when I met the men's families, they often spoke dismissively of presumed drinking and other "vicios" (vices) in the park. Some even asked me why I wasted my time with the men and warned me about becoming another park borracho, dismissing my "study" as another tall tale used to justify getting drunk in the park. I learned that the park was well established as a drinking site in the men's social circles and a frequent cause of problems and delicate negotiations within couples. In fact, one man's wife called the park a place of "perdición" (damnation).

Family obligations could serve as a convenient excuse to abstain from drinking or even to leave the park altogether. Family ties and commitments were also a source of differentiation between men who were more or less attached. As Locksmith explained regarding the times his wife came to the park looking for him: "It's a spectacle, but at least I have someone. La mayoría no tiene a nadie." (The majority don't have anyone.) During my time in the park, I also witnessed several men come to reject park drinking in favor of consuming at home. This shift usually resulted from having a nicer place and improved family dynamics.

While some men chose to avoid the park altogether because of the drinking, most were more strategic in circumventing potential problems, especially those who enjoyed other aspects of the park, such as playing soccer and seeing friends. For example, they would sit with a few guys who were casually drinking, even having one themselves, but leave once the crowd and commotion grew. To account for opting out, most of the men were adept at resisting beer invitations, relying on respectable reasons, usually family or work related. Some men took a more active role looking out for people who drank excessively and in policing other problematic behavior through various strategies, such as providing plastic cups, taking away car keys, holding on to money, and breaking up fights. Yet full avoidance remained the most effective strategy, since even the most sober, well-intentioned individuals could receive drinking citations or become entangled in drunken conflict.

"Para Convivir"

Beer drinking in the park proved irresistible to many. As the men often confided to me, they drank "para convivir," which I've taken to mean "for the sake of conviviality." Drinking brought the men together in ways they found compelling and meaningful. It constructed the park as a place where "things happened"; it was news making and revealing, even if the outcomes were sometimes disastrous. In fact, the volatility and unpredictability of these gatherings gave them a special sense of excitement and camaraderie. Doing deviant and risky things bound the group together and provided opportunities to test the limits of their new home, which the men could not necessarily do in other settings.

While group life at the park could presumably function without alcohol, drinking remained a vital way to mobilize interactions and friendships. And they needed to do this in a place where they felt in control, despite the risks. Like the park soccer games, beer drinking required a fair amount of organization, trust, and commitment to keep it going. Indeed, for these immigrant men, drinking was not an escape from the world, but instead a way to construct a part of the world as their own.[35]

Yet, as we have seen, drinking in the park created a series of problems for the men, which people drinking in commercial or private settings or who are less stigmatized in public spaces generally do not face. This paradox was not lost on me as I sat sipping wine with a local resident in his spacious home discussing these very "problems." The context and meaning of the men's drinking were entirely missing from local debates about the park and soccer field. Local residents and police officers did not see the men's park drinking in terms of more familiar, socially acceptable forms, dismissing it instead as criminal disruptions to public life. The illegality of beer drinking also distinguished it from soccer. Playing soccer, while perhaps stigmatizing and problematic, did not criminalize the men as much as their drinking, which could have serious consequences—problems that even abstainers had trouble avoiding.

Drinking created community by virtue of the common vulnerability it generated and the bonds that emerged from risky practices. The fact that drinking enlivened park life and facilitated friendships thus posed a dilemma for the men, especially for those whose identities and livelihoods depended on park ties. While most managed the pressures to drink para convivir, this high-stakes catch-22—drinking for the sake of conviviality—could, as we have seen, lead to problems that extended well beyond the park. Like the mixed meanings of the expression "jugadores del parque" (park players) discussed in previous chapters, the label "borracho del parque" (park drunk) was not without its sting and contradictions. And whether outsiders viewed the men's drinking as deviant or mundane, these meanings were hidden from them. Only by understanding the rich meaning and organization of this social world within its cultural context and in its full complexity can we truly appreciate what the men achieved and overcame when drinking beer together in a public park. For, at its root, drinking— like playing soccer—was simply a way for the men to be together and to feel as if things were "happening."

Fig. 1. Group photo during a Fourth of July day tournament.

Fig. 2. Action on the soccer field as others look on and wait their turn.

Fig. 3. Tamagás tending the grill.

Fig. 4. Caballo and son.

Fig. 5. Polo distributing jerseys to eager players.

Fig. 6. Zapata and Enrique sharing a laugh.

Fig. 7. Titi prepping a painting job.

Fig. 8. Filemón watches over as Coloccini cleans up a work site.

Fig. 9. Valderrama and Barba.

Fig. 10. Vino Tinto trying to restrain Darwin.

Fig. 11. Kathy and Zurdo.

Fig. 12. Polo holding court.

Fig. 13. Los jugadores del parque socializing with hidden beers by the recently fenced-in soccer field.

Fig. 14. The late councilman Bill Rosendahl inaugurates the new fence with park staff and a handful of his constituents.

Fig. 15. Team photo after a league championship victory, with coach Motor kneeling proudly in his customary Oakland Raiders attire.

Fig. 16. Los jugadores del parque.

4 * Fighting Your Friends

Nelson versus Tico

That Nelson and Tico were arguing during a midday soccer game was hardly surprising. The two men frequently quarreled on the field, and the clashes between their volatile temperaments were legendary. Despite this ongoing discord, the two men had never traded punches, preferring to spar verbally. On this day, Nelson was determined to settle the simmering tension with physical violence, even though he was almost a foot shorter and a hundred pounds lighter than the burly Costa Rican. Yet as soon as he moved aggressively toward Tico, several men blocked his path, urging him to "let it go." One man put his hands on Nelson's shoulder and calmly explained: "It's not worth it, brother! He's a brute, everyone knows that."

Tico, who at first seemed uninterested in fighting, soon demanded that the men "let him go" (déjalo), adding that he was going to teach the "little boy" a lesson if he "wants to fight." As expected, Tico's taunts further enraged Nelson, who aggressively tried to push past the men's clutches. Since the game had now been interrupted for a third time, several players pressed the interveners to let the two men fight. Yielding to growing pressure, the interveners' resolve weakened, and Nelson burst toward Tico, screaming: "¡Ven, hijo de puta!" (Come on, you son of a bitch!) A dozen or so more men formed an impromptu ring around the two adversaries as they exchanged a messy flurry of punches and kicks. Several men urged Nelson on. One supporter shouted, "¡Dale verga!" (Fuck him up!)

At first willing to let them fight freely, three men physically intervened when Tico picked Nelson up and prepared to slam him against a fence lining the field. In the commotion, Nelson fell to the ground, missing the fence by a few inches, and Tico delivered a quick succession of kicks to his head. As he moved to inflict more damage, several men forcefully pushed him away. Tico did not resist the interference, but loudly warned: "¡Nadie se mete! [Nobody get involved!] Let him fight. He provoked me!" Nelson, dazed but back on his feet, made a halfhearted attempt to counterattack, but relented when the other men blocked his path, putting an end to the short-lived fight. Several men crowded around him, offering their support and prognoses. A few even congratulated him for his efforts, patting him on his back, despite the defeat. Valderrama, with his arm around Nelson commented: "Don't worry, you fought like a man." Then, pointing to his battered nose, he added: "That's nothing, se acabó [it's over]."

Tico, for his part, walked in a circle, fuming yet triumphant. He was particularly incensed at the men who had stopped the fight and who had criticized his aggressiveness. Sensing that the crowd was turning against him, he reminded them that Nelson was the instigator: "He wanted to fight, everyone saw it. I told him not to." When someone informed him that he had probably broken Nelson's nose, Tico replied: "That's what he gets for getting involved in cosas de hombres" (affairs of men). Tico's summation, however, was far from the final word on the matter, as the men debated and dissected the latest park fight for weeks to come.

*

The fight between Nelson and Tico was one of fifty-four violent confrontations I witnessed during my time in the park. In addition, I heard about twice as many more fights, including some that occurred during my fieldwork and others from years before I arrived. I also observed and was told about numerous near fights. Approximately two-thirds of park fights occurred in the context of the soccer games, while the remaining third developed within the swirl of off-field interactions at the park. Some physical altercations were primarily a product of the moment—a hard clash on the soccer field or spontaneous disagreement over beer money—while others (like the fight between Nelson and Tico) revealed a deeper history, the culmination of brewing tensions and past problems.

Interpretations of what constituted a pelea or bronca (fight) varied, but the men frequently defined physical altercations in terms of putting hands on someone ("meter manos"), which the men acknowledged by warning others "not to touch me" ("¡No me toques!") or in seeking retribution for being hit. As one man put it to me, "If someone disrespected me [me faltó el respeto], you know that I had to put hands on him [tuve que meterle manos]." In contrast, the men rarely described an unanswered blow as a fight, and I never observed combatants attack people they knew who were uninterested in fighting beyond an initial shove. The majority of confrontations at the park never escalated into bodily contact, but hovered instead at the level of face-saving bluster and bravado. Even in the heat of the moment, the men tended to put the onus on others to throw the first punch ("¡Pégame!") and to find other respectable ways to avoid fighting.

Indeed, most of the men found it difficult to overcome the "confrontational tension and fear" of fighting, as sociologist Randall Collins found in his research on violence.[1]

I initially found this sporadic violence frightening and senseless, much as I had found certain aspects of the men's drinking at the park. Yet, to my surprise, the men also talked about the park as a relatively "safe" place to fight, at least in terms of physical injuries. This is not to say that the men did not occasionally hurt each other—black eyes, scratched faces, and chipped teeth did sometimes result—but nothing so serious as to require urgent medical care. Park drinking and fighting shared other similarities. Over time, I came to appreciate the ordered and performative quality of occasional park fights. As in Nelson and Tico's fight, I observed how violence in the park was controlled, monitored, and usually broken up before long, taming it in ways that didn't happen when fights broke out among strangers.

I also discovered an unexpected relationship between conflict and cooperation that helped explain why the men sometimes fought. The same context that fostered the formation of new ties at the park also provided a relatively safe space for tensions to boil over into a constructive kind of violence. Indeed, park fights typically settled rather than exacerbated conflict, and many men developed deeper relationships after trading punches. Tellingly, I never witnessed a single rematch at the park. By contrast, feuds that did not turn violent often simmered for months, even years. And, as when playing soccer and drinking beer together, fighting helped the men get to know one another and bond in meaningful, transcendent ways. Putting their bodies on the line was a way of acknowledging that their reputation and identity were at stake. In this way, fights had deep implications for the men's relationships and for the social world they created at the park.

Fighting Elsewhere

The men talked about park violence in relation to violence in other contexts. They pointed to the differences between the park and the calle (street)—another public setting occasionally the stage for violent interactions in the men's lives, especially for those who frequented rougher areas of Los Angeles. Not only did park violence contrast with the ruthless world of fighting described in studies of inner-city violence, but also with what the men experienced or anticipated away from the park.[2] Many of the men shared stories of vicious beatings and robberies that they heard about or to which they fell victim in other sections of the city, including where they lived. From fear of violence, they claimed to avoid certain areas and situations.

It was only after I followed the men into bars or walking the streets late at night that I observed firsthand how threats and behaviors actually differed outside the park—sometimes in ways that confirmed the men's mythic tales of Los Angeles violence, but also in other more surprising ways. I gradually discovered that park fights were one of a series of situations in which the men encountered and enacted violence.

For example, after hours of drinking in an infamous cantina, Locksmith became embroiled in an argument with someone sitting at the bar frequented by working-class Latinos. Although it wasn't clear to me why, Locksmith had clearly angered the stranger, who stood up from his stool and threatened to "matarte" (kill you) if he did not immediately leave. In the tumult, a large and increasingly impatient bouncer who had already intervened on Locksmith's behalf several times that evening grabbed him by the back of his jacket and forcibly expelled him from the cantina. As I helped him up from the sidewalk, Locksmith told me that the man at the bar had a knife on him, which is why he had left. He added that the same bouncer had pepper-sprayed him the last time he was there, which would have further decreased his odds of success. When I naively recounted the story at the park, many of the men scolded me for going to that cantina, especially with Locksmith, a known brawler. The message was clear: I was safe at the park but not elsewhere, and I was fortunate to have escaped unscathed. More importantly, as the men at the park explained, I was a fool to believe that bar fights resembled park fights.

Another time, I was walking out of a liquor store with four men from the park around 2:00 a.m. when we encountered about ten young Latino men they later identified as "cholos" (gang members). The area was dark and there was limited room to pass along the crowded sidewalk. Tough stares and defensive postures were exchanged as we crossed paths. "Accidental bumps," the triggers of many fights, were narrowly averted. Immediately after passing them, the young men turned in our direction and shouted explosive warnings and insults in both Spanish and English. The park men never broke stride and hurried to David's house around the corner. In the safety of his backyard, we nervously laughed about the encounter.

In both these incidents, the men avoided physical violence. Faced with uncertain odds and hidden variables, the men from the park assumed the worst and avoided potential harm. The peril and uncertainty of these events highlighted for me what was different about park fights. In these tense interactions with strangers, it was unclear how violence would unfold. Even if it was uncertain whether the man in the bar really had a knife and whether the young men on the street actually were cholos, their anonymity made these encounters feel all the more dangerous. Perhaps the men from the park simply were trying to save face by refusing to engage in conflict in an unpredictable situation where the risks were not clear. In any case, the odds were decidedly not in their favor. On the street or in bars, there was not the same expectation of restraint and control the men could count on at the park.

Some men even mocked park fights or renowned tough guys within a broader context of violence. For example, Bruja, who lived in a notoriously rough area of Los Angeles by MacArthur Park, loved to talk about the time Polo and Pisa visited him at his home. In contrast to their bold park demeanors, Bruja painted a very different picture of their behavior in his neighborhood: "You see Pisa here all big and bad. He was so scared he didn't want to go to a [local] bar." Instead, Pisa felt safer drinking beers in Bruja's home. As for the usually verbose Polo: "He barely said a word—calladito [completely silent]." Polo did not contest Bruja's account, adding: "Cálmate [Pipe down]. They kill you for nothing over there." Caballo, who had recently moved to a similar neighborhood in South Central Los Angeles, added: "Why do you think we still come here?" These stories and comments were especially instructive for men who had less experience in settings and situations that Bruja and others insinuated were "realer" in their violence. And even if he had exaggerated his friends' fears, Bruja explained their timid behavior in his neighborhood as a sign of the park's "softer" environment.

Yet anonymity can affect people in different ways. While it can be grounds for fear and a sense of danger, it can also prove liberating, even intoxicating. After a fight in the park, combatants usually negotiated the change in their relationship within the context of their shared past and presumed future together. But away from the park, men sometimes became the aggressors without concern for relating to their victims in the future.[3] For example, when a group of men stepped out of a bar in the early morning hours, Motor confronted a man walking by them, apparently for no reason. Although shorter and pudgier than his adversary, Motor repeated the provocative accusation, "¿Qué pedo?" (What's the problem?), as he urged the unsuspecting stranger to make a move. He seemed emboldened by the fact that he was drunk, with five of his friends standing behind him. As he probably anticipated, the unaccompanied man hurried past them without reacting to the challenge. While Motor's predatory behavior would have likely received censure at the park, the men laughed and encouraged his confrontational stance in this situation, embracing violence when the odds were clearly in their favor. Motor's actions were especially striking in this context, since he usually served as a "peacemaker," stopping fights in the park rather than provoking them.

Another incident I heard about from several sources also illustrates what seemed to be different about fighting strangers. On that occasion, after a steady afternoon of drinking beer at the park, half a dozen of the men went to a bar together. Soon after their arrival, they picked a fight with two strangers. The confrontation spilled out onto the street. In a scene vividly recounted for months, a park regular pulled one of the men out of a car—where he purportedly had gone to retrieve a gun—and repeatedly kicked him in the head, leaving him bloodied and apparently unconscious on the pavement. Like the individual Motor taunted in the incident recounted above, the men remained strangers before, during, and after the fight.[4] In contrast to conflicts on and around the field, where unprovoked violence was frowned on and usually prevented, the men shared many tales of violence away from the park in which they were the aggressors—some more believable than others.

In these accounts, the men revealed an enthusiasm for violence and a disregard for its consequences that I rarely observed at the park or heard about happening there. While park fights started for seemingly trivial reasons, they were not as arbitrary or aggressive as these confrontations elsewhere. For example, I never witnessed anyone at the park pick a fight, as Motor had, with an adversary who was clearly outmatched and uninterested in fighting. In any case, at the park onlookers would have intervened to prevent such an unequal match, especially when the aggression was unprovoked. By contrast, there were no such constraints in dealing with strangers.

Park fights generally differed from confrontations in bars or on the street, regardless of whether anonymity was experienced outside the park as a source of fear or freedom. This is not to suggest that the men were perpetual victims or perpetrators of violence as they traveled through the city—these incidents were actually rare—but to explain what was unique about fighting in the park. By following the men away from the park, I saw how their personas and demeanor changed as the possibility of violence increased or diminished. Away from the park, blustering fighters could suddenly become tame and forgiving, while customary peacemakers initiated unprovoked and remorseless violence. The impact of anonymity came to the fore much more powerfully as I witnessed how violence varied across situations.[5] As the men themselves acknowledged, fights are not all the same, but instead constitute a range of violent experiences. Understanding violence as a product of situations, not individuals, proved key to understanding what I observed in the park.[6]

Fighting in the Park

The fifty-four fights I observed in the park varied in tone and manner, although most were relatively brief and clumsy. Few physical exchanges lasted more than a minute, most only seconds, and punches and kicks rarely met their intended target, if they were executed at all. Moreover, the source of conflict was not always clear to me or others. The men frequently joked that they, too, had no idea why they fought or else pointed to reasons for fighting that emerged after the conflict had unfolded. For example, Secada explained to me that he punched Chino because he threw a beer bottle at him, even though this occurred well into their argument. The men often described the cause of past fights as over "pura mierda" (utter shit) or "tonterías" (silly stuff) and blamed alcohol or misunderstandings for accelerating the conflict.

While explanations of the reasons for fighting often proved erroneous or contradictory after the fact, there is little doubt that what the men routinely did together in the park contributed to the escalation of tensions. In particular, the daily soccer games could on occasion boil over into fights. For most of the participants, the games were competitive and hard-fought, which led to the passionate and hard-hitting play described in previous chapters. Yet because the line between aggressive and malicious play was fuzzy, the men sometimes took offense at their opponents' tactics. Usually only stern words or tough stares were exchanged, if apologies were not immediately forthcoming, but sometimes the spirited and litigious nature of the game led to fights. As Carlos put it to me in English, fights were "part of the game," adding an example from his own experiences to contextualize the physicality of play: "Like I tell my cousin, you're playing against me, you got the ball, and if I've got a chance to chop you down, I'll chop you down. That's just soccer—it's a passion." The men also used aggressive language—such as "ponga huevos" (show some balls) or "no tengas miedo" (don't be scared)—to motivate combative play. In some cases, this "passion" transformed physical confrontations over the ball into violent clashes.

Fights also happened as the men socialized after the games, often while drinking beer. As suggested in the previous chapters, these sociable interactions evolved in ways that tended to trigger park fights as well. The topics varied, but they often centered on park life, such as when rehashing past events or debating claims and status hierarchies on and off the soccer field. While usually festive and good-natured, these "character contests" occasionally escalated to the point of physical confrontation, especially when the men were agitated or intoxicated and, as a result, more sensitive to perceived slights that seemed to threaten their reputations.[7] As on the soccer field, the competitive and incendiary nature of park talk had the potential to provoke physical confrontations. Yet while the soccer games brought together all sorts of relations into conflict, off-field fights generally involved men with stronger ties and deeper histories together. And it was the nature of their relationships that made these conflicts so compelling and consequential in ways that structured and invigorated group life.

"¡Pégame!" (Hit Me!)

Despite the situational pressures built out of doing things together, park fights were hardly predetermined or an automatic outcome of conflict. Fights in the park were in fact rare, and crossing the line from verbal disputes to physical violence proved daunting to many of the men. Most men found it difficult to overcome their fear of using violence and of getting hurt in the process. Despite local limits and controls, fighting in the park could be upsetting and frightening. And even if men responded violently in the end, they were far more likely to respond nonviolently at first, even in the most hostile situations. In fact, only a handful of men were prone to fight at the park. Of the fifty-four fights I observed, thirty-one involved six of the approximately 150 men who interacted on and off the soccer field during my fieldwork. What I refer to as "near fights" were far more common.

Near fights involved situations in which men became entangled in animated and hostile conversations, which often included incendiary taunts and gestures, but without escalating to violent contact. In contrast to the playful tone of most joking and debating at the park, near fights—or "nonfight" fights—involved a degree of tension and perceived disrespect that foreshadowed the possibility of violence.[8] In many cases, potential conflict was resolved by one side deferring to the other—that is, objections were raised, after which one side apologized or backed down. The following example shows how tensions could be quickly resolved at the park:

> When Polo said he did not feel like working that afternoon, Motor kidded to the group of afternoon drinking companions that Polo was depressed because Filemón, his so-called lover, was visiting family in Oaxaca. Polo had laughed off this favorite park joke countless times before, even joining in the fun by playing along. But to everyone's surprise, Polo threatened to give Motor a "putazo" (punch) if he continued to insult him. Motor nervously laughed, not sure if he was serious, but changed his tune when it became clear that Polo was in fact offended and angry. Several men urged Polo to calm down (cálmate), and Motor quickly changed the subject: "Yeah, okay, hablemos de otra cosa [let's talk about something else]." He then abruptly left the circle of beer drinkers for another section of the park. When I later asked Motor why he left, he explained that Polo needed time to cool off and that his continued presence might have worsened the situation. He also

let me know that he did not take Polo's wrath personally and joked that he must be menstruating ("anda con la regla").

Although the men were not always as deferential as Motor after offending someone at the park, most potential problems were diffused in similar fashion. On the soccer field, this usually involved a simple "perdón" (sorry) or nonverbal gesture to excuse behavior and resolve conflict. It was also rare for someone to reject an apology and to seek physical retribution. Predatory, one-sided beatings almost never occurred at the park, whereas fights generally involved willing participants. Even when a person refused to back down when challenged by an agitated peer, physical violence still was usually avoided. In most cases, the men worked together to show a willingness and readiness to fight without crossing the line into physical aggression.

One of the most common and suspenseful near-fight situations at the park was triggered by the provocative taunt "¡Pégame!" (Hit me!)[9] I also heard English speakers shout, "Do something!" or "What are you going to do about it?" at a similar moment of tension. As the following example illustrates, these challenges took confrontations to the brink of violence, but only rarely did targets respond to the dare by throwing the fateful first punch.

> Irritated by Pikachu's incessant complaining, Roberto threw down his whistle in anger. When Pikachu continued to criticize his refereeing, Roberto rapidly approached him to the point that their noses were inches apart. Undeterred, Pikachu advised Roberto to watch from the sidelines or, better yet, to stay home. Standing firm, arms extended at his side in a defenseless posture, Roberto—nicknamed Ropero (Armoire) for his stocky build—responded by urging Pikachu to hit him: "¡Pégame, pégame, por favor pégame!" (Hit me, hit me, please hit me!) After two or three seconds of suspenseful inaction, three men stepped between the potential brawlers. Neither of the men resisted the interveners, and Roberto walked straight off the field, letting it be known he longer wanted to referee, adding, "Demasiada mierda" (too much bullshit).

Roberto later admitted to me that he suspected that Pikachu would not actually have hit him. And, as in this case, problems generally deescalated after a brief standoff, often with the help of onlookers.

Like "pégame," stern warnings and ultimatums also served as substitutes for violence in the heat of the moment. As the following example suggests, this was done in ways that asserted situational dominance over opponents while averting the risk of actual physical violence:

Problems mounted when Miguel asked Locksmith if he knew how to program car keys. Locksmith, true to his park nickname, said he could do it, but that it would cost $300. David, an airplane mechanic, interrupted his Salvadoran compatriot. Addressing the half-dozen men who were drinking beers together, he claimed that Locksmith was trying to rip off the young man and said he knew someone who could do it for half as much. Locksmith turned to David and proclaimed: "I'm an expert at this. This is what I do. I don't tell you how to fix airplanes, do I?" Then, referring to bruises the airplane mechanic had sustained after falling off his bike, Locksmith added: "I'm warning you, stay out of my business, or you'll look like you did earlier!" David replied, "Yeah, yeah. All you do is abuse people, I'm tired of it." Locksmith leaped from the top of the picnic table where he was seated and stepped toward David with his arms and hands spread apart: "What are you talking about?" Receiving no answer, he moved closer and closer to David as he repeatedly asked, "¿Qué? ¿Qué?" (What, what?), his eyes and forehead jerking toward David each time he asked the menacing question. David stood his ground but remained silent, as did the other men. After a brief stare-down, Locksmith muttered, "Lo sabía" (I knew it), as he sat back down on the picnic table. After a few moments, he broke the silence once again and, with a visible smile, quipped: "Otra reina del parque que quiere una nalgada." (Another queen of the park who's asking for a spanking.)

In some cases, the men tried to make good on their threats of violence, but yielded to crowd interference in ways that suggested they were not fully committed to fighting. They seemed to hope that a show of force would suffice to avoid fighting, while keeping their reputations intact. This was especially true when the antagonist anticipated that his exaggerated moves would go unanswered or blocked by others, as the following incident illustrates:

Valderrama and Huguito had been arguing for a good half hour. Valderrama felt that Huguito "ran his mouth too much." While Huguito was certainly garrulous and argumentative, most of the men gave Huguito a pass because of his age (mid-fifties), his small stature, and, most importantly, his entertaining personality. However, the Mexican-born Valderrama was not interested in placating Huguito, later explaining to me that the Colombian frequently disrespected Mexicans. When Valderrama made light of the fact that Huguito had recently lost his job—an insult that Huguito felt crossed the line—he threatened to "kick his ass." Valderrama laughed, implying that the fight would be unfair, at which Huguito raised his fists, challenging the younger and stronger man to fight. Valderrama continued to laugh and retorted:

"¡Ven, viejito!" (Come on, old man!) Huguito promptly charged toward him. While it's hard to know for certain, I suspect that Huguito anticipated that the five men standing between him and Valderrama would intercede as he made his way to Valderrama and a likely defeat. Sure enough, three men grabbed the well-liked Huguito and walked him toward another section of the park to cool down, laughing as they accompanied the fiery old-timer. Valderrama smiled as well, suggesting that he hadn't been offended by Huguito's aborted attack or taken it too seriously.

By urging their foe to hit them and then standing in a vulnerable or aggressive position, the men publicly signaled a willingness and capacity to fight. Like Locksmith and Huguito, men progressively upped the ante as they edged ever closer to physical contact. In other cases, men moved to a more suitable place for combat or indicated their readiness by removing clothing, lacing their shoes, or finishing their beer. But instead of attacking, they shifted responsibility for physical violence onto their opponent. At the park, throwing the first punch was a decisive move because it usually created a situation of no return.

As I repeatedly observed, the threat of violence served as a way to deter violence by creating a situation that allowed both sides to save face without fighting. Like bullfighters encouraging and then sidestepping the bull's attack, the men challenged each other as a way not to fight. These flirtations with violence generally worked because the men knew each other and the situational meanings of "pégame," even in the most hostile of exchanges. The men also understood that they would see each other again and would have to live with the fallout of an unexpected strike. In fact, some men were notorious for making empty threats—especially when intoxicated—but they were generally ignored in ways that a stranger would have had trouble overlooking. Those who took these challenges seriously were reprimanded for not recognizing the false saber-rattling. For example, for weeks the men had criticized Valderrama for fighting Mi Chavo, who most agreed was hot-tempered but harmless. In contrast, threatening someone whose intentions and character were unknown was considered risky. While idle threats and challenges were commonplace in the park, the idea of two strangers arguing nose to nose and baiting each other to throw the first punch seemed absurd to the men.

To diffuse tensions and avoid a fight, the men sometimes invoked their social status and disparaged that of their would-be adversary. For example, one man dismissed another's repeated putdowns and incendiary language by claiming, "I've got more important things to worry about than this drunk." In such cases, the reasons for nonviolence were due not to the conflict itself, but to the negative consequences that might result from fighting. Others suggested that their aggressor had less to lose by taking the moment so seriously. For example, one man resisted another's challenges by saying: "Why would I fight you? You're a drug addict, a nobody. All you do is fight. I've got a family, a house, a job. You've got nothing." By vaunting their superior status and character, these men felt they had already won. Describing in English a man who frequently fought in the park, Chino explained this to me in even stronger terms: "That's a person without love. He don't got no love. He don't got no wife. And you have to put that in your mind." In other situations, friendships were invoked to resist fighting. For example, when Polo threatened America, the latter responded quizzically: "Why am I going to fight you? Somos amigos [We're friends]." Men also cited a history of nonviolence to dismiss threats and accusations, as when Brazil told his would-be combatant to "ask anyone" if he ever played "dirty" on the soccer field. By making character assessments of this kind and invoking differences or common ground between themselves and their adversaries, the men were able to justify their refusal to fight and thereby avoid physical violence.

Most conflicts at the park, even the most heated, rarely escalated to the point of physical violence. While questions ("¿Qué?") and threats ("¡Pégame!") seemed to demand a response, the men generally avoided responding in a violent manner for as long as possible during confrontations at the park. With their reputation at stake, these performances were a way for the men to show that they were ready to fight, even if they were in fact reluctant to do so and anticipated that people would intervene. What appeared to be aggressive provocations—such as taunts to "hit me"— were actually measures intended to reduce the risk of physical violence. They were a means of social control, rather than a sign of its breakdown. However, near-fight situations would have had little meaning if they did not occasionally transform into real fights. The possibility of violence gave an edginess to park life, which would have been less compelling without it. Yet while bluffing and blustering could deter conflict and maintain respectability, it also put the men at risk of actually fighting.

Fighting over Moments and Relationships

There were occasionally incidents in the park where men did attack each other with the intent to inflict physical harm. As outlined in interactionist studies of violence, park fights generally followed a predictable pattern featuring a series of stages and turning points.[10] Opponents first refused to back down, even in the face of the perceived risk that violence might bring. Then, once this critical stage had been reached, the two opponents needed to agree to use physical violence as a means of resolving the conflict. In other words, fights required mutual consent. Even when apparent trivialities concealed more deep-seated tensions and perceived disrespect, the men had to provoke violent emotions in each other for the fight to happen—a threshold many of the men at the park found difficult to cross.

However, there was considerable variation in violent intentions and levels of commitment. Some men were out for blood—"I'm going to kill you!"—and had to be forcibly restrained, while others were content to "let it go" after a quick succession of halfhearted shoves. Whatever form they took, fights were characterized by deliberate physical contact, which the men acknowledged by warning others not to touch them ("no me toques") or by seeking retribution for being hit ("me pegó"). The violence of touch, if only attempted, transformed verbal conflicts into physical confrontations, which is why the dare to "hit me" was so provocative.

Rather than the result of past problems, park fights were often largely a product of the moment, triggered by the competitive nature of park life. The following incident took place during a soccer game:

> Although they were on the same team, Benny and Benzema had been arguing for much of the match. Benny appeared irritated that Benzema was not passing the ball to him, which he—a dark-skinned Jamaican playing with predominately Latino teammates—attributed to "racism." When Benzema missed a shot, and Benny again chastised him for being a "ball hog," Benzema confronted him and with little warning gave him a powerful kick in the calf and raised his fists for battle. Benny removed the mesh jersey over his shirt and lunged at Benzema, tackling him to the ground. As the two fought, players circled around them. When Ali tried to separate them, Tony blocked his path and said, "Let them fight." After a few more seconds of wrestling and errant strikes, Polo and others yelled from the bleachers to "break it up." Several men physically separated them, all of whom were lucky to avoid the brawlers' wild punches as they tried to stop the fight.

When I later spoke to the two young men, neither attributed the fight to past problems with the other, but instead to the heat of the moment. Even if his anger was grounded in a general frustration with what he perceived to be anti-Black racism at the park, Benny held no personal animosity toward Benzema from before the fight. In fact, the two men were even a bit surprised and slightly embarrassed that the fight occurred, and neither was interested in pursuing the matter, nor did they expect future problems. If anything, the fight became a source of humor and interaction between them, such as when Benzema playfully raised his clenched fists whenever he saw Benny after their frenzied fisticuffs. Similar spontaneous dustups happened off the field, including those sparked by spilled drinks or misfired jokes, when people were "cagando el palo" (annoying), as they liked to put it.

A smaller percentage of fights were more relational than situational in origin, rooted in tensions between individuals and often the culmination of several near fights. Nelson and Tico, for example, had argued for months before they finally came to blows in the incident described at the beginning of this chapter. The most drawn-out and dramatic physical confrontations in the park were generated by disputes over status within the group,[11] as the following incident illustrates:

> After playing their Sunday morning league game, many veteranos (old-timers) from the over-30 team reconvened at the park to barbecue and drink beer. The months-old argument between Locksmith and Ceja (Eyebrow) regarding who was the better soccer player promptly resumed as the men socialized. The debate between the two men, both in their mid-forties, involved current and past playing abilities. Ceja and Locksmith remained strong players, and arguments continued over who should wear the coveted number ten jersey. While most of his teammates regarded Ceja as the more talented player, Locksmith felt he was better and resented the praise Ceja received. As the argument wore on, Locksmith upped the ante and suggested they should fight to see who was stronger. Ceja had no interest in fighting, but repeatedly asked anyone who would listen not only who was a better soccer player, but who garnered more respect at the park. For Ceja, it was obvious that he scored higher in both respects.
>
> When Ceja eventually said something that Locksmith felt crossed the line, the latter stood up from the picnic table and signaled his desire to fight, adding, "¡Vamos!" (Let's go!), in case his intentions weren't clear. Ceja stood up and backed away from Locksmith, saying several times: "Mira, no quiero pelear." (Look, I don't want to fight.) Locksmith ignored Ceja's plea and slowly pursued him around the table. Four of their teammates grudgingly stood up, but soon backed away from the two men, realizing it was best to let them fight, especially as Ceja now appeared willing to engage. Locksmith charged at Ceja, who promptly threw his assailant to the ground. Now even more enraged but drunker than he realized, Locksmith jumped back to his feet and threw a wild punch at Ceja, who replied by dropping him back to the ground with a strong blow to the jaw. As Locksmith sluggishly pushed himself back up, two men intervened, indicating that Locksmith had had his opportunity and that the fight was over.

As this example shows, park fights were sometimes the result of preexisting problems, in contrast to more spontaneous clashes. Before trading punches, some men quarreled for months, even years. But when they finally did fight, the men typically sidestepped "pégame" posturing and launched straight into physical combat. And in such situations, the audience proved key in allowing fights to occur.

Crowd Involvement

According to Randall Collins, there are two primary means by which people overcome impediments to violence. The first—attacking the weak—was generally disapproved of by the men at the park, although condoned by them in other settings. The second—encouragement by onlookers—was crucial in these staged fights.[12] By their willingness to intervene or not, indeed by their very presence, the audience shaped the arc of the fight as the spectacle unfolded.

Most men anticipated intervention, and only on rare occasions did a crowd of onlookers unanimously "allow" fights to continue unimpeded. At the park, fighters could generally count on others to step in, often quickly, especially if they were decidedly winning or losing—safeguards they could not rely on elsewhere. Expected crowd involvement made the park a relatively "safe" place to fight. And whereas park fights were almost always one-on-one, multiple parties were typically involved in controlling clashes. However, the form and timing of intervention varied, as did consensus about how onlookers should influence the fight.

Some fights were broken up in an aggressive manner. For example, newcomers to the soccer games occasionally used or threatened forms of violence that park regulars viewed as extreme and unwarranted. In one case, a newcomer threw his opponent to the ground as they tussled for the ball and punched him repeatedly in the head as he lay defenseless on the ground. Five players rushed over and pushed him away as they admonished him for his violence. One man yelled: "What's wrong with you? Are you crazy? We don't do that here!" He then tried to attack the aggressor, but was held back by the others and finally relented when the now-frightened newcomer went to gather his belongings and left the field. Tellingly, the newcomer had struck a man who was given a pass for his reckless play by park regulars because they considered him mentally unstable or "loco," as many put it.

The men proudly shared stories about how they had policed park violence over the years. For example, I was often told about a problematic White South African player they had physically expelled from the park. According to Polo, "He hit one of the older players and didn't know that he was with us, so a bunch of us beat him up bad, and he never came back." The men also claimed that they had chased away a group of alleged "cholos" after they attacked two teenage soccer players. In these cases and others, park regulars made it clear that only certain forms and degrees of violence were tolerated there and that these aggressors had gone "too far."

The only free-for-all melee I witnessed at the park involved a group of Egyptian men in town for an event. During an increasingly tense impromptu soccer game between the two groups, the park regulars exhibited an uncharacteristic lack of restraint and eagerness to use violence. For example, one park regular struck an unsuspecting foe in the head with his clenched fist, an unprecedented sucker punch that continued past the point of defeat with a flurry of kicks. Here, the aim was not simply to win the fight, but to make a symbolic statement about who was welcome in the park.[13]

However, most park fights involved men with at least some history at the park and familiarity with each other. As for the onlookers, this was not an anonymous crowd, but a group of known others with particular relationships to the fighters. How the crowd responded communicated their view of the fight and the men involved. In many cases, onlookers intervened by stopping fights that were viewed either as unfairly matched or as avoidable and unnecessary. In contrast to more harmless or obvious forms of bravado, these situations involved fighters who appeared eager to fight and to inflict harm. Consider, for example, the following scene that took place during a soccer game, where Abel grew increasingly frustrated by Locksmith's seemingly malicious tackles:

> Abel put his fists in the air, urging Locksmith to retaliate as he walked toward him: "¿Quieres pelear, puto? ¡Bien, vamos!" (You want to fight, bitch? All right, let's go!) Four men quickly stepped in to block any contact between the angry men. Three of them directed their attention to Abel, the seemingly more enraged yet more reasonable of the two. Motor placed his hands on Abel's chest and quietly explained: "It's not worth it. Let it go! Your son is watching." And after reminding him about Locksmith's propensity to fight ("You know how he is"), Motor casually put his arm around Abel and walked him toward the sidelines. When Locksmith asked Abel where he was going, again questioning his character, Chino told him to be quiet: "¡Cállate, maje!" (Shut up, fool!), using a Salvadoran slur to silence his combative compatriot.

Onlookers were not always able to prevent fights. Some fighters evaded intervention. But more often, fighters were given a window of time and space in which to fight. For example, in Ceja and Locksmith's showdown recounted earlier, the long history of their relationship and the slow buildup of tensions caused onlookers to view the looming fight between them as reasonable, even necessary, and so let it happen. Most of these fights were quickly contained after it became clear that one of the combatants had clearly won, as we saw in the confrontations between Ceja and Locksmith and between Nelson and Tico recounted earlier in the chapter. However, there was not always complete agreement whether and when to intervene, as when Tony blocked Ali's attempt to break up the fight between Benny and Benzema.

We see therefore that the degree of consensus varied and that audience involvement was shaped by the way the combatants built up tensions. A long series of "pégame" (hit me) taunts and interventions to stop near fights put the men onstage and made everyone aware that something could happen. Indeed, simmering tensions and repeated threats of violence sometimes even led the crowd to encourage adversaries to fight. As the following example illustrates, crowd involvement did not always entail breaking up fights; instead, by "circling up," onlookers intervened by generating expectations for a fight.

> Problems between Mario Policía and Tico had been brewing for months. Yet in none of their many verbal altercations had punches been thrown. Mario Policía had always been the more reluctant of the two to fight. On this occasion, angered by a hard tackle on the field, Mario Policía showed an uncharacteristic eagerness to fight and approached Tico with his hands in the air and chest pumped out. Although several men were in proximity, they backed away, signaling that they would not intervene. The two men danced back and forth as the crowd gathered around, anxious to see the park heavyweights finally fight. Several men egged Mario Policía on, shouting, "Hit him!" Others advised him not to be scared. Tico threw the first punch, connecting to the side of Mario Policía's thick head, who quickly struck back at Tico. The two men aggressively swung back and forth, although few of their wild punches made contact or caused much damage. When both men appeared tired and uninterested in continuing the fight—trading more insults than punches—Polo stepped in to separate them, followed by several other men who led the fighters in opposite directions. Tico and Mario Policía both seemed content with the outcome and showed little interest in a rematch.

As these examples illustrate, spectators considered some fights at the park more justified and necessary than others. Some were actively encouraged, while others were discouraged or quickly broken up. Moreover, park fights took on new meaning in front of an audience, whose presence could intensify individual grievances and heighten the stakes. For example, while recurring tensions certainly prompted the fight between Nelson and Tico recounted in the opening scene, the crowd of animated spectators made it hard for them to back down once they began trading punches.

I often felt that the men fought less out of anger or animosity and more because they felt pressured to do so by the expectations of their peers. For example, Mario Policía explained to me that he was not so much enraged as compelled to fight Tico once he had committed himself to finally challenge his long-standing foe. Many men spoke of reaching a similar point of "no return," where they felt that they had to fight, regardless of what initially brought them into conflict. This dynamic explains in part why notorious brawlers found themselves in a disproportionate number of park fights. When tensions mounted, their foes were ready to fight, in contrast to the usual constraint shown in park conflicts. Men like Beavis, Locksmith, and Tico known for their violent behaviors found themselves prisoners of their reputations. "I fought because I was in a fight," Beavis explained to me more than once. At the same time, others seemed to back out of potential fights for fear of being unable to put on a good performance in front of their peers.

Thus, the presence of a crowd could affect the trajectory of confrontations in opposite ways. Onlookers offered physical safety through their possible intervention, but could also threaten a person's reputation through their disapproval. They made it simultaneously easier and harder to fight and withdraw. How the crowd intervened—whether by blocking, containing, or encouraging a fight—depended on collective understandings of the men involved and their past history. There was rarely complete agreement about which fights were permissible and why; instead, a general sense prevailed that there were indeed situations in which fighting was justified.

Fighting Your Friends

The men generally fought people they knew and interacted with afterward. For that reason, post-fight relationships had to be renegotiated—a key factor distinguishing park fights from more anonymous conflicts elsewhere. As could be expected, a few men remained bitter enemies after fighting, even years later. Araña, for example, claimed that he rarely approached Darwin, much less spoke with him, because of a fight they had had over fifteen years earlier. Like Araña, several men pointed to a particular fight when explaining to me why they did not associate with someone at the park. In this case, fighting was used as an explanation for a bad relationship, even though the fight had emerged as an expression of already-simmering tensions.

In most cases, however, the men actually developed more substantial relationships after fights, including those that were the most heated and violent. I repeatedly found that fights and the commentary that ensued linked the men in ways that led to deeper connections. The following example illustrates how intimacy emerged out of conflict at the park.

Mago and Pasmado were now trading jokes, despite having exchanged punches less than an hour earlier on the soccer field. Sitting around a picnic table with several other men, Pasmado claimed that Mago tried to squeeze his testicles when he wrestled him to the ground. Mago countered: "Yeah, because you didn't let me punch you." It was rare to see the two men interacting in this way, as they seldom spoke after the games, each retreating to their respective social circles. After their fight, however, they came together to discuss the incident, even recounting the fight in humorous ways for those who had missed it. The fact that Pasmado was fifteen years older and close to a foot taller than Mago made it particularly entertaining for the onlookers, especially since their fight was unexpected. While neither side accepted blame nor claimed defeat, there did not appear to be any lingering animosity between the former foes.

Through this interaction, Mago and Pasmado—with the help of onlookers—transformed their fight into a source of humor and goodwill in the hours and months that followed. Although they had interacted infrequently beforehand, they now talked regularly. Discussions were initially sparked by playful references to their fight. Others now spoke of the two men as a unit as well, drawing on the fight as a point of connection. Mago and Pasmado subsequently joined a long list of men forever linked by a park fight. Fights created a shared history in this case and in countless others, becoming part of the men's historical baggage at the park, which they carried with them as they interacted with others.

Some men avoided fighting by disparaging both the conflict and the relationship, implying that they couldn't be bothered or that their foe was unworthy of a fight. By contrast, men who did fight appeared willing afterward to overlook or move beyond past problems. For example, after publicly feuding for years, Tico and Mario Policía became much friendlier with each other following their fight described above. The same held true for Locksmith and Ceja and many other duos after they traded punches. When recounting their park friendships, the men often pointed to past problems, usually a fight, to explain how much they had been through and overcome with particular men.

During my second month of fieldwork, I experienced this bonding effect firsthand following a physical confrontation with Tico on the soccer field. While barely acquainted beforehand—which may explain why Tico confronted me in the first place after I fouled his teammate—the fight brought us closer together. In striking back, I communicated a willingness to engage and work out our differences on his terms. The conflict gave us a compelling topic of conversation; yet over time, our discussions went beyond the details of the fight. Through these exchanges, we built a deeper connection. For others, this fight became part of our shared history as well. For weeks, men playfully warned us to "watch out" (cuidado) whenever the other approached. The incident facilitated our growing friendship—an unexpected outcome that characterized many of the men's post-fight relations. In our case and others, the fight provided a more direct and immediate connection than our prior months of more distant and guarded interactions at the park. A few months after our scuffle, Tico made this clear to me as we were drinking beer together one afternoon. Casually putting his arm around me, he quipped: "You know I wanted to kick your ass when you first started playing here."

The inherent uncertainty of fighting—who would win, how the men would handle themselves, what the crowd would do, and so on—tended to trap the men in a state of conflict that only full-fledged fisticuffs could resolve. That is, once men communicated a mutual dislike and a willingness to fight, they made it increasingly likely that only fighting could resolve escalating tensions and insecurities. In contrast to the bluster and bravado that characterized most verbal conflict, there was something less ambiguous—and more honest—about engaging physically. And once emotions settled, tensions dissipated, which generally proved cathartic for everyone involved.

I often speculated that problems persisted between men because they had yet to fight. Park regulars seemed to recognize this as well when they urged others to let antagonists fight as a way to resolve persistent conflict.[14] In contrast, when others sensed that antagonisms were "pure show," they suggested alternative ways to diffuse tensions, usually humorous in nature. For example, when two men engaged in a series of what others viewed as empty threats, someone yelled out jokingly: "Give him a kiss!" In other cases, reluctant combatants were playfully urged to "buy a Chihuahua si tienes miedo [if you are scared]."

This is not to argue that fights settled all disputes. However, in most cases, the men's relationships improved rather than deteriorated after fighting, which is not what I expected. In fact, during my time in the park, I did not observe a single rematch between prior combatants, even among the few perennial fighters—clear evidence of the pacifying power of fights. The men felt no need to exchange blows again because one fight did the work of resolving the conflict between them. When I discussed this finding with the men, no one found it surprising. As Roberto explained to me, "After a fight, it's over," echoing Valderrama's words to Nelson cited earlier. Then, pointing to Pisa, who was socializing with a group of men on the other side of the park, Roberto added: "Look at Pisa over there. A lot of those guys tried to kick his ass at one point, including me, but todos somos amigos ahora [we're all friends now]." By contrast, in the case of fights that are retaliatory in nature, such as in gang violence, conflict is never over.[15]

Fight Stories

Relations also hinged on the men's reputations, which were in part established through park fights and the inescapable retelling and analysis that followed. Like soccer, fights gave the men something entertaining to talk about that sustained and invigorated hours of discussion. Fight talk was especially common immediately after a brawl, but stories and debates sometimes involved fights from months, years, even decades in the past. These narratives also communicated news and information to men who may have missed the fight or who were relative newcomers to the park. For example, when I returned to the park nine months after concluding my primary fieldwork, one of the first things I heard about was an epic fight between Araña and Valderrama. Fight stories reminded everyone that "things happened" at the park or, as Locksmith put it, fights were "part of the show."

How and whether the men fought served as concrete reflections of their character. The following case involved a relative newcomer to the park, which is what made it so compelling.

> Everyone seemed excited to talk about a recent fight between Gabe and Lebo. Lebo, a Black South African, was a longtime participant, while Gabe, a local "Gringo," had played in the games for only a few months. The fight drew a lot of interest because Gabe was said to have decisively punched Lebo in the jaw. Although Lebo was the aggressor, he did not fight back, according to witnesses.

Many regular participants of the midday games were surprised to learn of Gabe's willingness and ability to fight, especially since he was a bit of a mystery to the men. The fact that Lebo backed down was also noteworthy, since he was known for his confrontational demeanor. The general consensus that emerged from these discussions was that Gabe was not to be trifled with, whereas Lebo was all talk, as many had already suspected.

Fight stories often recounted incidents from years past, serving as rich components of the men's park-based biographies and identities. As the next example reveals, men were known at the park in part through past fights.

> As I was sitting with several men drinking beer, Motor pointed to Enrique and Landon—or Burro Panzón (Potbellied Donkey) as he was affectionately known at the park—who were walking side by side in our direction. Motor

asked me if I knew that Enrique had beaten up Landon at the park about fifteen years earlier. I replied that I did not know that, but found it hard to believe because Enrique, now in his early sixties, was barely five feet tall and remarkably friendly. In contrast, Landon was big, strong, combative, and almost twenty years younger. Motor and the others laughed at my predictable disbelief. Several proceeded to fill me in on the legendary park fight. Roberto concluded: "You don't mess with Tío [Enrique]. He's kicked some ass in the park." My astonishment prompted a lengthy discussion about other unassuming park brawlers. The men scanned the park for examples. Then when Rafa emerged from the parking lot, several men laughed and playfully shoved Polo. "Cuidado [watch out], Polo," quipped Roberto, "here comes Rafa!" Polo smiled but kept quiet as the men rehashed his renowned defeat in a fight with Rafa years earlier.

Fights gave rise to memories that contributed to the reputations of individuals, as well as to the solidarity and collective history of the group. For example, the incident involving invading cholos was frequently talked about in a way that said something about the group:

Whenever I asked the men about gangs in the park, they invariably discussed a legendary brawl between a group of park veterans and intruding cholos. The decade-old incident was sparked when Moncho—someone who was well liked and almost never fought—was apparently punched by a cholo when he tried to intervene on behalf of two teenagers they were harassing. This led over a dozen park regulars to attack the "invaders." While proud to vaunt their own involvement, the men gave special praise to Pinocho, who they said defeated five opponents by himself.

What this incident showed was the group's solidarity with one another and their desire to keep the park safe for its members. They claimed that it was thanks to this vigilant behavior that the park remained largely free of gang activity.

These stories not only invigorated group life but imbued park fights with greater meaning and drama. Like memorable soccer play, fights had "narrative payoff" at the park by creating "storied selves"[16] and memories that contributed to individual legacies and group lore. Many men were known at the park for a particular confrontation, and group history was sustained in part by several noteworthy incidents. These clashes were a central component of the men's park-based identities and histories, which is why they attempted to control how fights and near fights were remembered and talked about. In telling and debating fight stories, the men constructed an image of themselves and their relationships as they retrospectively made sense of what had happened. And as they did with tales of their soc-cer playing and drinking in the past, many older men claimed that while they no longer fought (or played or drank), they used to and urged me to ask others to support their claims. That is, fight talk—like stories of past prowess on the soccer field—was used to prove a masculine virility that they could no longer display in the present.[17]

Fights and fight stories operated in tandem at the park. Providing ma-terial for lively conversations and debates, these narratives enhanced the meaning of the incidents they commemorated. Fights continued to be waged in the retellings that followed, thereby shaping the context and understandings that others had if and when they themselves faced the weighty decision whether to fight or not. In this way, the behavior of potential fighters was influenced by knowledge of past confrontations and by a concomitant desire to have their own conflicts memorialized in laudatory narratives told to others in the future. I experienced this pres-sure firsthand when I was deliberately knocked over by someone during a midday soccer game. While enraged, I had no interest in fighting, but I knew if I did not respond to this clear disrespect, the men would have incessantly talked about my inaction—even cowardice—afterward. With this in mind, I gave my opponent a forceful shove, and—as I had hoped—we were pulled apart before serious punches were thrown. The stories I had heard about past fights compelled me to respond forcefully in the present. Sure enough, my near fight surfaced as an animated topic of conversation in the days that followed, especially as it was one of the few times I came close to fighting at the park.

Fighting to Prove Oneself

The meaning and consequences of fights went well beyond the actual event. As when playing soccer and drinking beer together, there was the sense that fighting exposed what was most essential and permanent about the men. By revealing aspects of themselves that were usually hidden, fighting helped the men "know" each other and build relations in ways that made sense emotionally.

Interpretations of a particular fight as a window into a person's character were mixed and often contradictory, especially since the men disagreed about the merits and morality of park fights. Some men had widespread reputations as problematic fighters. For many, their general propensity to fight—whatever the reasons—was criticized because it delayed soccer games, disrupted drinking sessions, and brought unwanted attention to the group. Several men claimed not to hire or recommend park brawlers for fears that their fiery behavior would carry over to the job site. By contrast, a few men were widely celebrated for a particular fight, such as Enrique's decades-old defeat of Landon or Pinocho's willingness to take on five alleged gang members by himself. Most men had less remarkable records, but could usually point to at least one moment of near or actual physical conflict at the park that they highlighted in discussions of fights at the park or when I talked privately with them.

I gradually discovered that far more important than the actual outcome of a fight was the information it generated—materials through which the men constructed and debated the reputation of those involved. As with drinking in the park—in which how much or little men drank was less important than how they behaved when drinking—fights created concrete data the men could use, along with other information, to evaluate themselves and others. The fact that fights were rare and hard to pull off made them all the more enthralling. Winning or losing was usually less important than showing a willingness to put their bodies and reputations on the line. Regardless of the outcome, there was something unambiguous about physical assertiveness, especially when contrasted to near-fight posturing.[18] Even when they lost, the men defined themselves as part of the group by their willingness to fight. Indeed, the risk of losing was balanced by the risk of losing face in front of their peers by refusing to fight.

Onlookers' reaction to a fight and their accounts of what had happened also made it possible to cast the incident in a positive light, well after the dust settled. Even the loser gained a degree of respect because of his willingness to fight, as the following field note suggests:

> As expected, all the men wanted to talk about as they sat on the picnic tables was a fight earlier that day between Mario Policía and Tico. The fight between the two park heavyweights was generally considered a draw, even though Mario Policía had a significant scratch on his neck. While Tico socialized with a few men on the other side of the park, Mario Policía sat with the largest gathering of men and seemed to revel in the attention. When Ivan asked him if he anticipated further problems with Tico, Mario Policía nonchalantly replied: "No, it was a fight. Fights happen." He then added, "What happens on the field stays on the field." While Mario Policía insinuated that the fight was "no big deal," he repeatedly asked others how they thought he had fared. The men generally praised his willingness to fight the combative Tico and said he did well. Mario Policía seemed relieved and proudly repeated several times that afternoon: "Tico won't mess with me again. Before he didn't think I would fight."

Like Mario Policía, many men pointed to an altercation or fight that, in their view, changed how other men perceived and related to them. Pinocho, for example, told me that he rarely got into trouble at the park because he had proven to everyone that he wasn't afraid to fight.

The decision whether or not to fight was made publicly in a moment of reckoning visible to everyone watching. Simply showing a willingness to fight communicated resolve and fortitude, as Henry succinctly put it to a potential foe: "¡Aquí estoy!" (Here I am!) Many men disclosed feelings of both fear and exhilaration when recounting park fights, especially the precise moments that transformed verbal conflicts into physical violence. It was therefore not surprising that Mario Policía and others revealed a sense of relief and self-satisfaction after crossing that climactic line, regardless of the outcome. Tellingly, most men remained at the park after fighting in order to bask in the attention and commentary that followed the confrontation.

In contrast, those who chose not to fight and who lacked a good reason for their decision were often viewed with suspicion. Untested, they had yet to reveal their "true self." One man even suggested to me that I needed to fight at the park to be "truly accepted" among the men. As when drinking beer and playing soccer, there was the sense that the men could not really "know" and trust each other until exposed under the most vulnerable of conditions. This was especially true for those who regularly created problems and threatened violence, but who refused to fight, as illustrated by the following exchange:

> Barba sparked a lively post-game discussion by asking: "What's wrong with Diego?"[19] The subject of his question had spent the day arguing with almost everyone—his teammates, opponents, and especially the referee. Several arguments led to near fights, and Diego was eventually kicked out of the game by Chino, the acting referee. Polo expressed exasperation with Diego's "chingaderas" (stupid antics) and worried they might lead to bigger problems. Motor told him not to concern himself with Diego because he was "all talk." Barba agreed and reminded everyone that Diego had never fought in the park, despite endlessly confronting and criticizing people. Mago half-joked that someone should fight him in an effort to "shut him up."

The men's objections to Diego's "chingaderas" suggested a deeper offense. In his reluctance to "meter manos" (put hands on someone), Diego signaled to the others that this group was not worth fighting over. That is, he was perceived to be above contributing in this way, made all the worse by his aggressive posturing. By contrast, those willing to fight communicated a deep commitment to what they had created at Mar Vista. Putting their bodies and reputations on the line, they contributed to the collective effort to show that their world at the park mattered. Unlike Diego, fighters paid their dues and trusted that others would reciprocate when necessary. Rematches were unnecessary because one fight did the work of reaffirming the relationships and identities at play here. Greater intrigue also accompanied clashes of fringe participants like Gabe because their commitment to the group was under question, which is why Diego's inaction generated such contempt. In short, the occasional fight between friends reminded everyone that this world was worth fighting over.

Controlled Violence

Why did the members of this tight-knit community—men who played and drank together and who enjoyed friendly, often jovial relationships— sometimes resort to aggression and violence? As with my questions concerning the men's beer drinking and soccer play, answers to these questions emerged slowly over time. The men's frequent bluster and occasional physical attacks had at first seemed senseless and scary to me, as no doubt they did to other newcomers and passersby. However, I gradually came to understand that fighting and the work of controlling and narrating the fights were part of what bound the men together. It was a process through which camaraderie was displayed, relationships reaffirmed, status negotiated, and social conflicts resolved. And through that process, combatants, onlookers, and storytellers relieved tensions, developed friendships, and generated collective memories.

Much like the Balinese cockfights described by Clifford Geertz, park fights served as a low-risk simulation of local life—a way of doing violence without getting hurt.[20] Like the rooster in a cockfight, controlled violence served as a stand-in for tensions and conflicts between the men. But rather than reflecting the culture of the people as a whole, park fights conveyed rich biographical information about the individuals involved, revealing much about their character and relationships with others. What on the surface appeared chaotic and reckless emerged as an orderly, productive way to resolve the challenges of developing and sustaining deeper connections in a new place.

In the next chapter, I explore how the men's work lives were affected by the relationships and reputations they formed during these fights, as well as by playing and drinking together.

5 * Working Connections

One afternoon about two years into my research at Mar Vista, I joined a group of men sitting at picnic tables by the soccer field. Most of them had just finished playing soccer in the midday games. As I walked over, Mi Chavo hopped in Moncho's truck. As I suspected, he was off to buy beer, which Polo revealed by accusing me of timing my arrival to avoid contributing money. I smiled and responded that he could count on "mis dos pesitos" (my two dollars) for the next beer run. Polo shook his head and replied, "Otro güey que no trabaja." (Another guy who doesn't work.)

Even two years after the economic recession of 2008, good employment opportunities remained scarce for many of the men. That afternoon, Polo was complaining about an overbearing supervisor and claimed he was prepared to quit if he persisted with his "mamadas" (bullshit). When someone questioned his seriousness, Polo replied that he could find work at another restaurant "en dos toques" (in the blink of an eye). Araña told Polo he should be thankful he had a job, as it had been over a month since he himself had laid tile. Valderrama, a general handyman, commented that there was plenty of work in construction so long as you were willing to work "por pesos" (for cheap). Barba challenged these familiar gripes: "Hay jale [there is work], but Araña doesn't want to work. He prefers to drink for free in the park." Araña fired back by pointing out the precariousness of Barba's own situation, who—despite working full-time at a supermarket—was sleeping in his "pinche combi" (fucking van).

As the men talked, Titi remained unusually silent and morose. I knew from previous conversations that he had been struggling to find steady work as a painter. He was trying to set out on his own, rather than work for his brother or other contractors. However, going solo was proving more difficult than he had imagined, despite his years of experience. His expression warmed with the buzzing of his cell phone resting expectantly on the concrete table. He seemed even more pleased when he recognized the number of the incoming call.

Titi stood up and answered the phone in English: "Hello." With one hand on the picnic table, he listened to the voice on the other line and replied: "No problem! Yes, yes. Okay, goodbye." As soon as he hung up, he motioned to Mi Chavo and spoke in his native Spanish: "Let's go, I've got to see un cliente." Polo interjected: "Don't go, Mi Chavo! He was just talking to his vieja [old lady]," implying that his exaggerated talk in English was a ruse to impress the men. Titi ignored Polo's jab, but when Araña asked him where he was headed, he told him to mind his own business. Titi added that he didn't want any "drunks" on his crew, which everyone understood to be a clear crack at Araña, who was always looking for work as a hired hand. As the two men walked toward Titi's van stocked ready with painting supplies, Araña yelled out: "Cuidado [careful], Mi Chavo"—a face-saving and not-so-subtle warning for the "ayudante" (helper). Polo interjected with his own jibe at the departing duo: "Come back with beer!" On cue, Titi shot back: "Busquen trabajo, culeros." (Look for work, assholes.)

*

The world of work was never far removed from the park. Even though many men claimed to come there to escape their workaday lives, intersections between work and play abounded. Work was a frequent topic of conversation, during which the men often complained about problems with bosses or clients and about a general lack of opportunities. Yet as they socialized, they also talked shop and vaunted their achievements and adventures at work. The steady flow of people to and from jobs and phone calls from employers made work feel ever present, especially since cell phones allowed the men to remain "on call" while at the park. Men arriving in clothing stained with dirt and paint as well as vehicles stocked with tools and supplies identified them as workers, as did nicknames like Carwash, Locksmith, Mata Rata (exterminator), and Pisa Muerto (morgue attendant) and iconic park insults like "go heat up the soup" or "go paint toilets." In any case, most of the men were familiar with their peers' employment schedules that kept them on the move. Fixing cars or equipment in the parking lot and planning projects at the picnic tables were other ways the workplace flowed into the park. Moreover, as many of the men worked nearby, the park provided a convenient pit stop or respectable waiting post between jobs. But long stretches in the park could signal a lack of employment—a humiliation exacerbated by the recurring taunt to "look for work."

However, these indicators of employment (or lack thereof) only dimly reflect the close interconnections between park life and the men's work lives. As detailed in previous chapters, what the men created and sustained in the park facilitated the development of relationships and reputations that spilled over into the men's labor. They came to play and unwind, but found that the park provided a vital space to network and generate employment opportunities. Many of the men who met in the park worked together, referred each other for jobs, and exchanged work-related information and resources. Most of these concerned low-paying jobs in restaurants, construction, gardening, and cleaning—positions filled with fellow Latino immigrants. The park also became a place for many of the men to combat the isolation and drudgery of their work, giving them a unique space to construct and revel in meaningful interactions and rewarding relationships.

This chapter explores the men's work lives and their connections to the park and beyond. I focus primarily on labor in private homes, in which I was able to participate and observe projects firsthand, in contrast to other employment sectors (such as restaurant work) that tended to be off-limits and knowable only through interviews. By shadowing the men at work, I saw how social relationships and informal arrangements organized their labor. I also grew to appreciate how an increasingly vital sector of the contemporary economy was filled by immigrant labor in private homes, where—in contrast to the park—the men and other workers like them were welcomed and depended upon.[1]

Immigrant Labor

In Los Angeles and many other parts of the country, certain tasks historically carried out by middle-class and some wealthier homeowners—tasks such as painting, housecleaning, gardening, and childcare—are increasingly done by hired help. Immigrants commonly do this work and are often employed "off the books." Today private homes, rather than factories, serve as major economic points of entry for new immigrants.[2]

This shift in hiring practices is well documented in the research on domestic workers.[3] Less well understood are the types of paid services provided by the men from the park, such as small-scale construction, painting, and gardening jobs.[4] Yet, as with nannies, their work is critical in keeping the culture and economy of Los Angeles afloat. Indeed, in many communities, immigrant labor has become indispensable to the maintenance of smoothly running households and affluent lifestyles. Today's "hourglass economy" generates—and depends on—low-paying jobs,[5] including in restaurants, another major source of employment at the park.[6]

Despite the ubiquity of immigrant labor in Los Angeles, prospective workers and their clients face many challenges in this informal economy. Like any client, homeowners seek to maximize quality and minimize costs, both economic and social. Whereas companies in the formal economy—like painting firms, for example—are publicly accessible and provide institutionalized credibility and legal recourse, they are often much more expensive than off-the-record workers due to greater overhead, licensing fees, insurance costs, and mandated wages and benefits. These requirements also make them less flexible and less adaptable to shifting economic conditions and to the evolving needs of clients.

Anonymous day laborers present different challenges. While usually cheaper, they offer few safeguards to clients if the work goes badly. Moreover, the prospect of selecting workers at a formal or informal hiring center and bringing them in and around one's home can prove daunting for even the most adventurous homeowner. Like day laborers themselves, clients face fears and uncertainties interacting with strangers in an unregulated labor market, be it over theft, negligence, or other forms of abuse.[7] In fact, studies of day-labor sites show how workers and employers try to transcend the competition and anonymity of these sites by establishing more familiar and permanent employment relationships.[8]

While formal companies and day laborers can and do meet homeowner needs, the men served a more intermediary position in the labor market: workers who neither work in the formal economy nor deal with clients as complete strangers. They avoided the heavy costs of regulated companies, as well as the risks of anonymity. However, these work arrangements did not develop automatically or without effort. For in contrast to friendships formed in the park, the relationships between these workers and employers involved people separated by considerable social distance played out within the physical proximity and private spaces of clients' homes. The site of production was also the place of consumption, raising the stakes and providing leverage for both parties.

The Work

During the final three years of my primary fieldwork, I observed fourteen men from the park at work. On roughly half of these jobs, "ayudantes" (paid helpers) from the park assisted. In total, I observed thirty-four jobs over a three-year period. In twenty-five of these projects, a range of new tasks or "extras" were added to the original labor agreement as the work progressed. Several of these expanded jobs lasted over a month, although most projects were completed in under two weeks.

The work primarily involved maintenance and home-improvement jobs, including construction, painting, cleaning, gardening, and renovation projects. The size and format ranged from small-scale or repeat tasks (such as fixing a fence or repainting a bedroom) to long-term arrangements (such as weekly gardening or pool maintenance) to large-scale projects (like remodeling a kitchen or repainting an entire home). In many cases, the men had worked for clients for several years, even decades, although I observed initial and onetime encounters as well. Work relationships often began with small, short-term tasks, but then developed over time into more substantial, long-term arrangements.

I primarily shadowed the men at work in West Los Angeles. Occasionally, they serviced multimillion-dollar homes in the most exclusive sections, such as Beverly Hills, Brentwood, and Malibu. But more typically they worked for middle- and upper-middle-class White homeowners in and around Santa Monica, Venice, Pacific Palisades, and Culver City. As I drove around with the men, this area became a monument of sorts to their professional careers as they pointed out various homes they had worked in over the years—some within a few blocks of the park.[9]

In addition to location, the jobs shared several other characteristics, notably the fact that the men generally worked directly for the homeowner, rather than for a third party, such as a contractor or property manager. The men described this job arrangement as "por mi cuenta" (on my own). Many of the men had experience working for compañías or as ayudantes but preferred working independently. Although this work could be sporadic and uncertain, they found it more lucrative and enjoyed the freedom and flexibility that came with being self-employed. However, working on their own did require them to constantly look for new jobs—what sociologist Mary Romero referred to as "finding *casas*" in her study of domestic workers.[10] Unlike their friends employed in restaurants, they did not work for a salary on a regular schedule.

Chango's career arc followed a familiar path from apprentice to entrepreneur.[11] He started painting with his father, who taught Chango the trade over weekends and summers. Seeking greater independence and new experiences after finishing high school, Chango began working for other contractors and spent over a year with a commercial painting firm. But by his late twenties and with a growing family at home, he was anxious to set out on his own. Feeling confident in his skills and start-up funds, he embarked on this new chapter in his professional life. By the time I met him in his early thirties, Chango was well established as an independent painter, moving from one casa to the next.

Like other independent contractors, Chango sometimes needed to hire additional workers. These ayudantes were almost always people he knew, rather than anonymous workers encountered on the street. The contractors I met at the park often employed the same helpers, most of whom they knew from Mar Vista. Seven ayudantes from the park accompanied the men on jobs I observed, and two helpers not associated with the park were hired as well. Like Chango, most men had begun their careers as ayudantes, working as apprentices under a more seasoned professional.[12] Occasionally, men who typically worked on their own would work as helpers. The vast majority of these shifting arrangements and relationships were tied to the park.

The work was generally "informal" in that it was not regulated by or reported to the government.[13] Usually the parties relied on verbal agreements and cash payments, although contracts were sometimes produced and services paid with personal checks. Although federal and state regulations do apply to this type of work, I never sensed that either party was aware of or concerned with these guidelines. Neither party secured permits for any of the projects I observed, although the men acknowledged that some jobs did require formal approval. In some cases, they took special efforts to avoid inspection; in other cases, they claimed to have lost out on jobs because they were unable to secure a permit or to meet other licensing or insurance requirements. I never observed any clients openly inquiring about the men's legal status when negotiating the fee or scope of work.

How the men secured work varied, but these jobs almost always involved some sort of referral or recommendation either from a client or a fellow worker. Few of the men actively solicited work from strangers through business cards, advertisements, or employment agencies. The helpers generally worked for someone they knew as well, rather than seeking work at day-laborer centers. Clients, in turn, typically hired someone they knew or recommended either by friends, neighbors, or colleagues or by people they had employed for other jobs.

Friends and Family

Taking Titi as a paradigmatic case, we see how a variety of personal ties could generate work opportunities. It was his mother-in-law's recommendation that led to the phone call he received in the opening vignette. She recommended Titi to paint the inside of a condominium apartment she had cleaned for over twenty years. Another referral came to Titi through a former soccer teammate, who recommended him for a job painting two bedrooms in a home where he was installing new windows. And Motor— another friend from the park—urged his client to hire Titi to paint a kitchen he was in the process of remodeling. In all three cases, the recommendations led to Titi securing the job.

Titi's work history reveals the value of ties to people who work in private homes. Indeed, the more people the men knew with such clients, the greater the potential for referrals. As working-class Latino immigrants, their social circle tended to include people who did similar "brown-collar" work, although not all networks were of equal value.[14] Although the men drew referrals from other parts of their lives, the park became a key networking site, especially because it brought together men who did similar work.

Chances for referrals were also high because of the various jobs that unfold in the life of a home, as well as the need for regular maintenance. Along with shifting cultural expectations, the pressures of a competitive real-estate market produce a steady supply of work as well. Upper-class clients regularly asked their working-class hires for recommendations for maintaining their homes. As the clients suspected, the men almost always knew someone who could do the work, if they did not offer themselves as candidates for the job. Moreover, they could usually count on the work being done well at low cost, which is what drew them to this intermediary sector of the labor market in the first place.

For example, as Titi was painting a wall above a fireplace, his client asked him if he knew someone who could install a new gas fixture, adding that she was tired of not having a working fireplace. Titi replied that he did, although he admitted to me that at the time he wasn't sure who could do the job. But the following week, he returned with Raul, a plumber he knew from the park, and the two men installed a new unit, splitting the earnings in half. The client later explained that she asked Titi about the fireplace because she was worried that a "company" would be too expensive. She added that she didn't want to deal with "all the hassle" of finding someone and negotiating the terms by herself. In fact, she told Titi to "take care of it" and did not ask him how much it would cost. To her relief, Titi knew someone who could do the job at an affordable rate.

Referrals were usually made in response to client requests, but were also offered in anticipation of their service needs. Workers often made suggestions—and subsequent referrals—for work that might be less noticeable to the client. For example, Valderrama mentioned that his brother-in-law, a gardener, frequently brought issues (such as a rotting fence or a cracked wall) to the attention of his clients. Similarly, when Titi noticed that a client's gutter was leaking, he told him he knew someone who could repair it. Talking with me later, the homeowner expressed gratitude for having had the problem identified and fixed. When I asked him what he would have done without the recommendation, he explained: "I'm sure I would have found someone to take care of it, but it would have been a pain and taken a while." He later joked: "I probably wouldn't even have noticed it, like a lot of things around this house." Indeed, I often saw men working on a job recommend a friend or relative to fix problems the homeowner had put off handling or hadn't even noticed.

However, a referral did not guarantee employment. I observed several men who missed out on jobs, despite having received a strong recommendation, usually due to scheduling conflicts or disagreements over fees. The referral merely opened up the possibility of work by bringing the two parties together. Yet hiring through word of mouth offered the advantage of lessening the uncertainty that came with anonymity and the men's unregulated status. Not only do people tend to trust people they know—which is why they ask for recommendations in the first place—they also recognize that the recommender's reputation is on the line, which is especially important if future work is at stake. The stakes of the referral became apparent when clients talked fondly of the recommender when negotiating a new hire. For example, meeting Titi for the first time, his client gushed about how much she loved his mother-in-law, Gladys, who cleaned for her, and how happy she was to help out her family. The client later told me in confidence that she trusted Gladys's judgment, but also knew she would "keep an eye on" her son-in-law. After the job was completed to her satisfaction, she presumably expected Titi—who by then had earned her trust—to serve the same role in supervising Raul on the fireplace project. As in other workplaces, the referral was leveraged as a source both of information and control.[15]

*

Referrals were rarely made strictly for benevolent reasons. The men making the referral expected to be compensated, although the form of compensation varied. In some cases, a cash payment was offered. For example, Locksmith usually gave around ten dollars to doormen he knew at several Santa Monica high-rises when they referred him to residents locked out of their apartments. In another case, Pow Wow gave Barba fifty dollars for a job he helped him win. When I asked Barba what would have happened if Pow Wow had not paid him, he replied: "Nothing, I just wouldn't have recommended him anymore."[16] As Barba was a sociable man who mingled in different social circles, Pow Wow would have lost a valuable contact. In this way, Barba underlined the importance of maintaining relationships with well-connected people.

Reciprocity was more typically achieved through subsequent referrals rather than through cash payments. The prospect of future employment was what most motivated the men to recommend others: "Hoy por ti, mañana por mí." (Today for you, tomorrow for me.) Valderrama explained his decision to refer fellow workers in these terms: "If I help someone [get jobs], they'll help me out later with work." This form of exchange was most common among those whose work lent itself to helping others. For example, Beto (a carpenter), Chicas (an electrician), and Caballo (a plumber)—all friends from the park—frequently referred each other to clients, either in the course of doing a job or when contacted by a client. Like the exchanges and associated obligations built around beer drinking at the park, the trading of job referrals indebted the men to each other and deepened their relationships. Generally, there was a double bonus in these exchanges since the referral benefited their friends and employers, thereby increasing their status and future prospects with both parties. Understandably, the men were excited when their friends obtained work as it could lead to opportunities for them. For example, when I told Martín that Titi had been contacted for a new painting project, he replied: "Ojalá [hopefully] he gets it," knowing this could mean work for him as a helper.

Referrals did not go smoothly every time. There was always a delicate balance between helping out a friend and making sure that person would do a good job; indeed, even a skilled worker could behave inappropriately, showing up late or offending the homeowner in other ways. A bad referral could have disastrous consequences for everyone involved, as illustrated by a falling out between Titi and Motor over a job gone sour:

> As Titi was repainting a home, the client asked him if he knew someone who could install new kitchen cabinets. Titi recommended Motor, having worked with him before on a similar job. Recently, the two men had been socializing more often after Titi had begun playing for the soccer team Motor coached. Motor agreed to take on the job, happy to have found work after a brief stretch of inactivity.
>
> The client purchased the cabinets, and Motor went to work installing them. The two men rarely interacted because instructions were passed through Titi. When Motor finished, the client said his wife was unhappy with how they looked. She wanted them positioned differently. He claimed that Motor had not followed his instructions and that he would not pay him until the cabinets were moved. Titi relayed the news to Motor, who was already growing anxious about being paid for three days of work. Motor pushed back, arguing that he did exactly what Titi said the client had requested. He refused to move the cabinets until he was paid for the work he had already done. In the meantime, unbeknownst to Titi, the client found someone else to do the job, and Motor was never paid.

Despite making this "bad" referral, Titi was nevertheless fortunate to avoid the worst-case scenario in which both workers were fired. Instead, as more typically happened in these cases, the client continued to hire the first one for work—as he had already proven himself—but no longer asked for his suggestions.

Consequently, with fewer opportunities to recommend people, Titi's own chances of receiving referrals declined. As the men depended on the exchange of referrals, it was therefore in their best interest to offer reliable recommendations to their clients, at least to those with whom they wished to remain in good standing. Similarly, those referred were under pressure to perform well if they hoped to be recommended again for jobs in the future. Like their clients, the men used the prospect of future referrals as a means to motivate their protégés and to keep them in line. For example, Titi told Motor that there would likely be much more work with the client to whom he was recommending him "si termina bien" (if it ends well). Yet the job, as we learned, did not go well, after which Titi chided Motor: "You lost a lot of work with that guy!"

At the same time, there was sometimes trepidation about introducing a potential competitor to a client. Indeed, many of the men were adept at different home-improvement tasks or at least professed to be. For example, Titi (a painter) preferred to recommend Motor for carpentry jobs, rather than Valderrama, because the latter was also a skilled painter. By contrast, Titi claimed that Chango no longer employed him on his painting crew because he was worried Titi would "steal his clients." Chango laughed when I asked him if this was really the case, but he did not dispute Titi's allegation. While these two men remained friends, I knew of several relationships that soured due to pilfered work. So it was hardly surprising that the men were very careful in choosing whom they recommended to their clients.

Building Reputations at the Park

The park represented a key social setting for the men to sort out many of these concerns. As the opening vignette shows, the men often talked about their work as they socialized. Through these stories, the men learned about each other as workers—information they later used to make decisions about whom to hire or recommend. As expected, tales of referrals or hiring arrangements gone bad garnered special attention. For example, it took several years for Coloccini to restore his reputation after Barba told everyone at the park he bungled a job he had helped him secure. Barba later told me he was angry with Coloccini because the client—who owned several apartment buildings—no longer asked him to recommend workers, thereby depriving him of fees for referrals and also reducing opportunities for recommendations for himself from those he might otherwise have recommended. Similarly, after Secada was caught by a client taking a shower in her home, Araña, who had hired him, was immediately fired. Subsequently, many men refused to employ Secada as a helper. But culpability was not always clear or uncontested. For example, Secada claimed that Araña made up the shower story to avoid paying him. Similarly, following the kitchen cabinet debacle, outsiders disagreed over who was at fault; some felt that Titi was responsible for the miscommunications with the client and therefore should have paid Motor out of pocket for his work.

As these cases suggest, workers' reputations were an important and guarded source of currency at the park. In lieu of firsthand knowledge, the men's performance and behavior on the job were the grounds on which referrals or hires were based. It is therefore hardly surprising that the men aggressively promoted and protected their standing as workers. This meant making sure others knew they were working, which was always in doubt when they were at the park. The men communicated this verbally, but also by arriving in vehicles stocked with supplies and in clothing stained with dirt or paint. When possible, the men also took their breaks at the park. Phone calls with clients, especially when conducted in English, were another way to signal active work lives. Although these moves were not necessarily deliberate, their implication was brought into focus when others joked that these phone calls were only simulations of the real thing, as Polo did when mocking Titi's phone conversation recounted at the opening of the chapter.

Work histories took on a more forceful and strategic tone in the men's storytelling. As they socialized, they were quick to publicize successful jobs and wealthy clients—a strategy evident in the following exchange:

> It was late afternoon on a Tuesday when Valderrama pulled into the parking lot. Manuel, his regular helper, was sitting in the passenger's seat. Valderrama hopped out of his truck and walked straight over to the group of men I was sitting with by the picnic tables. He was wearing jeans, boots, and a flannel shirt, all of which looked dusty from a hard day's work. Valderrama said hello and exchanged handshakes with most of the men. He then sat down and exhaled deeply as he stretched out his arms and legs. He seemed relieved to be sitting down.
>
> After surveying the scene, Valderrama blurted out to no one in particular: "What a day!" Filling the silence, he reached out to Martín, a fellow construction worker: "Hey, Martín, remember that job in Brentwood by the school? I'm working over there. We're fixing a stone wall by the entrance." Sensing he had Martín's attention, he continued: "Puros millonarios [nothing but millionaires] over there. They have a pool, security guard, de todo [everything]! But the owner wants it exact. He's European." Gaining momentum, he turned to another colleague in the business: "Motor, you should see the wall, pura calidad [top quality]." Martín and Motor nodded their heads in approval, but the latter then cautioned: "Don't forget to finish it," alluding to a well-known situation from a few years earlier when Valderrama failed to complete a job he was working on with Motor. Valderrama laughed and responded: "We're almost done. We could have finished today, but there's no rush. Hopefully there's more work."

As with Valderrama, the stories the men shared about their work tended to involve bigger jobs and more affluent clients. Like their friends who worked in restaurants, the men felt better about serving important people, so they had a personal interest in elevating the status of the people for whom they worked.[17] They tried to gain status by association, not only to boost their self-worth, but also as a way to promote their skills. In borrowing prestige from their clients, they built themselves up as prestigious workers and therefore as worthy of being recommended by their peers.

But like much that was said at the park, these statements tended to be met with scrutiny and suspicion. For example, several men questioned Titi's claims about the new job mentioned in the opening section and joked that he had actually been hired to have sex with the elderly client. Workers relied on their powers of persuasion, but also called on companions to corroborate their statements. With most of the men working alone or in pairs in isolated homes, stories were a key way to publicize their work experience in order to increase their chance of being hired or recommended for other jobs.[18] As Valderrama did with Manuel, the men often engaged me in conversation about their work when socializing with the other men, asking me to tell the others about the fanciness of the home or the particularities of a client. I suspect that one of the reasons the men were willing to take me along to their jobs was in order to use me as a more neutral source of corroboration.

*

In addition to stories about the men's work, park life—as we've learned—provided ample opportunity to evaluate their character in ways that affected the men's hiring practices and referrals. For example, Beavis felt that he was denied work as an ayudante because "I get into too many fights." Several men told me that they did not hire or recommend one man for jobs because they had seen or heard about him stealing at the park. Several men were excluded from employment deals because of their heavy drinking, for fears that they would show up drunk or not at all. Others were shunned because of their failure to adequately reciprocate in dealings with their peers. For example, when I asked Pachanga why he refused to work for a notorious freeloader at the park, he replied: "How am I going to work for him? He never puts in money for beer!" Sensing that I did not understand the connection, he clarified: "If he doesn't pay *here*, he's not going to pay *there*!" Park interactions also put pressure on workers to behave on the job, as Robert explained when questioning rumors claiming that a park regular failed to pay his assistants: "How are you not going to pay someone you see at the park every day?"

By contrast, men who handled themselves well at the park—whether on the soccer field or drinking beer together—were more likely to be considered for jobs. For although they came to have fun, they recognized the opportunities that could arise from interactions with a large group of men in similar lines of work. Most men also preferred to work with friends since this helped pass the time, despite the occasional complications. Like an invitation to drink a beer together, hiring or recommending someone for a job solidified and deepened relationships at the park. For example, when I commented to Roberto during a return visit to L.A. that Polo and Motor seemed to be spending a lot more time together at the park, he responded: "It's because Polo's working with Motor now," the former having decided to take a break from decades in the restaurant industry. As in this case and many others, bonds built at the park and on the job became mutually reinforcing and facilitated a range of employment opportunities.

Referrals from Clients and Their Circle of Friends and Neighbors

Referrals also came from the men's existing clients, who represented another key means of networking. Often these recommendations were requested by clients' friends or neighbors who needed people to service their home, but had yet to find qualified and trustworthy workers to do the job. For example, several clients explained to me that their friends were always looking for "good help." In the crowded and largely unregulated informal labor market, finding "good help" could be difficult, which is what made recommendations so valuable. A referral based on firsthand experience offered them assurances that the job would be done well. It also provided information about cost, another source of uncertainty. Moreover, in contrast to recommendations for restaurants or movies, the stakes were high, as one client emphasized as she negotiated with a prospective hire: "This is my home. I live here and need the work to be done correctly." A referral from a trusted adviser helped allay these concerns.

All fourteen of the men I followed said they received work through client referrals. For example, the painting job Titi secured through his mother-in-law resulted in the client referring him to three of her friends, two of whom ended up hiring him. She even invited friends to her home to meet Titi and to see his work. Months later, one of these new clients told me that she was "so happy" to have met Titi because "he's done such a good job" painting her apartment. I observed a similar development with Chango. A client invited two of his friends to meet him and to inspect the finished job. Chango ended up painting their homes, which expanded his clientele and earnings.

Several of the men pointed to a particular client who had been especially helpful in introducing them to new clients. For example, Chango attributed his heavy workload to referrals from a longtime client who owned a paint store and who recommended him to many of her customers. Similarly, Motor secured a series of jobs in an apartment complex after doing work for someone he met playing soccer at the park who recommended him to his neighbors. A particularly striking example of networking through clients concerns Araña, who obtained a number of jobs through members of an extended family he had worked for over the previous two decades. The depth of his connections to that family became clear when I observed him installing kitchen tiles in the home of a man Araña had known as a child when he was working for his parents.

The men's affluent, primarily White clients dwelt in very different social circles from them and consequently had access to a wider range of people outside the men's networks. By putting the men in contact with other homeowners, these "weak ties" expanded the men's opportunities.[19] This was especially true of the better-connected and more motivated clients. These links were crucial, given that these clients had only so much work to do and money to invest in their own homes.

The men also told me stories about clients trying to poach them when they were working as ayudantes, just as their colleagues suspected. For example, Pasmado told me about a client who surreptitiously asked for his phone number as he discussed a future job. The men believed clients did this because they assumed that so-called helpers would be less expensive than their bosses. They also had the comfort of having seen the men at work in their home. Notwithstanding the potential for greater earnings and autonomy, the men said they were careful about sharing their contact information because allegations of job poaching could tarnish their relationships and reputation, as previously explained. Despite these risks, several men told me that they developed more independent relationships with clients after initially meeting them as hired hands. Like Valderrama, most of the men got their start as ayudantes, and this was one way to strike out on their own. Clients' underhanded moves also show the lengths to which they would go to secure cheap and dependable labor for themselves and their friends. Yet at the same time, they expanded the men's reach into untapped networks.

*

The visibility of the men and their work proved to be another valuable source of referrals. The fact that the homeowners' friends and neighbors saw the men on the job gave prospective clients an opportunity to observe and interact with them. As with referrals from employees and friends, these interactions lessened some of the costs and uncertainties involved in the hiring process. Instead of choosing a stranger through advertisements or at a day-laborer center, the chance to talk with the men and observe them at work gave a prospective client confidence that the job would be done well for a reasonable price.

Over the course of my research, I observed sixteen neighbors approach the men about potential jobs in their homes. Clients usually spoke directly about the work, but sometimes began with small talk, without making specific reference to a job. The men quickly realized that the neighbors were "feeling them out," which explains why they never ignored or dismissed these onlookers, no matter how distracting or strange these encounters may have seemed. Here's an example of one such encounter:

> As Güero—a gardener—was packing up his equipment, a White man in his mid-forties walked by with his dog. The man stopped and stared at Güero for a bit and then blurted out: "Muy caliente" (very hot) in accented Spanish. Güero smiled and replied, "Sí," as he returned to his work under the scorching sun. The man then asked Güero in English if he had just worked at the home in front of which he was parked. Güero answered yes and set down the hedge trimmer he was in the process of repairing. The man took this opening to explain that he was looking for someone to do his yardwork. Güero nodded and responded, "Okay." Güero went into his truck for a piece of paper to write down his given name (Francisco) and phone number. He handed it over to the man, who was being pulled away by his dog. As he departed, he shouted out: "We'll talk later."

While prospective clients usually approached the men on the edges of the work site, it was not uncommon for people to enter their neighbor's home to observe the work firsthand and speak with the men, even when the homeowner was not around. As with encounters on the street, the men did not appear startled or at all bothered by these intrusions, perhaps because the intruders were generally White and appeared to live in the area.

All the men I followed said that they had independently secured work with a client's neighbor or with someone simply passing by the client's home. They admitted that not all conversations led to work; but, well aware of the rewards their visibility could bring, they appreciated the potential of these interactions. As Güero explained, "My work is my best advertisement." It was therefore not surprising that the men seemed to spend considerable time and energy perfecting sections of their work visible to passersby, especially in walkable neighborhoods. For example, when I asked Motor why he was redoing a part of a fence the client would not be able to see, he replied with a wink: "Para los vecinos" (for the neighbors), which he later confirmed was in the hope of attracting new business. For the same reason, the men rarely changed out of work clothes stained with paint or dirt, as they recognized this as another way of advertising their skills. Thus, rather than *lower* the visibility associated with their status as immigrant workers, the men tried to *heighten* it by lingering near the job site and calling attention to the quality of their work.[20]

Not all jobs provided the same visibility or opportunities. Those whose work kept them more hidden from public view engaged in other strategic forms of self-promotion in the hope of publicizing their work. For example, Enrique made a point of leaving supplies and equipment in and around his truck to identify himself as a pool cleaner, which was harder to see since he worked in backyards. This became apparent when I noticed him speaking with a client's neighbor. When I asked Enrique how the neighbor knew he cleaned pools, he responded, "You see that net? I always leave one sticking out the back window." In this case, the neighbor explained that he had just moved into the neighborhood and was looking for someone to clean his pool. Enrique gave the man his phone number and, several weeks later—having "caught" the client with his net—added the home to his route.

When I asked Enrique why he did not post a sign and phone number on his truck—which seemed a more straightforward way to share his information—he replied: "Porque no vale la pena." (Because it's not worth it.) Like Enrique, few of the other men had business cards or any identifying information on their trucks or their work clothes. Some claimed to have advertised this way in the past, but had not found that it attracted much business. In any case, these more formal signs of organization might have made them appear more expensive and regulated. There was a certain benefit for their business to appear informal, small scale, and presumably undocumented in the eyes of their clients, as when Titi's client asked for help from one of his "friends" to fix her fireplace. Publicizing a company name and phone number on one's truck or work clothes would have disrupted this image. Moreover, clients and workers alike appreciated the value of referrals—rather than more indirect methods—to initiate work arrangements. In fact, some clients later confided to me that they had not seriously considered initiating a project until they saw the men at work, which suggests that the prospect of finding someone to do a competent job represented a barrier overcome by the visibility of the men.

That these men secured work through referrals should be of little surprise, especially to migration scholars who repeatedly show the significance of social networks in employment outcomes. Indeed, a common theme in migration studies is the mobilization of interpersonal ties by immigrants to further their material interests.[21] The men secured work through multiple sources, which together formed a dynamic web of relations that expanded with every successful project. However, as we shall see, the most noteworthy and illuminating aspect of the men's work proved to be the consequences of networking on the job.

Networking on the Job

Referrals figured prominently in workplace dynamics, both in terms of how the men viewed and carried out their work and how clients attempted to motivate and control their labor. For example, the men claimed to take on projects and even lower their fee in the hope of securing future work. For reasons that often escaped my attention, they looked beyond the requirements of any one task when deciding which projects to pursue, how much to charge, and how to conduct themselves on the job.

The prospect of further employment and greater earnings was always on the men's minds as they negotiated with clients and completed a given project. For example, as Titi painted the interior of the condominium apartment referred to in the opening vignette, he repeatedly told me that he expected to paint the exterior of the building, which he pointed out needed a fresh coat. In fact, it became a running joke between us every time we went outside for him to tell me: "I'm going to paint this building." He later told me that he was motivated to take the inside job in the hope of securing the more lucrative outside job. Although it turned out that the residents were not ready to repaint the exterior, Titi eventually won a job painting several rooms in another unit, thanks to the client's recommendation.

For a different client, Titi agreed to do a small-scale painting job in the expectation of getting hired for additional work he felt was necessary, given the condition of the home. As he anticipated, the initial $500 job to paint the front porch led to the much larger $9,000 contract to paint the entire home's interior. Like Titi, the men were eager to secure employment in homes that appeared to require substantial work, even if meant beginning with smaller, less profitable projects. The wealth and aspirations of clients were also taken into account. For example, when pursuing the initial porch project, Titi told me with a big smile that the client "tiene mucha plata" (has a lot of money). Similarly, Valderrama explained his interest in a potential job because he had heard that the client bought and sold houses. By contrast, some clients were found to be stingy or short on funds and thus not worth cultivating.

The prospect of more lucrative jobs affected not only the men's choice of projects, but also the quality of their work. For example, when I asked Titi why he was being especially diligent repainting a closet, he replied: "She'll see me doing a good job and recommend me to her friends." As mentioned earlier, Motor explained that he took extra care installing the fence around a multi-unit condominium, knowing that both the client and other residents would be watching. Based on his past experiences, he believed that once the client's neighbors saw the quality of his work, they would consider him for their own projects. Sure enough, a second resident hired him to fix a bedroom door, and a third hired him to install a shelving unit. The last time we spoke, he had completed three more jobs in the same twelve-unit complex as he further established himself as a skillful and dependable handyman.

The quality of the men's work, however, was not always clear to the client. Often they were not able to perceive or appreciate the effort and skill involved. Consequently, the men took pains to draw the client's attention to less conspicuous aspects of their labor in order to highlight their diligence and expertise. They made the quality of their work more visible to earn approval for the job at hand, but also with an eye toward the future. For example, when painting the condo, Titi regularly called the client over to show her various problems he was fixing or challenges he was facing in executing the job. In one instance, he asked her to stand on his ladder to inspect a small crack in the ceiling that he was in the process of filling. "A lot of painters come and just paint without looking," he explained to her. "I take my time and do it right." This interaction served not only to highlight the quality of his work, but also to assuage the client's growing concerns over how long the job was taking.

Like Titi, the men often asked clients to inspect their work and compared themselves favorably to less skilled or less careful workers in order to tout their services and justify what they charged. And, like Titi, they also employed a range of other tactics to showcase their talents, including more indirect strategies, such as making elaborate gestures to cover and protect furniture or leaving expensive materials in full view for clients to see, even if they didn't actually use them on the job. Similarly, several painters told clients they bought materials from an upscale shop in Santa Monica, when they really bought cheaper alternatives from Home Depot. Above all, they were always careful to maintain clean and tidy job sites. At times, the men employed more duplicitous strategies to impress their clients, such as taking shortcuts without informing them, concealing problems, or taking longer on tasks to make the work seem more involved in order to increase their fee. For example, Motor surreptitiously removed part of a railing to maintain a level fence, and Pow Wow concealed a scratch on a floor using a colored marker and putty. In one of the more extreme cases, a man I shadowed filled a garbage bag with dirt from outside, which he then claimed to the homeowner to have cleaned off the window frames and blinds. As Güero explained, it was important to "mantener" (care for and cultivate) the client, and there were a variety of ways to do this, some more underhanded than others.

The men also explained that they adjusted their pricing in relation to what the job might bring. For example, Titi claimed that he could have charged $7,000 for the condo painting job. But hoping a lower fee would lead to additional jobs in the building and worried about being outpriced by someone else, he decided to charge only $5,000. By contrast, Titi confided to me that he inflated his price on a different job because he did not expect it to lead to subsequent work. Similarly, Motor offered a relatively low price on the fence job because it was his first project at the site, correctly anticipating that it would lead to other work, provided he did a good job.

The men also considered the long-term prospects of a particular client. For example, Valderrama agreed to charge one client a low rate because, as the owner of several apartment buildings, he had provided a steady supply of work for him over the previous fifteen years. These jobs became especially important as Valderrama struggled to find work with other clients during the economic downturn that began in 2008. In fact, whenever we discussed his work history and prospects, Valderrama quipped, but only half-jokingly, that this key employer "better not die!" When dealing with their regular clients, the men offered special treatment in addition to inexpensive rates. For example, Chango served regularly as a handyman for one family, and Motor did frequent work for the owner of a dozen rental homes. In both cases, the work was not always lucrative and could interfere with other projects, but the men always gave them priority. At first, I was perplexed to see them leave a job or the park to attend to their clients' needs—sometimes for something as small as a blown fuse or burned-out lightbulb. However, I grew to appreciate how important these clients were to the men because of the steady work they had provided over the years. In cases such as these, seemingly trivial tasks were understood as part of larger endeavors.

*

For the most part, the men's approach to their work coincided with clients' interests. Clients wanted quality work at a reasonable price, which explains why they initially hired the men and subsequently rehired or referred them to others. That many of the men were skilled in a variety of trades—or usually knew someone who could do the work they could not—was crucial for securing the various jobs that unfolded in the life of a home. Chango's work for a key client over twelve months illustrated this diversity and consistency of ventures: at this client's home, he repainted two bedrooms, rewired a bathroom, delivered and installed a large bookcase, and removed a small tree from the backyard.

The alignment between the men's skill and affordability, on the one hand, and the clients' needs, on the other, was hardly surprising. More surprising were the ways clients deliberately exploited the possibility of future work as a source of leverage and control. For example, when negotiating costs with Titi, the client repeatedly mentioned: "I know people with money." When installing the fence, the client tried to lower the price by suggesting to Motor that the other condominium residents would want his services, especially with his recommendation. One of Güero's prospective clients made a similar point as they were negotiating a bimonthly gardening contract: "Everyone knows me here. I'll help you out."

Clients also used the prospect of future jobs to motivate the men to do their best work. They understood that the workers had longer-term interests and tried to leverage their best performance by tapping into their ambitions. It was a game of persuasion played by both parties, but with different goals and resources. For example, as one of Titi's clients was inspecting his work, she reiterated that if he did a good job, she would be sure to refer him to her "rich friends." She then added: "Trust me, they know I'm picky," implying that her recommendation carried weight. Similarly, after a decorator helped Chango secure a painting job with one of her wealthy clients, she told him in front of the homeowners: "This is good for you. Make sure you do a good job." We see a similar approach used by the client who hired Motor for the fence project discussed earlier. After inspecting Motor's handiwork, the client joked that he would soon be working all over the neighborhood—a prediction he then fulfilled by introducing Motor to a neighbor who needed a broken window frame fixed. This, as we saw, led to several other projects in the same building. In the case of longtime clients, the prospect of future work could go unspoken, but nevertheless motivated the men to do their best. For example, when I asked Valderrama why he was redoing a section of a wall for one of his main clients, he replied, "He would eventually see [the problem], and then I'd be in trouble." Valderrama and the others knew the risks of losing a valued client.

Extracting "Extras"

While referrals opened up the possibility for future work, "extras" were often a sure way for the men to increase their earnings. By "extras"—a term used by the men—I refer to work added to the initial job agreement.[22] In most cases, the men were financially compensated for this additional work, although clients were adept at extracting free labor as well.

Given the nature of the home and workplace, the possibilities for supplemental work were ever present. Most homeowners had a long list of home-improvement needs apart from what they actually hired the men to do. Some predated the men's arrival; others emerged over the course of a project. Motivated by the men's presence and know-how, clients regularly asked them to take on additional tasks. These tasks were generally small and seemingly minor. For example, one of Titi's clients asked him to do a variety of chores as he painted her condominium, a job that took approximately three weeks to complete. Over the course of two consecutive days, she asked him to change a lightbulb, hang a picture frame, water a plant, empty the trash, watch her dog, retrieve boxes from storage, and help her unload groceries from her car. The client prefaced each request with some version of "since you're here." Some of these tasks she certainly could have done herself, but others—like changing a hard-to-reach light bulb and hanging a heavy picture frame—would have been too difficult for her to do. But for Titi, these were relatively simple undertakings, especially with the help of a tall ladder and a strong coworker. Hiring someone for these menial jobs, however, would have seemed outlandish.

As I observed with Titi and several other of the men, clients often asked workers to do unpaid jobs around the home unrelated to the project for which they were hired. For example, as Motor was removing an old fence around an apartment complex, one of the residents asked him if he could remove a dozen wood planks from her back porch. This request was more substantial than most, taking us around twenty minutes to remove and dispose of the rotting wood. The client's visible relief suggested that she felt unable to remove the rotting wood herself. Yet for Motor and his helper, moving the wood was relatively easy; moreover, he had his truck to haul it away. In this case, as in many others, the men possessed the strength, skill, and equipment to take on tasks their clients could not. Motor agreed to the work without any mention of pay, but after we finished, he told the resident that she should call him if she needed any additional assistance. Later that day, she asked Motor if he could fix an uneven door. In this case, she paid him $100 for two hours of work.

I was repeatedly struck by how frequently and nonchalantly clients asked the men to do work beyond what they were initially hired to do. They seemed to believe that hiring workers for one job entitled them to complimentary assistance on other household tasks, some of which they could have done themselves. The men's informal status was key, in contrast to formal companies, where everything had a contractual rate and protocol. Differences in race, class, and citizenship might also have emboldened clients to make these requests, as did dangling the prospect of future work and recommendations to other potential clients.

The men generally attended to their clients' wishes, although in private they sometimes expressed frustration over these intrusions. For example, after a series of interruptions, Titi's helper exclaimed: "I wish she'd leave us alone." He found her frequent requests invasive and sometimes draining; but most of all, they interrupted the work they had been paid to do and kept them from moving onto other paid projects. But Titi told his helper not to worry because "it keeps her happy" and because he was counting on her recommendation to her "rich friends." Like Titi, most of the men were willing to take on minor—often easy—unpaid tasks in order to ingratiate themselves with their clients in the hope of gaining additional paid work.

While clients were more likely to initiate side jobs, the men themselves sometimes volunteered to take care of tasks separate from what they were hired to do. This work was usually minor as well, as when Valderrama asked a client if he needed help moving garbage bags to the alley or when Titi offered to repair the latch on a door. In cases like these, the men capitalized on their superior knowledge and capability, as well as cultural expectations about their subservient position, in order to curry favor with their clients. Most of the men's clients took for granted free labor of this kind. Yet always with their eyes fixed on the future, the men viewed these unpaid tasks and their subordinate position within a broader and potentially more lucrative frame of exchanges. Like their clients, they exploited their informal status, which gave them the flexibility to execute their work and fees on a case-by-case basis. By doing these favors, they transformed the relationship, creating an expectation of reciprocity in the future.

*

Taking on extra work was not simply a way to keep clients happy. Extras also regularly surfaced as a key source of additional revenue. But in contrast to unpaid labor, most of these paid projects were anticipated and initiated by the workers. They also grew out of the work the men were hired to do, in contrast to the more disparate tasks described above. By altering the home, whether in small or substantial ways, new possibilities for payment often emerged. Some men even lowered their bids or agreed to smaller projects in expectation of expanding the scope of work and making more money as the job progressed.

The mutability of the scope of work was evident in many jobs I observed or heard about from the men. For example, Chango was hired to paint adjoining living and dining rooms. He encouraged the client to add crown molding, but she declined. She felt it was unnecessary and was worried about the added costs and complications. However, after the client saw the bare walls and rooms emptied of furniture—a requirement agreed upon for the job—she agreed that crown molding would look better and consented to the higher price. Chango later explained that he had not initially pushed for the more expensive project because he was confident she would agree to it once he emptied the room. I asked him if this often happened, and he responded with a sigh: "¡Siempre es lo mismo!" (It's always the same!)

On some projects, unexpected complications emerged that also increased the costs. For example, Chicas was hired to install a new light and heating fixture in a bathroom. The job seemed relatively straightforward, and Chicas negotiated a price of $100 plus materials. However, in the course of removing the old unit, Chicas identified a problem that required fixing. He explained to the client that the wires needed to be replaced and recommended installation of a separate breaker for the unit. The client agreed to the expanded work, which increased the cost to $300.

As with Chicas, clients sometimes had to take workers at their word when agreeing to additional work and pay. In such cases, the men depended on their reputation and powers of persuasion to convince the client, who at first might have been hesitant and distressed at the thought of increased costs. The average client's ignorance and lack of skills also worked to the men's advantage, since skilled homeowners might choose to do the work themselves. Regarding the bathroom job mentioned earlier, Chicas told the client that he had installed a similar breaker and wiring system in his own home. Similarly, to convince a hesitant homeowner to add crown molding in her living and dining rooms, Chango claimed that this was a standard feature in the homes of many of his clients. More typically, the problem was more or less self-evident, especially when pointed out and explained by the workers. For example, when Chino Julio removed the carpeting in a client's house in order to refinish the wood floor underneath, he discovered damaged floorboards throughout the small home. When he called to explain the problem, the client asked him if he could simply repair the wood or fill in the gaps with putty. Chino Julio replied that this was not feasible and urged the client to come see for himself. After seeing all the damage, the client consented to the additional work. As he left to return to work, he yelled out: "Just let me know how much more it's going to cost!"

New tasks often emerged due to the very nature of home-improvement projects. Once work began, clients tended to see their homes in a new light, which sometimes convinced them to agree to additional work they had initially declined or not even contemplated. As we have seen, empty rooms and torn-out carpeting presented new possibilities. The intrusive quality of renovation projects encouraged additional work, particularly those that required significant construction. Once clients saw holes in the wall and their furniture displaced, they often consented to expanded projects. They realized that doing additional work separately would have been much more expensive and disruptive. I frequently heard clients utter a version of the comment "since you've started" to explain their decision to consent to additional work and increased costs. Comments like these seemed to echo the logic behind that other common refrain "since you're here" that motivated clients to request uncompensated side jobs.

As these different examples show, most of the men anticipated the possibility of extras, which motivated them to take on jobs that may initially have appeared small scale and low paying. In some cases, they doubled or tripled their earnings through additional work. Expanded projects also solidified their reputations as capable workers and led to future work and referrals. They were investing in their future, since the job they had in hand was not the one they needed to worry about.

Extras were the only way some workers could substantially increase their pay. Unlike their bigger competitors, independent contractors in this informal economy could not take advantage of economies of scale, relying instead on more intermittent gains. For example, Güero and Enrique supplemented their regular work for companies with side jobs. Güero charged around $200 a month for weekly gardening jobs, Enrique a bit less for cleaning and servicing pools. Yet both men supplemented these monthly paychecks thanks to the occasional extras that emerged. For example, Güero added annual and biannual upgrades to his weekly assignments (such as cleaning gutters, planting flowers, or trimming trees) that earned him additional money. Similarly, Enrique augmented his earnings through more periodic tasks, such as emptying pools for deeper cleanings, repairing broken tiles, or fixing filtration systems. However, in order to obtain these extras, the two men needed to hold on to the weekly jobs, which they claimed were not very lucrative on their own.[23] Not surprisingly, they were frustrated by the clients who never went beyond the primary agreement.

Although additional tasks often increased the overall costs of projects, clients did not hesitate to exploit workplace conditions to advance their interests. In addition to receiving free labor for relatively minor tasks, they expected and generally received a discounted rate for more substantial extras—an arrangement that lowered the cost in comparison to what they would have paid to hire someone separately. A case in point is when Titi identified a leak in the kitchen ceiling of a client who asked him to check all the accessible pipes. With the kitchen walls and ceiling already opened up, this was a relatively simple task, so Titi agreed to check the pipes at no charge. To the client's great relief, Titi's brother found and fixed the source of the leak in another section of the house. Thanks to him, the client received a free inspection of his pipes—and peace of mind. Hiring a plumber to do this job from scratch would have meant much higher costs, not to mention all the inconvenience. Had Titi and his brother found additional leaks, they presumably would have earned additional money to fix the problems.

As in Titi's case, I frequently observed the clients taking advantage of work in progress to attend to issues not included in the original scope of the project. Some requests were related to the task at hand; others were less connected but made possible by the work. For example, as Valderrama was digging holes to build a backyard wall, the client asked him to lay plastic tubes for a sprinkler system he eventually planned to set up. Valderrama agreed to do the work free of charge, even though it required digging several additional holes. On a different job, Motor was asked to run wiring along a fence he was installing. Like Valderrama, Motor did the work at no additional cost, hoping to impress his new clients. Attaching the wire was not difficult, and the clients were pleased to have outdoor lighting without having to find someone else to install it and pay for their services. As Valderrama, Motor, and the others knew well, work in private homes was an evolving and negotiated endeavor, and they were adept at dealing with clients' changing needs.

Working Connections

On balance, this chapter presents an optimistic account of the men's world of work. It highlights their autonomy and capacity for negotiation, as well as the freedom with which they made themselves and their work visible in public. The men had something to offer that their customers lacked: namely, know-how that might not require formal schooling but that generally entailed a certain level of competence and certainly more skill than their clients possessed or were prepared to acquire.[24]

The more I learned about the men's work, the more I came to appreciate the significance of the phone call described at the beginning of the chapter. For Titi and other men at the park—especially those involved in home-maintenance and home-improvement work—employment opportunities were structured by their social relations. In a world that prioritized personal connections and referrals, Titi's excitement over the incoming call was understandable. This could be his big break, which is why his mother-in-law—despite their differences—had recommended him for the job. With these high stakes in play, Titi's face brightened at the voice on the other line, and he agreed to meet with the client right away to discuss the project. His enthusiasm proved prescient. After establishing himself as a capable and trustworthy painter, the client recommended him to several of her friends and neighbors, some of whom hired him for their own painting projects. And, as we have seen, Titi ended up doing a range of additional jobs in their homes as well—some paid for, others done for free.

*

The work experiences recounted in this chapter stand in sharp contrast to other, more common depictions of low-wage immigrant workers. For example, immigrants working as babysitters, housekeepers, or for cleaning services are usually more or less interchangeable with parents, relatives, or non-immigrant caretakers. By contrast, because the upper-middle-class lifestyles or aspirations of the men's clients have often committed them to investments requiring long-term maintenance, their relationship to the men tends to be ongoing and not one-off as it would be had they hired a day laborer. This mutual interdependence helps explain why the economic recession of 2008 was not totally disastrous for the men.

Despite their ingenuity and hard work, the men confronted challenges and setbacks working in the home-improvement sector of the economy. They faced stiff competition from other workers, which tended to drive down wages.[25] The pressure to find work and maintain equipment proved burdensome as well—a main reason why some men preferred working for companies or in restaurants. An unregulated work environment and social differences with their clients could also be marginalizing and lead to the men's exploitation. They were hired for their willingness to work, which sometimes forced them to accept unfair working conditions, including from clients who believed they were purchasing the right to have the men perform whatever tasks they stipulated. The men also found themselves barred from more lucrative projects because they lacked the necessary permits, licenses, and insurance policies, which confined them to smaller-scale work where these qualifications and credentials were not required. In this way, their marginal status was a double-edged sword that both facilitated and constrained their opportunities. Imperfect English also ruled them out from jobs that required more prolonged or complex communication. Thus, while pleased to be working on their own—and no longer as ayudantes—the men faced numerous roadblocks in their efforts to climb the socioeconomic ladder.

Perhaps most importantly, not all networks were created equal, nor were they permanent. Just as social connections could expand and increase opportunities, networks could also be unreliable and transitory.[26] For example, while Motor boasted that "people call *me* now" to explain his heavy workload, Martín lamented that his contacts had retired, died, or moved away. And, as Titi's case revealed, it takes time, perseverance, and lucky breaks to start out on one's own. Despite these challenges, the men adapted in creative ways to create greater demand for their services. Most notably, they negotiated referrals and extras on the job to survive in a competitive, often precarious labor market.

Workers as People

When following the men at work, my thoughts inevitably returned to the park. This was due in part to the men themselves, as they often talked about goings-on at the park as we worked together or as we strategized ways to return in time for the midday soccer games or post-match beer drinking. I was constantly reminded how these worlds of work and play were intertwined. In ways I heard about but later confirmed firsthand, the park served as a place to build the relationships and reputations that helped many of the men secure employment. Others relied on the park as an arena to find hired hands they could count on, often on short notice. While this chapter focuses on work in private homes, I learned of similar network-based hiring practices in restaurants, another primary source of employment at the park. With many of the workers limited by their credentials and immigration status—as well as by a competitive labor market and isolated work environment—the park emerged as a key networking site and source of stability in the men's lives.[27] So, in contrast, to the men's oft-repeated lament "el parque no paga" (the park doesn't pay), time there could indeed pay off.

As we have seen, few of the men held traditional nine-to-five jobs. Their employment situations tended to be precarious, requiring them to be "on call" for phone calls that might or might not come. The park solved the problem of what to do while they waited by allowing them to pass the time in a meaningful way. Like other precariously employed individuals who seek refuge in coffee shops or libraries, playing soccer and socializing at the park helped fill the time between jobs, while also providing connections that helped the men find work.[28]

But for the Mar Vista soccer cohort, the park represented much more than simply a convenient pit stop and useful networking site for immigrant workers. More importantly, it became a place for the men to enrich their lives. Here they could be *someone* in ways they couldn't necessarily be at work. At the park, they participated in a social world where they were viewed as *people* valued for their history and for achievements beyond their abilities to wash dishes, lay tile, or mow lawns. My visits with the men on the job gave them an opportunity to share this world with their employers, who seemed to wonder how I knew them. Polo revealed the significance of these exchanges when I ate at the restaurant where he worked. He came over to my table with several waitresses and encouraged me to tell them about his soccer-playing exploits. In return, he touted my prowess on the field and my studies at UCLA. Like Polo, many of the men I accompanied on the job made a point of explaining to their employers that we knew each other from playing soccer together at the park. I sensed the employers' curiosity and the men's satisfaction as they relayed this information in ways suggesting that this was the first time they had communicated an identity beyond work to them.

*

Not surprisingly, the relationship between the men's work and what they had created at the park was entirely absent from debates about the soccer field recounted in the concluding chapter. While some local residents were sympathetic to the men's need for recreation, many others felt that their presence was bringing disorder and disrepute to the park and surrounding area. But neither side in the debate seemed to appreciate how park life enriched the men's work opportunities, in ways comparable to White men networking on the golf course, over drinks at a bar, or at a professional luncheon. Even the men's family members failed to appreciate the importance of socializing at the park, including Valderrama's brother, who refused to hire "los borrachos del parque" (the park drunks), as well as several spouses who urged me to avoid the park and spoke disparagingly of it to my wife.

Yet I always suspected there was a deeper, more sinister reason for outsiders' aversion to the men's presence and activities at the park. To put it bluntly, the working-class Latino immigrant men were seen as "out of place" at the park during "normal" working hours because they were expected to be working. It was not only the men's foreignness that provoked this backlash, but what was perceived as their idleness. In fact, I often heard field critics question why the men were not working, as when one local resident wrote over email: "Don't these guys have jobs?"[29] Police officers posed similar questions when interrogating the men at the park.

The hostility the men faced for "playing" in the park contrasted sharply with the warm welcome they received as workers in people's homes— including by homeowners living only a few miles from the park. As workers in people's homes, their presence and activities were not only embraced, but actively sought after and relied on for all the reasons explained in this chapter. In fact, most homeowners seemed to have a marked preference for foreign-born Latino workers, which my presence appeared to disrupt—and hence their apparent relief when they learned I was not a "real" worker. Yet despite the substantial social and cultural differences separating the men from their clients, these relationships depended on trust and involved close interactions behind closed doors. Workers saw their clients at their most vulnerable and in their most private domestic spaces. Clients, for their part, spoke fondly of the men, even in familial terms, and occasionally offered them "gifts," usually household items and clothing they no longer had use for. And even if colored by their social differences and the constraints of employer-employee relations, over time these relationships often developed a degree of comfort and familiarity, as conversations about work led to questions about the worker's family and country of birth.

The men did not receive the same welcome at the park, where their foreignness and working-class status were perceived as threatening, rather than as reassuring and appealing. There, they became "bad hombres." At the park, the men interacted with local residents from a distance, becoming visible and menacing in ways they were not when they were working in people's homes. In fact, the stigma associated with "brown-collar occupations" seemed to accentuate differences that made them unwelcome in the park but approachable on the job.[30] By contrast, I never sensed that Latina immigrant nannies faced resentment of this kind when they came to the park with their charges from the neighborhood; parkgoers and neighbors seemed to understand that they were there simply doing their job.[31] This disjuncture between the worlds of work and leisure points to the enduring dilemma faced by immigrant workers. As Swiss playwright Max Frisch famously noted in an essay about foreign workers' feelings of alienation, "We asked for workers, but people came."[32] Immigrants are desired for their labor, not for their social presence, and the men I studied broke that bargain by socializing as *people* in the park.

Conclusion

As I finished writing this book, President Trump stoked a familiar fear. On the eve of the 2018 midterm elections, Trump warned the public of an "invading" caravan of Central American migrants making its way to the southern border. Reminiscent of his "bad hombres" rhetoric that launched his presidential campaign, he described the group as made up of "a lot of young men, strong men, and a lot of men we maybe don't want in our country."[1] Here and elsewhere, Trump sought to dehumanize the migrants to justify hostility against them in order to score political points. Cable news played along by broadcasting images of the caravan slowly making its way toward the border, where the group was eventually met by riot police and tear gas. Many of the people among them looked like the men I had come to know in the park.

While at times Mar Vista felt worlds away from the fearmongering and nativism that resurfaced with Trump, similar anxieties were evident in the attitudes of Mar Vista residents toward the soccer players. Viewed as a threat to the park, the Latino men also seemed to represent broader concerns about changing demographics in the area. Yet most park neighbors had little interaction with the men or understanding of what drew them to the park and what they did there. This distance fed into fears that were exploited to justify limiting access to the park. Years before candidate Trump incited supporters with promises to "build the wall," Mar Vista residents pushed to build a fence around the soccer field.[2]

Fencing the Field

In June 2005, the city installed an artificial turf soccer field at the Mar Vista Recreation Center to replace the bumpy, worn-out grass field that had been informally used for decades by Latino immigrant men to play soccer. As previously discussed, the new field created challenges for the veteran park soccer players. It also precipitated problems for residents living near the park, but of a different kind. Area homeowners voiced concerns over an alleged increase in noise, street parking, traffic, loitering, trash, vandalism, and crime. There were also more subjective and alarmist discussions of the park and neighborhood's deteriorating "nature."

One neighbor described these changes to me in this way: "Just the number of people and the quality. I hate to say quality, it sounds so snobby, and I don't mean it to be, but it is. It was the nature of the park being so different." When I pressed him on what he meant, he explained: "I walk there with my kids and there's like three hundred people all speaking a language I don't understand and milling around and just kind of behaving in a way that is unfamiliar." He maintained that his school-age daughters no longer felt safe in the park because of field-related activity.

Perceived threats to community and family were conveyed through photographs circulated in the neighborhood and to city officials that included pictures of garbage, discarded beer cans, and large numbers of predominately Latino men in and around the field. One such image showed Latino men playing soccer on the field, with a caption that read: "What parent will ask these men to stop so he can play catch with his child?" Moreover, "these men" were often portrayed as unapologetic lawbreakers, such as in the following observation shared over email by a local resident with her collaborators: "During the last holiday weekend, I observed a person walking into the park with a case of Corona beer, making no attempt to conceal it."

In interviews, residents spoke with fear and anger about the impact of the new field on their everyday lives. One neighbor claimed that he no longer felt comfortable having friends over for a barbecue. Another was concerned that she would never be able to sell her home because of its proximity to the field. She then laughed at the ridiculousness of her situation: "They kick the ball over and then expect me to kick the ball back over; they yell at me to throw it back!" Like her, many described an "out-of-control situation" most sensationally captured in the flyer below. It was this provocative handout left on my professor's windshield that had initially triggered my interest in the park.

LIGHTS = LAWYERS, LAWSUITS & LITIGATION
The Mar Vista Artificial Turf Field . . .
Failure to install 10' fence customary for Los Angeles
artificial turf fields (20' in Santa Monica)
Failure to observe Prop K guidelines
Children cannot sleep at night in their homes
Failure to respond to reasonable resident requests
Turning a quiet residential neighborhood into a

> WEST SIDE STAPLES CENTER
> Parks Department failure to supervise during peak use/crime
> LAPD failure to respond to urgent calls from residents trapped
> in a lawless, Wild West environment
> Failure to do anything about open drug and alcohol use
> **Do City Officials and Departments care about residents?**

Encouraged by this growing chorus of complaints, field critics urged their neighbors to sign a petition to address these concerns. They argued that the park was "too small and too close to residential homes to adequately support the amount of traffic [the field] has invited." Endorsed by the homeowner's association and signed by 130 area residents, the petition demanded that the park "reduce hours of operation, in order to remedy the negative impact its current use is having on the surrounding neighborhood." On the advice of park officials, residents launched a campaign calling for fencing around the soccer field.

Although calls for a fence provoked opposition, including allegations of racism and NIMBYism, they were eventually heeded. In September 2010— five years after the field's opening—the city enclosed it with a twelve-foot-high fence. When residents referred to the new enclosure, they presented it as a welcome park improvement and as a symbol of community cohesion. They rarely mentioned the heated debates and divisions that preceded its completion. The Latino soccer players were also absent from these discussions, as they had been from the very beginning of the field's history.

Playing in the Shadows

The city installed the artificial turf soccer field at the Mar Vista Recreation Center at the request of local residents, especially those active on the Park Advisory Board (PAB).[3] The field replaced what many of them remembered as an ugly blot on an otherwise appealing landscape. It is notable that none of the people involved in planning the project had actually played soccer in the park.[4] In my conversations with them, it became clear that they had envisioned the field as an aesthetic improvement for a persistently unkempt section of the park and as a resource for area youths. Since users of the field were not part of the process, those pushing for the project were not in a good position to anticipate the social consequences of what they were proposing. While eager to improve the appearance of this section of the park, neighborhood advocates did not foresee how much "outsider" interest and adult activity the artificial turf field would invite or the problems this might pose for some local residents.

Moreover, there appeared to be no historical precedent regarding neighborhood opposition from which to draw. Prior to the opening of the new field, there had been little publicly voiced objections to the presence of the Latino men who, for decades, had played soccer and socialized in that space. For example, when I asked a local resident about soccer play that predated the new field she responded: "I never even noticed it." Her response corroborated what the players themselves told me: that before the turf field the neighbors never even seemed aware of their presence in the park. Park administrators confirmed this perception in official documents, one of which claimed that "prior to construction, the grass area was open and used primarily as a picnic area."

However, everyone I spoke with acknowledged that Latino immigration had transformed use of the park well before the opening of the new field. Indeed, it was heavy use of the old field by Latino immigrant men that had in part precipitated the installation of artificial turf. Moreover, neighborhood complaints that were eventually aired regarding activities around the new field echoed past descriptions of behavior around the old dirt field: large gatherings, beer drinking, and boisterous interaction. As one player remarked: "They didn't care about us until they put in the nice field."

Once demands for fencing were made public, other local residents began to question the motives of their neighbors. A member of the Park Advisory Board told me: "It didn't take long to figure out that maybe it was the people who were playing soccer [rather than the noise] they had issue with. Obviously, there was something more going on." The councilman's field deputy assigned to the area suspected that "there was that shift in the environment of the park, and I think, for the neighbors, the soccer field just amplified an issue they were already having with that park." Like her, many pointed to the growing Latino population on the "changing Westside" as the source of unrest. Perceptions of prejudice were especially galling given the area's self-image as liberal and tolerant.

By contrast, park officials had from the start predicted pushback from local residents. Based on their experiences in other parts of the city, they understood that in a White and affluent area like the Mar Vista neighborhood, some homeowners might express discomfort or opposition to the increased presence around the new field of Latino men who were flocking to limited park space throughout the city to play soccer. To mitigate anticipated problems, the city had surrounded the new turf field with a hastily designed six-foot-high chain-link fence before the field's official opening back in 2005.

A new park director assigned to Mar Vista after the first fence was installed explained to me that her predecessor fenced in the field so staff could control its use, based on the assumption that, without a fence, it would be difficult to manage when and by whom the field was used, which they expected to be a playing population some residents might find problematic.[5] In other words, park officials seemed to understand residents' fears and prejudices better than they did themselves and accurately anticipated those concerns before they were even expressed. In fact, they installed the fence without community input to avoid having to face awkward questions about outsiders coming to the field. However, it did not take long for local residents to complain about the underhanded way that first enclosure had been constructed, as well as its aesthetic shortcomings and negative implications for the neighborhood's reputation. Less than two months after its controversial installation—well before the field became a problem for some local residents and tested the neighborhood's standing as open and progressive—the city removed the fence only to replace it with another fence twice as tall five years later.

Further exposing the shifting and disingenuous nature of the opposition was the fact that this group largely ignored commotion and noise in other sections of the park, such as the outdoor basketball and tennis courts that generally attracted a non-Latino playing population. Moreover, activity on the soccer field did not appear to dramatically alter neighbors' use of the park. Some field critics admitted to me that they continued to use other areas of the eighteen-acre facility, as they had before. Few expressed any interest in using the field itself. And few spoke of any face-to-face contact—much less direct conflict—with field users. Most importantly, perhaps, they rarely had any direct evidence that the soccer players themselves were responsible for purported field-related problems, be it noise, parking, trash, or vandalism.

Yet hearing from or identifying the "culprits" seemed beside the point for aggrieved residents. For example, in a rare instance of the players' interaction with park neighbors, several participants in the midday games offered their assistance to a nearby resident whose exterior wall had been vandalized with gang graffiti. Although she politely declined their offer to repaint the defaced wall, her frustrations with the field boiled over when the men stressed that the midday soccer players were not responsible for the vandalism:

> I know it's not you guys, but it's all connected. It's everything. I'm sick of it, this field has brought too many people to the park. I go out in the morning every day and the garbage cans are filled with beer. People are out here all night on the field. There are too many people at the park.

The fact that soccer players were not listened to or invited by local residents to community meetings regarding the field made it difficult for them to present their side of the story. Had they been able to speak for themselves, rather than being misperceived on the basis of provocative accounts and photographs taken from a distance, they might have been able to change the tenor of the debate.[6] In fact, the only attempt at accommodation I observed was the decision by administrators to post park rules in both English and Spanish. Nearby residents did not seem to know or care about the men's efforts to curb problems on and off the field. Indeed, proponents of restricted access to the field seemed to resent the appearance of soccer players at later community meetings. As one person put it, "Suddenly a whole bunch of sweaty guys are showing up at the meeting who have no idea what's going on."

The general absence of the Latino soccer players at community meetings and the neighbors' lack of direct contact with them seems to have relegated them to figments in the imagination of people on both sides of the debate. Whereas proponents of restricted access to the field tended to portray the absent players as rowdy lawbreakers abusing a public resource, advocates of open access reimagined them as "hardworking family men" who had both a need and the right to use the public field. However, it's unclear how many of them knew or understood the men whom they had reduced to either criminals or laborers. Moreover, there was much more at stake than realized by those debating a fence and what the park represented for them. Restrictions on field use and other forms of exclusion and intimidation threatened the rich interactions and relationships described in this book. Indeed, while it was neighborhood grievances that had originally drawn me to the park, it was the soccer players themselves who captured my attention and who deserve to be brought out of the shadows.

Fútbol and Friendship

By offering a close-up portrait of this group of Latino immigrants at play in a West Los Angeles park, I hope to foster a better understanding of what they have created and confronted there, as well as empathy for these men and others like them. Like all newcomers, they have had to create spaces for interaction in which to build and sustain community. But as working-class immigrants, they could not take friendships or opportunities for granted; instead, they have had to overcome the strangeness of their new surroundings. They have done this by coming together to have fun, creating a familiar environment in which to live rich, meaningful lives. In the process, they have generated relationships and other resources that help solve the practical problems associated with immigration, but that sometimes create conflicts with their family and friends, as well as with park neighbors.

In general, local residents, passersby, and city officials did not have the same understanding of park life as the players. For example, the beer drinking and fighting that may have seemed disorderly to outsiders actually served as community controls, rather than leading to the breakdown of community. The broader context of how and why the men socialized in this park was also invisible to onlookers, most of whom wondered why they were not working or why they did not get together in bars or backyards. Lacking this information, outsiders tended to perceive and represent the situation on and around the soccer field as unruly, even dangerous.

To challenge and help correct these misguided impressions, I have tried to present sufficient data to allow readers to judge for themselves whether my analyses and conclusions seem valid. At the same time, I have tried to be transparent about the limitations of my research, as well as the truth of what I found. I have shown the men fighting, drinking, and cursing because this was a regular part of park life. Although these representations may embarrass some who advocate for this population, my goal was never to use the men as moral or political props. Regardless of readers' views on immigration reform or border enforcement, my aim was to present this group of soccer players as complex people trying to make a life for themselves under difficult circumstances.

Moreover, building meaning and comfort into their lives is an ongoing process. It unfolds through interactions that solidify into stable relationships at the park while also responding to shifting political and economic contexts over which the men have little control. While going to the park every day made it hard for me to perceive the subtle ways the scene was shifting before my eyes, time and distance away from the park allowed me to see this process with greater clarity. My return visits helped me realize how the story of los jugadores del parque is continually being rewritten.

Rudy and Michelada

During my short-term return visits to the park after finishing graduate school, I invariably encountered people who were strangers to me, but who were well known to the others. On one occasion in May 2014, my visit happened to coincide with Rudy's return to the park after a lengthy absence. The old-timer's homecoming was given an enthusiastic reception by the men, several of whom were quick to introduce us, knowing my interest in park history. I, too, was eager to meet Rudy, whose name had occasionally come up in the men's stories.

According to Polo, Rudy was the finest soccer player from El Salvador ever to have played at Mar Vista. In a rare moment of consensus, Motor and Zapata nodded their heads in agreement, and Motor recalled a legendary goal his compatriot scored in a league final. Caballo joined in and asked Rudy if he remembered their old battles, which sparked a spirited discussion of players, teams, and matches from that period in the park's history two and three decades earlier. Now in his early sixties, Rudy did not dispute or downplay the men's praise and seemed to revel in the attention. As their enthusiasm swelled, Polo yelled over to Ivan to come meet the living legend and insisted to the latest park hotshot that Rudy would have dominated him in his heyday. Ivan smiled, having heard these old-timers' tales many times before, and promptly turned the tables on Polo: "¡Bueno, saca las chelas para tu ídolo!" (Well, then, bring out the beers for your idol!)

Later that afternoon, I asked Rudy why he rarely came by the park. He explained that since moving from West Los Angeles to more distant Palm-dale, it was harder for him to visit. Later in our conversation, he explained that a serious knee injury and years of hard partying also accounted for his withdrawal from the group. While I didn't doubt the men's assessment, Rudy—potbellied and walking with a limp—appeared far removed from his playing days as one of the "best ever." After discussing his past exploits, I asked him what he thought of the action on the soccer field that afternoon. Rudy replied that he was happy the games were going strong, but felt that they weren't as "duro" (rough and tumble) as the soccer play in his heyday.

Four years after meeting Rudy, I encountered a player at a very different stage of his park career. Michelada had only recently started coming around. Although he had not made it to that week's Sunday league game, he soon joined the group of viejitos for the customary post-match festivities at the park. I did not recognize him, but he was warmly greeted by the others, several of whom asked him why he had missed the game. He explained that he didn't have a ride, but someone joked that he hadn't shown up because he was embarrassed to be understudy to Huguito—the beloved but washed-up old-timer who played ahead of him. Michelada laughed and playfully bowed in Huguito's direction. Signaling all was forgiven, Moncho tossed him a beer, but not without poking fun at the youngster's stylish new haircut.

I introduced myself to Michelada, who also seemed intrigued by the attention I was receiving from the group. After responding to his questions about my own park history, I asked him how he had come to join the group. He explained that Nelson, with whom he worked, had invited him to play with the old-timers about a month earlier. The two men had bonded over their love of the game while preparing food and washing dishes together at a Santa Monica restaurant. Having arrived from Gua-temala less than a month earlier, the twenty-four-year-old told me that he was excited to have found an opportunity to play soccer and to meet new people. That Sunday, he was at the park for the first time without his

Honduran coworker. He said that he also enjoyed playing in the midweek games when his schedule permitted. When I asked if he knew other people in Los Angeles, he replied that he was living with his brother, but did not know many people beyond those he had met in the park. I asked him if he was happy to have discovered the park and he answered: "¿Claro, qué más quieres?" (Of course, what more could you ask for?)

*

Although I was meeting Rudy and Michelada for the first time, their presence and interactions with the group made sense to me. Having spent years in the park, I recognized familiar patterns and processes in their stories. Even without knowing Rudy, I understood how an old-timer like him could reinsert himself seamlessly into a social world he had not visited in years. He had a place in this community so long as his legacy lived on in the memories of his former teammates. And while he no longer resembled the soccer star of yore, his return had clearly invigorated an otherwise mundane gathering at the park.

By contrast, Michelada was just starting out, but his swift integration into park life also matched what I had witnessed over the years and experienced myself. Like others drawn to the park, Michelada did not have a ready network of people with whom to socialize and unwind after recently moving to Los Angeles. Through a friendship at work born out of a shared passion, he had found the park, along with all the relationships, resources, and experiences it offered. The men embraced the newcomer as companion and teammate and used his entry as yet another source of intrigue and interaction. His arrival with a Michelada beer in hand that first day contributed an amusing nickname to the scene, and jokes about him serving as Huguito's understudy offered a fresh source of entertainment and meaning. Months later, I learned that Michelada had continued to visit the park, often without Nelson, and that he had changed jobs, thanks to a tip from someone he had met at the park. He had even found a ride from a teammate to the Sunday league games.

Through the examples of Rudy and Michelada, I also saw the problems that could result from time in the park. Years of soccer play and heavy drinking had taken their toll on Rudy, not to mention threats to family and work life we did not broach. Michelada may confront similar challenges managing his commitment to the park and his other goals and responsibilities. In fact, he hinted that the pull of the park had already created strains with his brother, who preferred to attend church during his free time. Yet park life would not be the same without these risks—perils that Rudy knew all too well and that Michelada was just beginning to understand. As I had seen with many others, both men exhibited an irresistible attraction to the fun and camaraderie of park life.

Rudy and Michelada were two of the many jugadores del parque I met while conducting research for this book. Like the others, they arrived with their own backstories, personalities, and ambitions. What made the comparison between them so interesting was the fact that I met them at opposite points in their park careers, with Michelada in the early stages of creating the types of bonds and memories that ensured Rudy's smooth reintegration. Each in his own way contributed to the dynamic, meaningful world detailed in this book. Together with an evolving cast of newcomers, regulars, and old-timers, they built and sustained a community of play that helped them overcome the strangeness of their new home. Here they forged new identities, relationships, and possibilities.

Social Tying

Actively participating in park life gave me a rare opportunity to look more closely at the taken-for-granted processes by which immigrants make social connections in new places. At the park, they found a community of men in similar situations and with shared interests who helped them meet the demands of their new lives. But as my study also shows, having fun together in a public place is a significant accomplishment, because it takes a great deal of cooperation and creativity to sustain interaction and to control the space.

For working-class immigrants, having fun may be even more important than for others, as this is the one outlet for doing what they want, with no one bossing them around. For example, in contrast to governing practices common in organized religions, the men themselves determine how to organize their activities, without guidance from a book or leader. Moreover, having fun helps the men solve other problems, even though solving those problems did not prompt their coming together in the first place. The search for fun and sociability creates a community that both diminishes the costs of migration and creates new resources that facilitate settlement. To feel grounded in their new country and thrive there, the men leaned on another at the park.

Although the men have come together in a place they have made familiar and that meets many of their needs, it is not an environment they fully control. As we have seen, social networks are not created equally or effortlessly. In forming and sustaining social ties, different groups face different kinds of opportunities and constraints. To repeat one of the central findings of my study, it is not always so easy to play together. This generalization about social interaction is especially pertinent to this particular group of men, given their lack of economic and political resources and their unequal position in relation to authorities and to neighbors around the park.

To fully comprehend people's connections—and how these connections generate advantages or disadvantages—we need to better understand the contexts in which they are made. This transformative process is often missing from migration studies, which tend to focus more on the consequences of social networks than on their formation. Even the more probing studies generally fail to show *how* migrants make fresh ties in new places over time. As opposed to seeing networks as emanating from preexisting relations, this book shows how people create a framework for forming new connections and pays special attention to the role of soccer and public parks in this dynamic process.

Despite the unique features of this case, I imagine that gatherings of Latino immigrant men to play soccer and socialize in public parks elsewhere follow similar patterns, practices, and constraints. A focus on the active process of social tying—rather than on the taken-for-granted effect of social ties—provides a conceptual lens for making sense of these familiar scenes. I hope my findings will encourage migration scholars to look more closely at the contingent nature of network formation and to examine how newcomers fully realize their personhood in other less conventional sites of interaction. This may involve going beyond traditional gatekeepers and mixing more deeply with immigrants as *people* in their everyday lives. For the heart of this story is what the men actually did and accomplished together in the park—experiences, which due to their interactive and spontaneous nature, would be difficult to capture through more distanced methodologies.

Parks as Social Infrastructure

In *Palaces for the People*, sociologist Eric Klinenberg offers an insightful look at the important role that public spaces play in fostering individual and collective well-being. His book concerns the "physical places and organizations that shape the way people interact," which he calls "social infrastructure."[7] When these spaces are robust, they can determine whether or not people feel connected and supported. Such spaces are particularly important for the young, elderly, and disadvantaged because they have fewer options for sociable gathering places. Klinenberg joins others in showing how this social infrastructure is under threat due to neglect and hostility.[8] This degradation and assault on public space, he argues, contributes to growing inequality, division, and discord.

My book offers clear evidence in support of Klinenberg's belief in the promise of communal spaces. Like many public parks, the Mar Vista Rec-

reation Center is a vital gathering place and refuge for working-class immigrants who have limited options to socialize elsewhere. It has provided
the men in my study a place to interact and to develop bonds of friendship
and mutual support. A shared passion for soccer brought together this
diverse group of participants and led them to meet people they probably
would not otherwise have encountered at work or in their neighborhood.
The fact that the park was open, free, and relatively accessible was key
to fostering these developments, much as Klinenberg found in his study
of public libraries.

There was a sense of inevitability to these outcomes at Mar Vista. For as
Klinenberg writes, "People forge bonds in places that have healthy social
infrastructures—not because they set out to build community, but because
when people engage in sustained, recurrent interaction, particularly while
doing things they enjoy, relationships inevitably grow."[9] Yet friendships
only felt inevitable because of the work the men did to create and sustain
the shared projects that brought them together in the first place. The soccer
games, sideline chatter, and post-match gatherings were not preordained
but instead contingent accomplishments. Moreover, as we have seen, the
men faced various challenges—many internal to the group—in sustaining
this world. Parks or libraries do not automatically *do* anything by themselves.[10] They only provide a more or less inviting space for people to do
the work of creating the type of community described in this study—a
community that was not inherently good or inclusive, but molded to the
needs, talents, and personalities of its members.

While Klinenberg downplays these inner struggles and the role they
play in bringing people together (or pushing them apart), he points to the
types of external pressures on public life identified in my study. As we have
seen, the immigrant men I studied faced threats from local residents and
city officials who tried to limit their access to and use of this public space.
This was due in large part to who they were and what they were doing—in
contrast to less stigmatized users who faced fewer obstacles socializing in
this park and in other social settings. As my research underscores, when
people think about public spaces, there is often a desired and undesired
public. The men adapted as best they could; however, coming together
required compromise and concessions.

The Mar Vista Recreation Center in Context

Despite these challenges, the men benefited from several distinctive advantages in creating the social infrastructure needed to foster community
in *this* park. As men, they were freer to socialize in this space than the
women in their lives, whom I rarely saw at the park and who as a result

could not benefit from the social interaction and resources there. I never had a good sense of whether these women found comparable gatherings elsewhere, but other studies suggest that gender norms and inequalities may confine immigrant Latinas to the domestic realm, making it harder for them to generate new connections.[11]

Another advantage the men enjoyed at the park was that it was a safe and an attractive space, especially compared to some of the more dangerous and degraded facilities in the area. Police and community involvement were a mixed blessing, bringing benefits as well as scrutiny. The relative accessibility of the high-quality artificial turf soccer field was particularly unusual. The men exhibited a strong attachment to this park, which helps explain their tenacious hold on to this rare gem and why some who moved to more distant parts of Los Angeles continued to return there. The men often spoke of the park's many charms—its trees, wildlife, and cool breezes, not to mention the dependable presence of familiar faces and excitement. Some even dreamed of being buried in the park or having their ashes scattered on the soccer field after they die. Long tenures in the park provided a sense of comfort and claim to this space. Old-timers used this history to legitimize their use of the soccer field and to galvanize group interactions. And, as we have seen, newcomers were quickly assimilated into the scene, over time creating their own memories and connections to the park.

The park also attracted individuals with particular interests and sensibilities that some might consider aggressively masculine or unhealthy in certain respects.[12] Most enjoyed playing soccer and drinking beer and found these ways to pass the time familiar and engaging. Although some of the men socialized at the park without playing soccer or drinking beer, many of the activities the men engaged in there could prove alienating and risky. For example, several men stopped visiting the park once they could no longer play soccer, while others stayed away to keep from drinking alcohol. Many were friends or acquaintances of men who avoided the park altogether, preferring to spend their leisure time at home or elsewhere. Changes in schedules and responsibilities also made it difficult for some men to visit the park. Others experienced developments in their lives that made the park a less attractive option, such as a new relationship, a new job, or a change in residence. But for those who enjoyed these activities and could carve out free time, the park offered a space to revel in the company of their peers.

The politics of the neighborhood and of Los Angeles more broadly also affected the men's activities at Mar Vista. Local residents encountered a series of unexpected challenges when they tried to limit access to the soccer field, including hard-to-stomach accusations of racism. Upper-class Whites in other areas do not always face the same resistance. For example, nearby San Marino gained notoriety during my fieldwork for restricting Lacy Park to locals on the weekend, which many interpreted as a blatant measure to keep outsiders from visiting the picturesque park.[13] Whereas some Mar Vista residents may have welcomed a bold move of this kind, it was not possible in their neighborhood, legally or politically. Moreover, despite the scrutiny that the soccer players and their cohort received at Mar Vista as Latino immigrants, it was much easier to be out in public there or elsewhere in Los Angeles than it might have been in other parts of the country. In an immigrant and sanctuary city like L.A., they were safer and less conspicuous than in less diverse, less welcoming places.[14]

My move in the summer of 2013 from Los Angeles to rural Virginia brought home the uniqueness of what the men had created in the park. Although my family relocated to a town with a sizable Latino immigrant population—part of what migration scholars refer to as "El Nuevo South"—I have yet to encounter anything that resembled what I found at Mar Vista.[15] In Harrisonburg, as in Los Angeles, Latino families frequent local parks and there's a flourishing Spanish-speaking soccer league in town. However, Latinos do not socialize in parks in male-only groups as they did in Los Angeles. In fact, my new Latino neighbors in Virginia explain to me that they do not feel comfortable or safe socializing in public parks and that they prefer to get together with their friends in their homes. They claim to avoid drinking in public parks because of heavy policing and public scrutiny. When I tell them about the social world at Mar Vista, they seem envious and acknowledge that, for the time being, a similar scene is not possible here. I wonder about what is lost for Latino immigrants in places that have a limited social infrastructure.[16] I sense that they are more bound to their homes and less likely to meet new people or to access the opportunities that come with an expanded network. Yet despite the strength and longevity of the scene at Mar Vista, the community the men created there remains somewhat precarious. In fact, I always left the park uncertain of what I would find when I returned.

An Uncertain Future

In researching this book, I was always sensitive to measures that might restrict the men's ability to assemble freely in the park. Indeed, it was rumors of plans to limit access to the soccer field that initially drew me to the park. While the fencing that resulted did not dramatically impede the men's use of the field, limits on open access gradually increased over time. For example, once the fence was installed, park officials began locking the field when the office was closed for holidays, as well as before sunset on weekends (5:00 p.m. on Saturdays and 3:00 p.m. on Sundays), even though many people remained in the park at these times. Play by permit also increased over the course of my research. Groups paying to use the field included soccer clubs and other sports organizations, such as youth lacrosse and Ultimate Frisbee groups. Permitted users tended to be White and young, in contrast to the more diverse participants in the pickup soccer games.

These changes minimally affected the midday games I studied, but they reflect rising restrictions on more open, informal play at this park and in other parks throughout the country.[17] Like the installation of fencing, issuing permits has become a means to control who has access to public space, which tends to adversely impact poorer and more stigmatized users. I'm not sure what the players would do if they lost access to the field during their usual midday playing time. Their limited involvement in the fence debate and in other policy discussions suggests that it would be difficult for them to counter these restrictions. In any case, the need for permits would radically alter the spirit and effect of a more open and negotiated system of play. Indeed, the arguing and uncertainty that characterized the men's games seemed to be half the fun.[18]

Threats to the men's use of the park went beyond limiting access to the soccer field. Although the police were present throughout my research—and viewed as a menace by most—their surveillance and patrolling of the park may intensify. In fact, a growing homeless population in the park in the final years of my fieldwork attracted greater police attention. A similar uptick in police presence occurred in 2011 after members of a gang pushed out of nearby Stoner Park reconvened at Mar Vista. In both cases, the men I studied were targeted more than usual by the police, and some even chose to avoid the park during this period because it was "demasiado caliente" (too hot). While I sensed that the park was a relatively low priority for the LAPD during most of my time there, future developments could increase their patrolling. Given the men's visibility due to their drinking and appearance, police expansion into the park would likely create problems for them, even if they had nothing to do with what initially drew more officers to the park. As we saw in chapter 3, guilt and innocence do not always matter in determining who receives alcohol citations.

*

The changing political climate could also heighten the men's sense of vulnerability. While the politically liberal leanings of the area[19] suggest that most locals would probably resist the deliberate targeting of Latino immigrants, the controversy over the soccer field exposed lingering prejudices and underlying tensions over the demographic changes described earlier in the book. Some might welcome tougher policing. Shifts in immigration enforcement at the federal level could also trickle down locally, causing Latinos everywhere to feel more vulnerable. Knowing that L.A.'s designation as a sanctuary city does not guarantee their safety may lead some of the men to avoid public spaces altogether—a tendency increasingly common in other parts of the country.[20]

If the nativist sentiments reignited by Trump and fear of xenophobic attacks targeting Latinos[21] continue to push immigrants into the shadows, social scenes like the one described in this book might well become more uncommon and less vibrant. Yet the creation and preservation of welcoming public spaces can ensure that immigrants develop supportive networks in an environment in which few such networks are generally available to them. Since we have done nothing to eliminate the structural need for immigrants in this country, the flow of migrants will undoubtedly continue.[22] But what will their experiences be like without vital opportunities for social interaction and networking like those described in this book? What would have happened if los jugadores del parque had never had a chance to come together in the park? It's hard to know. Many of the men claimed to have had limited social lives before meeting in the park, just as those who left the area bemoaned the lack of a similar scene in their new home—a problem I have witnessed firsthand among Latino immigrants in rural Virginia.

Without the group at the park, Valderrama might never have overcome the loneliness of his new home. I also doubt whether Polo would have spent years organizing the midday pickup games, experiencing all the status and headaches that came with it. And would Motor have found a comparable crop of talent to coach to multiple league and tournament championships? Similarly, without the pickup games, Chepe and Junior might not have followed their fathers to the park, where they acquired the skills to become college soccer players—a signal of upward mobility that brought pride to all the players. Old-timers like Rudy would not have a place to bask in memories of his glory days, just as newcomers like Michelada would not have discovered a scene that would prove fulfilling for years to come. For these men and others, the park became a place to build a sense of who they were, separate from their identities elsewhere or their country of origin. Moreover, without the activities in and around the soccer field, many of the men would have lost one of the primary places to hunt for jobs—from dishwashing to landscaping to construction. And like the many ayudantes and lavaplatos, my own career as a sociologist might have been less productive and far less rewarding had I not encountered this lively scene.

*

Changes within the group eventually may have an even greater impact than external pressures on the social world the men have created at the park. Many park regulars are aging out. They are finding that playing soccer and drinking beer are difficult to continue in old age, especially after a lifetime of playing and partying at the park. Other life changes and commitments are pulling away some men, including those displaced by gentrification and rising housing costs on Los Angeles's West Side. In the past, new recruits like Michelada have replenished the ranks, sustaining a pattern of socializing that stretches back decades in the park. But not all current newcomers share the same needs and interests. For example, there is a new cohort—led by young men who began coming to the park as boys with their fathers—who were raised in Los Angeles. While they intermingle with the old-timers and respect what they've created and sustained over the years, certain tensions have surfaced. Old-timers allege that these youngsters have a different orientation toward the park. According to some, they are "only in it for themselves" (sólo por ellos). In a conversation captured in the course of a tape-recorded interview, Polo and Caballo vented their frustrations concerning the newest arrivals:

> Polo: Look at Chepe, he knows about this history. He knows that it's our tradition, and he likes it. He has always enjoyed it, but he doesn't do the same [no hace lo mismo]. Nor does Ivan. They do not want to make friends. Son fríos, sólo por ellos. [They are cold; only in it for themselves.] They are more American. They were born here. We were not. When we saw someone new, we said: "Hey, come! Play! ¿Qué pedo? ¿De dónde vienes? [What's up? Where do you come from?] I'm Mexican, I'm Salvadoran. Ah, ¡bienvenidos [welcome]! Come, we play every day." Well, they are different. So, this surprises me because they live here, and they should make more friends. I do not see this anymore, no lo veo [I do not see it]. Los gabachos [the White guys] have another show. When I arrived, people here treated me well. Tortuga treated me well, Zapata, the mechanics, everyone. "Come, Polo! Come, come! Do you want a beer?" "Yes, yes!" Ivan and Chepe are not like that.
> Caballo: Ellos no vienen inyectados de este ritmo. [They don't come filled with the same enthusiasm.]
> Polo: Exactly, qué bueno que me entiendes [I'm glad you understand me]. That's the point. And when others come, nos vamos a perder esto [we're going to lose this].

Although Polo and Caballo failed to mention that they, too, have confronted criticism from some *older* old-timers, they were correct in recognizing the changes that Chepe, Ivan, and other newcomers were bringing to the scene. While I personally did not find the newest generation to be "colder," they do have more options than their elders to socialize and hence are less bound to the park for making friends and having fun. Most have access to expansive networks both at school and at work. They also feel more comfortable in bars and restaurants, where they also gather. In this way, they are "more American" and more like the gabachos. For them, the park is less a place to meet new people and find personal meaning than to play soccer and pay homage to a colorful world they knew as children. If anything, I was struck by how much time they *did* spend in the park. Like many second-generation immigrants, Chepe and Ivan have a foot in two worlds, and their movements within and beyond the park revealed the singular role that the activities in and around the soccer field played for their fathers' generation.[23]

Unlike these dozen men who began coming to the park as children with their fathers, most of the newcomers to the soccer field have little interest in socializing after the games. To borrow from Caballo's eloquent observation, "ellos no vienen inyectados de este ritmo," which literally means "they don't come injected with this rhythm." Unlike their predecessors, many of these newcomers are not working-class immigrants from Latin America, but a mix of US-born Latinos and other social groups. While Chepe's cohort loosely carries on the traditions started decades ago, I may have happened upon a scene in its waning moments.

Welcomed but Excluded

None of these developments should be surprising. Social worlds are never static, but constantly evolving. Cities have many spaces that host brief forms of social life that fail to take root or to become institutionalized How these social worlds arise, their uses, and whether they endure or fade away reflect the changing, often ephemeral nature of public life.[24] These developments and transformations are hardly new. Indeed, the story of Los Angeles has been one of constant growth and change.[25] This study provides one window into this ever-changing landscape.

The question is: What kind of life will immigrants be allowed to live in public spaces? Although they are welcomed as low-wage workers in the neighborhood and elsewhere, their presence in public parks seems to upset the social order. At the Mar Vista Recreation Center, the men in my study were visible and perceived at times as threatening in ways they were not as busboys, painters, or gardeners. In fact, the very qualities that rendered them appealing as low-wage workers (foreign-born, Latino, and presumably undocumented) made them unwelcome to some at the park.

The men understood this tension firsthand, which they expressed by taunting slackers to "look for work" or when they joked about a notorious critic of their presence at the park who hired a crew of Latino men to build a wall around her backyard—a barrier they suspected she erected to shield herself from Latinos in the park. As Barba quipped, "¡Ahora le gustan los latinos!" (Now she likes Latinos!) In similar fashion, Donald Trump was decried as a hypocrite for simultaneously smearing and hiring Latino immigrants (including a number of undocumented ones). Yet unbeknownst to outsiders, the park became a place for the men to build the connections that allowed them to do the work their clients did not want to do themselves.

Mar Vista provided the men a space in which to build a life with purpose and possibility, including the social tying and access to employment opportunities they were more comfortably associated with in the minds of park neighbors. It was also in the park that los jugadores del parque held on to their humanity in defiance of their broader dehumanization, reconfirming that the separation between workers and people is difficult to sustain, except for migrants in the most isolated and temporary of migrations.[26] Rather than pushing people out of parks and into the shadows, we should join together to build a viable social infrastructure that best serves the needs of all segments of society. Indeed, what kind of world would it be for immigrants who lacked opportunities to live rich, meaningful lives?

A Sad but Grateful Farewell

While ethnographers often leave the field with ambivalence, I departed with sadness. Ironically, the park gave me a career that sent me thousands of miles away. While sad to go, I am forever grateful to the men for welcoming me into the park and letting me tell their stories. Participating in park life allowed me to observe, but also to experience firsthand the order and meaning of their world. Yet before the men were willing to accept me and allow me to study them, I had to earn their respect and trust. I accomplished this over time through my interactions with the men—playing soccer, socializing afterward, or accompanying them away from the park.

Reciprocal exchanges also helped build relationships: the men offered me access to their lives and, in return, I provided resources of benefit to them—translating forms, offering rides, representing them at community meetings, or simply lending them my cell phone. Power dynamics were at play, as they always were at the park. Any researcher doing work with structurally disadvantaged populations is forced to reckon with his or her relative power and privilege. There is no one right answer to the ethical challenges that inevitably surface. Between active advocacy and withdrawing from the study altogether, the balance I sought was solidarity. By portraying the men's experiences at the park with as much specificity and honesty as possible, I've tried to honor what they were able to overcome and accomplish in that time and place. And the men's willingness to participate in my study showed their solidarity with me.[27]

I had many moving experiences along the way—the fun and fellowship I have tried to capture in this book. Some of these were moments of high emotional energy, but I was equally taken in by the everyday scenes at the park. There were fewer greater joys at that time than playing in the midday soccer games or listening to the men's stories over shared beers. While I was ostensibly at work, the park was a welcome respite from my other responsibilities. I found data, but also joy in the warmth and revelry of park life. However, this project was not without its challenges. Like the men, I dealt with injuries, hangovers, and strains on my relationships away from the park. But these, too, were part of the story and a source of affinity and cohesion. In this way, I joined the men in managing the ups and downs of this vibrant world.

While my experiences were unique in some respects, deep engagement in the life of the park helped me better understand what the men were seeking to create there. Like Michelada, I was once a newcomer to this social world; like Rudy, I can only hope to return to Mar Vista, surrounded by friends who share memories of all we did together there. This book is my attempt to portray as accurately as possible the rich and complex social world the men graciously allowed me to share. I hope they see themselves in this book and continue to have a place to call their own.

¡Que vivan los jugadores del parque!

ACKNOWLEDGMENTS

First and foremost, I would like to thank the many jugadores del parque who participated in this study. This project would not have been possible without their willingness to let me observe and experience the social world of the park. Their sincerity, trust, and friendship made this book possible and transformed me both as a person and as a scholar. *Fútbol in the Park* is my earnest attempt to convey and pay tribute to what the men create and confront in their daily lives. I hope they will recognize the situations, spectacles, and struggles I describe as their own and sense my gratitude when they come across their names on the printed page. I extend a special gracias to Polo, a giant in the pantheon of primary informants.

I also wish to thank all the various park activists, neighborhood residents, city employees, and local politicians who met with me to share their views and experiences regarding the park. I am equally grateful to the men's employers who put up with my presence and nagging questions. Though some may disagree with parts of my analysis, I hope they all recognize that my book was carried out with the best intentions.

My wife and two young children contributed in important ways to this research as well. I thank them for their willingness to join me in my field-work, which generally involved socializing with the men at the park or on nearby soccer fields during Sunday league games. Maureen graciously opened our home to many of the men over the years. Her warm presence helped me develop fuller relationships with the men. Our two children, born in years three and five of fieldwork, played a similar role. There's no doubt that my role as a husband and father helped shape the arc of this project, and I hope they all see their contributions to this book.

Maureen, Marcel, and Alana also provided me with the love and reassurance I needed to complete this project. It was not always smooth sailing—especially given problems sometimes associated with the park—but they never stopped encouraging me, including during the seemingly endless years it took me to finish writing this book. A special debt of gratitude and appreciation is reserved for my wife, who not only tolerated my time away at the park, but left her family and country to come with me to live in Los Angeles. I can never thank her enough.

It is now well over a decade since I first arrived at Haines Hall, home to the Department of Sociology at UCLA. It proved a welcoming and stimulating environment to pursue this project. I owe much of my development as a sociologist and ethnographer to Jack Katz. While the book's shortcomings are entirely my own, this project might have followed a very different path were it not for his guidance. His attention to the intricacies of social interaction and his insistence that my claims fit my data pushed me to dig deeper and go beyond the original contours of the project. While Jack was often my fiercest, most devoted critic, Roger Waldinger proved to be my biggest champion at UCLA. He saw promise and potential in the project well before I did. It has been a tremendous privilege to have been trained by Professors Katz and Waldinger, whose intellect and scholarship are unparalleled. I trust that they will see their imprint on this book throughout. I thank them both for their mentoring and support.

Stefan Timmermans has served a guiding role for many years, most recently as editor of the University of Chicago Press's Fieldwork Encounters and Discoveries series, of which I feel so honored to be a part. Rubén Hernández-León provided similar support, especially in response to numerous tricky translation questions. In addition, I thank Robert Emerson, as well as Anastasia Loukaitou-Sideris, Rebecca Emigh, Ching Kwan Lee, Andreas Wimmer, and David Halle.

I also greatly appreciate the rigorous training I received in the MA Program in the Social Sciences at the University of Chicago, which offered me and so many others a jump-start into academia. I am especially indebted to John MacAloon, director emeritus of the program. Finally, I express my warmest thanks to Christina Gómez, who first introduced me to the power of the sociological imagination and has continued to encourage me years after I left her dynamic classroom at Dartmouth College.

I reserve much of my gratitude to my fellow graduate students at UCLA. Our innumerable discussions about research and fieldwork were a tremendous source of inspiration and assistance. In particular, I thank all the students associated with the Ethnography Working Group, an incubator of so many excellent ethnographies. I express my deepest thanks to Michael DeLand, my twin sociologist of pickup sports. Mike has improved many of the pages in this book through his keen insights and gentle guidance. Iddo Tavory, Jooyoung Lee, and Forrest Stuart were phenomenal role models during graduate school. Iddo, in particular, has gone beyond the call of duty in supporting my development. Caitlin Patler and Elena Shih were also instrumental figures during my graduate studies and beyond. A bicoastal writing group with Michael DeLand, Laura Orrico, and Rocío Rosales kept me motivated with feedback and deadlines. I also wish to thank Thomas Soehl, Pamela Prickett, John O'Brien, Nahoko Kameo, Nazgol Ghandnoosh, Curtis Jackson-Jacobs, Andrew Deener, Eli Wilson, and Neil Gong, along with Benjamin Gebre-Medhin and Jonathan Gordon, two dear friends turned fellow sociologists. Jon in particular was always available to discuss the ups and downs of academia and life. For their friendship throughout this project, I also thank Reg Laing, Eli Carter, Michael Ammons, and David Kang, as well as Alec Banks and Haji Outlaw, childhood friends who provided a couch to sleep on during my return visits to Los Angeles.

My book is the product of my personal relationships but was made possible thanks to a number of different funding opportunities. Most were provided by UCLA in the form of fellowships and teaching assistantships. For its material and administrative support, I thank this great public institution and hope that it can continue to prosper in uncertain times. I also thank UC MEXUS for supplying a small grant to transcribe interviews. In addition, I express my deep gratitude to the state of California for providing my family with crucial Medi-Cal assistance during the birth of our two children and in the formative early years that followed. Without this temporary aid, this project would have been far more difficult. I hope that the taxpayers of California continue to provide for families in need.

The task of turning my research into a book took place at James Madison University. For creating a supportive environment in which to meet this challenge, I thank all my colleagues in the Department of Sociology and Anthropology, especially Beth Eck and Liam Buckley, who have headed our department with poise and skill. In addition, I wish to acknowledge Chris Colocousis, Jonas Hart, Joshua Linder, and Shaun Wright for their feedback and good humor. I have also benefited from the help of colleagues at other institutions, chiefly Colin Jerolmack. From the day I first heard about his project on pigeons, Colin has been a source of inspiration and direction. I also thank Joanna Dreby, Jonathan Wynn, Randol Contreras, Eric Klinenberg, Sergio Chávez, and Jennifer Doyle for their comments and suggestions. I remain indebted to Elijah Anderson as well, who invited an upstart sociologist to present at a distinguished ethnography conference at Yale University in 2014. The generous feedback I received there confirmed that this project was worth completing. I had a similarly encouraging experience several years later presenting at the NYU Ethnography Workshop, thanks to an invitation from Lynne Haney and Iddo Tavory.

I am also grateful to the many scholars I have met or communicated with briefly over the years and from whom I have drawn enormous inspiration, including Pierrette Hondagneu-Sotelo, Cecilia Menjívar, Robert Smith, Mario

Small, Mitchell Duneier, Douglas Hartmann, Gary Alan Fine, and Randall Collins. In addition, I thank the good friends I've made in Harrisonburg, Virginia—especially Nico—for keeping me entertained and grounded as I tackled the tenure clock and book-writing deadlines. Finally, I express my profound appreciation to all the teammates and coaches with whom I have played soccer over the years, including my hometown clubs Pele Stars and JaHbat F.C. This book is in part my attempt to make sense of these personally engrossing and transformative experiences.

Publishing with the University of Chicago Press has been a fantasy come true. I am deeply honored that this book received an advance contract from the late Douglas Mitchell, thanks to Jack Katz's generous introduction. Although we never met in person, Doug's wit and enthusiasm for this project shared over email lived up to his reputation as a champion of immersive, innovative ethnography. Elizabeth Branch Dyson has proven a terrific successor in steering this project to completion. Her patience and attentiveness have greatly improved this book. For her editorial assistance, I also acknowledge Mollie McFee and other staff members involved in this project. In addition, I thank the generous reviewers of this manuscript, as well as dozens of anonymous readers of related articles. Finally, I wish to express my heartfelt thanks to senior manuscript editor Erin DeWitt for her careful and thoughtful editing.

I close by thanking my family. Above all, I express my deepest gratitude to my parents. If I am an academic, it is largely because of my mother, Mary Seidman Trouille, who taught French literature for many years and whose comments on the manuscript were invaluable. From an early age, she instilled in me a passion for knowledge and scholarship, a path set forth by her pioneering mother, Virginia Crosley Seidman. I type my grandmother's name with great respect, as she played an outsize but nameless role as senior manuscript editor at the University of Chicago Press, where she edited countless books, including several groundbreaking studies in sociology. During this era, the Press had a policy not to acknowledge in print the immense contributions of those working "behind the scenes." I feel deeply honored to carry on this family tradition of scholarly endeavors.

My father, who has his own immigrant story to tell, showed me the value of hard work and determination—skills and sensibilities that helped me become an academic. Together, my parents provided the symbolic and very real safety net that allowed me to focus my energies on being a student over *many* years of study, an advantage not all my classmates shared. My book is the end result of my parents' unconditional love and support, for which I am forever grateful. I also thank my two amazing sisters and their families for their love and encouragement. My Tico family members were additional sources of affection and levity during this long process. In particular, I thank mi suegra, Doña Olga. Without a doubt, this book would never have been possible if not for her unfailing care and cariño. I hope that this book serves as a small token of my immense gratitude to all the people who have supported me over the years.

NOTES

Introduction

1. Arreola 2004; Davis 2001; Flores and Benmayor 1997; Sandoval-Strausz 2019; Valle and Torres 2000.

2. Dolgon 2005; Doyle 2018; Figueroa 2003; Meneses and Rabadan 2015; Nelson 2016; Pescador 2004; Poblete 2015; Price and Whitworth 2004; Quiroz Becerra 2014; Santos-Gómez 2017; Tuohy 2018.

3. Foer 2004.

4. See page 172 in the conclusion for the full text of the flyer.

5. Chavez 2008; see also Flores and Schachter 2018; Pickett 2016.

6. For comparable examples of community concerns over the perceived threat of "outsiders," see Anderson 1990; Kefalas 2003; Nicolaides 2002; Pattillo 2007; Rieder 1985; Suttles 1968.

7. On the "gendered racial removal" of Latino immigrant men, see Golash-Boza and Hondagneu-Sotelo 2013. On "bad hombres" as a form of racialized and gendered discourse, see Silber Mohamed and Farris 2020.

8. On the value of empathy in ethnography, see Small 2015. However, on the limits of empathy, see Bloom 2017.

9. For diverse takes on the contemporary challenges and choices facing ethnographers, see Cobb and Hoang 2015; Fine 2019; Katz 2019; Ray and Tillman 2019; Rios 2015; Small 2015.

10. On how Latino immigrants are framed in popular media, see Chavez 2008; Haynes, Merolla, and Ramakrishnan 2016; Menjívar 2016; Santa Ana 2002; Silber Mohamed and Farris 2020.

11. See, for example, Abrego and Schmalzbauer 2018; Dreby 2015; Hondagneu-Sotelo 1994; Hondagneu-Sotelo and Avila 1997; Schmalzbauer 2014; Segura and Zavella 2007; Villalón 2010. The richness of ordinary middle-class White experiences has also been well documented. See, for example, the work of Fine 2002, 2009, 2015. On the importance of examining the full humanity and complexity of the people we study, also see Hunter et al. 2016; Kelley 1996; Scott 1990; Small 2015.

12. McKinney 1966; see also Du Bois and Eaton 1899. On the contemporary relevance of "Chicago School" ethnography, see Abbott 1997. For a critique of this approach, see Burawoy 2000.

13. For a rich and diverse selection of ethnographic examples, see Duneier, Kasinitz, and Murphy 2014.

14. Anderson 1923; Anderson 1978; Bourgois 1996; Contreras 2013; Duneier

1999; Goffman 2015; Horowitz 1983; Jerolmack 2013; Lane 2018; Lee 2016; Liebow 1967; Low 2010; May 2001; Pattillo-McCoy 1999; Stuart 2016; Suttles 1968; Whyte 1943. For a more general discussion of public hangouts and forms of sociability associated with "third places," see Oldenburg 1999.

15. See, for example, Stuart 2016.

16. See, for example, Anderson 1978; Duneier 1992.

17. Jerolmack and Khan 2017; Tavory and Timmermans 2009.

18. While there have been several qualitative studies of Latino immigrant men looking for work on street corners (Fernández 2018; Ordóñez 2015; Purser 2009; Turnovsky 2006; Valenzuela 2001; Walter, Bourgois, and Loinaz 2004), there has not been the same ethnographic focus on them socializing as *people* in public (but see Horowitz 1983). Indeed, most "street-corner ethnographies" have been written about Black or White men. However, there have been several ethnographic studies of Latino immigrants in other settings and situations. See, for example, Abrego 2014; Andrews 2018; Chávez 2016; Dreby 2010, 2015; Estrada 2019; García 2019; Holmes 2013; Hondagneu-Sotelo 2001; Keller 2019; Mahler 1995; Menjívar 2000; Rosales 2020; Schmalzbauer 2014; Smith 2006; Zavella 2011; Zlolniski 2006.

19. On mining puzzles and surprises in ethnographic research—an abductive approach used throughout this book—see Jensen and Auyero 2019; Katz 2001; Mears 2017; Timmermans and Tavory 2012.

20. Boyd 1989; Massey et al. 1987; Tilly 1990.

21. The importance of networking is hardly unique to migrants (see Desmond 2012; Fischer 1982; Stack 1974). However, the ties they forge are shaped by the special circumstances created by moving across borders and settling in new places (Massey et al. 1987).

22. For a similar critique, see Chávez 2016; Del Real 2018; Flores-Yeffal 2013; Hagan 1998; Krissman 2005; Mahler 1995; Menjívar 2000; Portes and Sensenbrenner 1993.

23. Durand and Massey 1992; Massey et al. 1987.

24. Hernández-León 2008; see also Chávez 2016; Fussell and Massey 2004.

25. Menjívar's book *Fragmented Ties: Salvadoran Immigrant Networks in America* (2000) was especially helpful to me in developing my critique of migrant networks as uniformly stable and supportive. See also Bashi 2007; Cranford 2005; Flores-Yeffal and Aysa-Lastra 2011; Mahler 1995; Ordóñez 2015. But regarding the continuing, albeit contentious, significance of origin-based networks in some low-wage employment sectors see, for example, Rosales 2020.

26. Piore 1979; see also Hondagneu-Sotelo 1995.

27. Polo's story is corroborated by Deener's (2012) study of Venice, California. He found that Latino immigrants socialized at Penmar Park during this time because they felt unsafe at the nearby Oakwood Recreation Center that was perceived to be controlled by African American gangs during a period of intense gang violence (Umemoto 2006). In this small way, Deener's decision to identify—and not mask—the places he studied helped to advance my research (see notes 67 and 71).

28. Emirbayer and Goodwin 1994.

29. Massey et al. 1987.

30. Gomberg-Muñoz 2011; Hagan 1998; Hondagneu-Sotelo 2017; Hernández-León 2008; Menjívar 2000; Smith 2006; Waldinger, Popkin, and Magana 2008; Zepeda-Millán 2016.

31. Cranz 1982; Goodman 1979; Hardy 1981; Riess 1989; Rosenzweig 1983.

32. For close ethnographic studies of other sporting scenes see, for example, Brooks 2009; DeLand 2018; Fine 1987; Grasmuck 2005; Kidder 2017; Klein 1993; May 2009; Wacquant 2004.

33. Goffman 1983; see also Collins 2004; Fine 2012; Rawls 1987.

34. Blumer 1969; Goffman 1967; Mead 1934.

35. For a similar approach to studying network formation as an interactive and transformative process, see Clawson 2005; Crossley 2010; Desmond 2012; Feld 1981; Fine and Kleinman 1983; Gibson 2005; Goffman 2019; Mazelis 2017; Ray 2016; Small 2009, 2017; Smith 2005; Torres 2019; Wittel 2001.

36. Collins 2004.

37. Gans 1962.

38. Hjelte 1977.

39. Tam, n.d.

40. Bobo et al. 2000; Charles 2004.

41. Alarcón, Escala, and Odgers 2016; FitzGerald and Skrentny 2021; Hamilton and Chinchilla 2001; Waldinger and Bozorgmehr 1996.

42. Joassart-Marcelli 2010; Wolch, Wilson, and Fehrenbach 2005.

43. Klinenberg 2018. See also Latham and Layton 2019.

44. For a more focused discussion of "Latino masculinity," see Cantú 2009; Donaldson et al. 2009; Gutmann 2006; Hondagneu-Sotelo 2017; Mirandé 2018; Montes 2013; Pribilsky 2012; Ramirez and Flores 2010; Smith 2006; Walter, Bourgois, and Loinaz 2004.

45. Dreby 2010; Hondagneu-Sotelo 2014, 2017; Schmalzbauer 2014.

46. Abrego 2014; Hamilton and Chinchilla 2001; Menjívar 2000.

47. Cornelius 1998; Cranford 2005; Waldinger and Lichter 2003.

48. Kalleberg 2011.

49. For comparable studies of people using nicknames in other small group settings, see Brandes 1975; Fine 1979; Skipper 1986.

50. Hondagneu-Sotelo 2014, 2017; Loukaitou-Sideris 1995; Main 2013.

51. Chavez 1998.

52. In 2014, according to the Pew Research Center, in Orange and Los Angeles Counties there were one million undocumented immigrants who together comprised 22 percent of the foreign-born population and 7.5 percent of the total population in these areas.

53. With the men's permission, I had initially planned to tell their stories of "illegality." However, I gradually came to appreciate the danger of disclosing their legal status or even of delving into their individual experiences as undocumented immigrants. (See Contreras 2019 on the dangers of unmasking in ethnographic research.) Los Angeles may be a sanctuary city (Maya 2001; Papazian 2011), but the risks have intensified in today's polarized climate and tomorrow's uncertain future. In any case, I did not always have a good sense of the men's legal standing, either because some were uncomfortable divulging the full details or because others seemed to be in a state of "liminal legality" they themselves could not explain (Menjívar 2006). For a more focused discussion of Latino immigrants' experiences of living without documentation, see Abrego 2006; Andrews 2018; Coutin 2003; Dreby 2010, 2015; Enriquez 2020; García 2019; Gomberg-Muñoz 2011, 2017; Gonzales 2015; Menjívar and Abrego 2012; Patler 2017; Rosales 2020.

54. I played Division I college soccer and remained a competitive soccer player throughout my time in the park.

55. I have spent considerable time in Latin America and predominately Latino immigrant settings in several US cities. Often these interactions were based around a shared interest in soccer. Thus, despite its idiosyncratic qualities, the Mar Vista games represented a familiar cultural and social setting. I believe my personal and professional comfort with similar gatherings helped ease my integration into the group at Mar Vista (Trouille 2008, 2009). While always an outsider, my marriage to a woman from Costa Rica, with whom I had two children during my fieldwork—all of whom got to know the men from the park—also helped bridge my social and cultural distance from the men. (On the relationship between family and fieldwork in ethnographic research, see the collection of essays in Brown and Dreby 2013.)

56. Anderson 2011.

57. Whyte 1994.

58. Having made clear from the beginning that I expected to work "for free," I was never paid for this work, but the men would often treat me to lunch or beers at the park as a token of their appreciation.

59. Kusenbach 2003.

60. See DeLand and Trouille 2018 and Trouille and Tavory 2019 on the value of looking across time and in different social contexts.

61. On the tenuous relationship between accounts (i.e., what people say) and action (i.e., what people do) in qualitative research, see Jerolmack and Khan 2014.

62. Sensing the men's interest, I set up a private (and now-defunct) website to catalog and display my photographs. The men often talked about the photographs at the park, and many told me that family and friends in Los Angeles and elsewhere enjoyed viewing them as well. As Barba remarked, "We're famous in Yalapa," referring to the small Mexican village from which he had emigrated twenty years earlier.

63. I received signed permission forms from the men pictured in the photos, except from some of the men in the two large group photos. Unfortunately, I was unable to track them down to ask for their signed consent. However, as they had agreed to participate in my study and their faces are less distinguishable in these group shots, I decided to include them without their explicit approval in order to give a more complete picture of the gatherings at the park. I also double-checked with one of the men concerning a photo about which he might have second thoughts, despite his initial enthusiasm for its inclusion. As I suspected, he asked that I not publish the potentially embarrassing photo—further evidence that informed consent in ethnographic research is an ongoing process (Plankey-Videla 2012).

64. I translated the Spanish into English with the assistance of editorial staff at the University of Chicago Press and several Spanish-speaking colleagues, friends, and family members. Their suggestions proved especially helpful in translating the men's more colloquial words and phrases in their particular context.

65. On the everyday language of Latino immigrants, see Lauria 1964; Limón 1989, 1994.

66. The fact that I did not include the men's full names gives them a degree of "plausible deniability" in case of unwanted attention or scrutiny, as other scholars faced with this issue have maintained (Contreras 2019; Pacewicz 2016; Reyes 2018b). Moreover, I identify many of the men by nicknames used only at the park—an aspect of park life that pseudonyms could *not* have meaningfully replicated (Lahman et al.

2015). In addition, I never identified individuals when recounting incidents or stories that might embarrass or harm them in some way. While not possible in all cases, I showed many of the men passages in the book where they were mentioned (Duneier 1999). This was to elicit their feedback, but also to see whether they found the material in any way problematic. Although their comments often helped me refine my descriptions and analysis, at no point did the men ever ask me to change or remove material from the book.

67. On the benefits of greater transparency in ethnography, see Duneier 1999; Guenther 2009; Jerolmack and Murphy 2017; Scheper-Hughes 2000.

68. See, for example, Duneier 1999; Liebow 1993; Myerhoff 1978.

69. In the course of my research, I interviewed a range of actors connected to the park, including area residents, community activists, city administrators, and politicians. I also observed numerous meetings about the soccer field and, from 2010 to 2012, served on the Mar Vista Park Advisory Board. When a position opened up, several board members urged me to apply because "you're always here," as one person joked. As it turned out, I was the only person who applied, and my application was accepted. Yet I do believe they were eager to have someone on the board who was younger and more closely connected to the soccer field. To construct a local history, I used a variety of primary sources, including accounts of activities that predated my arrival. To supplement public records that I personally gathered, several contacts graciously handed over stacks of materials—including flyers, reports, photographs, and hundreds of emails that helped me piece together events and reactions to events I had not observed firsthand.

70. When I began reaching out to local residents and park staff in early 2008, debates about the soccer field and proposed fencing were at their apex. In order to encourage their participation in my study during this contentious period, I chose to offer them anonymity. Although I didn't have the time or interest to build close relationships of the kind that facilitated my fieldwork with the men at the park, most people involved in the field controversy were willing to speak with me. As previously mentioned, several provided me with stacks of materials (emails, flyers, photos, and reports) related to the matter—a treasure trove of materials I did not anticipate receiving. It is unclear to what extent the promise of confidentiality may have encouraged their participation, but I am grateful for their help.

71. Regarding the difficulty of concealing the site of one's fieldwork, see Reich 2015; Walford 2018. As for the benefits of site disclosure, see Burawoy 2003; Duneier 1999; Jerolmack and Murphy 2017.

72. Trouille 2014.

73. On the application and advantages of "reflexive ethnography," see Eason 2017; Flores 2016; Reyes 2018a; Stuart 2018.

Chapter One

1. In his study of Mexican immigrant culture and community on LA's Westside, Leonard Melchor (2014) identifies Mar Vista Park as a field used by Latino soccer teams in the 1970s and 1980s.

2. Mar Vista was the third public artificial turf soccer field installed in Los Angeles, after Griffith Park Recreation Center and the Ross Snyder Recreation Center. By 2020, there were twenty-one such fields (https://www.laparks.org/synthetic-turf -fields). At the time of its opening, the field at Mar Vista was the only one operated by

the Los Angeles Department of Recreation and Parks that offered free and open play at certain hours of the day. See García, Flores, and Pine 2002 for an earlier study on soccer fields and equity in Los Angeles.

3. Strauss 1978.

4. Anderson 1999; Lofland 1973, 1998.

5. For example, the Santa Monica airport field located a few miles away was restricted to permit use and generally locked and empty when the men played at the Mar Vista field.

6. The fact that chapter 1 deals with the organization of the soccer games is hardly surprising, since it reflects the allure of the scene and my experience there as a participant observer. It is what initially sparked my interest and served as the focus of my early research (Trouille 2013), whereas other aspects of park life required more time and a deeper engagement to access and understand. However, studies of inter-actions in public space often remain at this more surface and ethnomethodological level of analysis (i.e., how people do things), without digging deeper into how the site connects to other aspects of people's lives and biographies (see, for example, Morrill, Snow, and White 2005; also see DeLand and Trouille 2018).

7. Low, Taplin, and Scheld 2009; Robins, Sanders, and Cahill 1991.

8. Anderson 1978; Jerolmack 2009.

9. Lyman and Scott 1967.

10. Collins 2000, 26–27.

11. In a different setting, Turnovsky 2006 shows how Latino immigrant day labor-ers resist the first-come, first-served custom of day-laborer centers, in preference for a more negotiated, malleable setup on la parada (the street corner). See also Purser 2009.

12. Anderson 1999.

13. Hall 1959.

14. See Edgerton 1979 on how beachgoers stake out territory and minimize their interactions with strangers.

15. Regarding the social significance of queueing and waiting, see Bourdieu 2000; Schwartz 1975.

16. The use of an appointed referee at Mar Vista contrasts to pickup basketball games where players typically call their own fouls (DeLand 2013; Jimerson 1996).

17. Garfinkel 1967.

18. Goffman 1967, 2–3.

19. Duneier and Molotch 1999. See also Gardner 1995.

20. Cavan 1963, 27.

21. Anderson 1978. See also May 2001.

22. Anderson 1999; Horowitz 1983; Suttles 1968.

23. See Britton 2008 on "third parties" and the use of public space.

24. See Zukin 2009 on the "paradox of public space."

25. Suttles 1968.

26. Erikson 1961.

Chapter Two

1. See Goffman 1961 on games as "world-building activities."

2. Huizinga 1949 famously argued that games exist in a "magic circle" that separates them from everyday life. See also Goffman 1961 on "rules of irrelevance" in games.

3. Goffman 1961.

4. The section heading was inspired by the title of Erving Goffman's influential essay "Fun in Games" (1961).

5. Collins 2004; see also Birrell 1981. See also Durkheim's ([1912] 1995) analysis of how religious gatherings can intensify, electrify, and solidify shared experience and group identity, which he famously defined as moments of "collective effervescence."

6. See Hendricks 2006 on play as "expressive behavior."

7. On the relationship between humor and difference, see Jerolmack 2013; Reid 2015.

8. See Kornblum 1974 on "back-fence cosmopolitanism."

9. Regarding the integrative function of "joking relationships," see Radcliffe-Brown 1940. See also Coser 1959.

10. While some scholars view comments like these as expressions of racism and homophobia, others suggest that fans at professional soccer matches draw on the diversity of players and teams in this way to drum up support and enthusiasm. For this second view, see Ben-Porat 2001, 2014; Crabbe, Solomos, and Back 2001; Müller, Van Zoonen, and De Roode 2007.

11. On the relationship between humor and biography, see Fine and De Soucey 2005; Roy 1959.

12. Goffman 1961 makes a similar point about the source of fun in games. He writes: "While it is as players that we can win, it is only as participants that we can get fun out of winning" (37). See also Fine and Corte 2017.

13. Motor's experience is reminiscent of Csikszentmihalyi's well-known descriptions of becoming lost in the "flow" of the moment (1974). For Motor and others, this was part of the game's appeal, although the world beyond action on the soccer field was never far removed.

14. On how the self becomes immortalized through sport, see Schmitt and Leonard 1986. See also Perinbanayagam 2006.

15. On how watching television can become a shared resource for interaction, see May 2001.

16. Anderson 1978; Jerolmack 2013.

17. On how males bond and construct "masculine" and "heterosexual" identities through "fag discourse," see Pascoe 2011. See also Burn 2000. However, for men who might have been "in the closet" at the park, these "gay jokes" were presumably less a source of fun and solidarity, but instead a cause of resentment and pain. But my sense is that the sexual banter "worked" because they believed that the recipients were not actually gay, nor did it reflect deep-seated animosity toward gay people. And with no openly gay men among los jugadores (as far as I knew), it was hard to test this hypothesis about the conviviality of "gay jokes." For additional context, see Carrillo 2017 on the experiences of Mexican immigrant gay men in the United States.

18. Goffman 1981, 46.

19. On male mentorship in sports, see Brooks 2009; Sacha 2017.

20. Smith 2006.

Chapter Three

1. Research on contemporary Latino immigrants, while frequently referencing alcohol and hinting at its significance, often fails to interrogate the subject fully (see Chávez 2016, 138; Menjívar 2000, 182; Smith 2006; but see also Limón 1994;

Ordóñez 2015). Or this research tends to treat alcohol primarily as a form of self-medication and source of social and health problems (see Holmes 2013, 98; Worby et al. 2014). By contrast, there has been considerable scholarly attention given to the drinking practices and settings of earlier, non-Latino immigrant groups (Koren 1899; Kornblum 1974; Light 2013; Powers 1998; Rosenzweig 1983) and to those of working-class Whites (Cavan 1966; Desmond 2007; Halle 1984; Kingsdale 1973; LeMasters 1975; Spradley 1970), African Americans (Anderson 1978; Bell 1983; May 2001), and Native Americans (Lurie 1971; Spicer 1997; Weibel-Orlando 1985).

2. Douglas 1987, 3.

3. For example, an eighteen-pack of Modelo cost roughly twenty dollars at a convenience store, whereas one Modelo cost around five dollars at the cantinas the men occasionally frequented.

4. See MacAndrew and Edgerton 1969 on the social and contextual meanings of "drunken comportment."

5. See Menjívar 2000; Smith 2006.

6. See Brissett 1978; Karp 1980; Prus 1983. On the social organization and effects of marijuana use, see Becker 1953; Zimmerman and Wieder 1977.

7. London 1913, 106.

8. At the time, Chicharito (Little Pea) was the most famous soccer player from Mexico.

9. See Brandes 2010 on how men in Mexico joined Alcoholics Anonymous not so much to fight alcoholism but to find friends, which became harder once they stopped drinking, given that the basis of their friendship had been drinking together.

10. On the stigma of drinking "alone," see Topper 1985.

11. See also Brandes 2010; Gutmann 2006; Lancaster 1994; Lomnitz 1977.

12. See Ordóñez 2015.

13. See Allison 1994 on how female hostesses in Japanese bars facilitate and expedite relaxed conversation. See also Hoang 2015.

14. Turner 1976.

15. Goffman 1967.

16. Goffman 1967.

17. See Brandes 2010 on how Mexican men in Alcoholic Anonymous redefine their masculinity through similar stories.

18. Anderson 2011.

19. Gouldner 1960.

20. Mauss 1967; see also Bourdieu 1990; Schwartz 1967.

21. "Pachanga" means "boisterous party" in Spanish slang.

22. On the "moral economies" of drug addicts, see Bourgois 1998.

23. On how drinking occasions are framed as a "time-out" from normal sober behavior, see MacAndrew and Edgerton 1969.

24. See also Hoang 2015; Mars 1987. Also see Alice Goffman 2019 on how social occasions can prompt unexpected turning points and transitions in people's lives.

25. Lomnitz 1977.

26. Reticent police officers informed me that they surveyed the park on periodic patrols (alcohol representing one of several concerns) and also in response to direct calls from the public about men drinking in the park. A member of the park staff told me that they typically received one to two complaints a week from other park users about alcohol consumption that the staff then relayed to the police.

27. The fine for public alcohol consumption changed over the course of my fieldwork. In 2008 it was $185, and by 2017 it had risen to $225.

28. See also Goffman 2015; Rios 2011; Stuart 2016.

29. While beer was the most prominent intoxicating substance consumed at the park, roughly 20 percent of the men regularly smoked marijuana at the park. Like the beer drinkers, they consumed openly, although always with a cautious eye for the police and other threats. A few men used crack and cocaine, but always in their cars or other discreet locations. While I never directly witnessed anyone using these harder substances, I heard rumors of its use and occasionally saw what I presumed to be its effects.

30. Although I observed and heard about multiple cases in which the men's drinking created legal problems beyond a misdemeanor alcohol citation, I was not always aware of the precise reasons for these developments. For example, I don't know exactly why one of the men was sent back to jail after initially being detained for suspected drinking or if another really was arrested for unpaid parking tickets. But to maintain good relations with the men, I did not press them on their cases beyond what I was told or overheard. That said, most men understood that beer drinking could lead to more serious problems with the police, even if they were uncertain of the specific causes.

31. The matrícula consular is an identification card issued by the Mexican government through its consular offices to Mexican nationals living outside of Mexico.

32. In 1979 the City of Los Angeles passed Special Order 40 prohibiting LAPD officers from questioning individuals for the sole purpose of determining their immigration status. For a discussion of how this mandate has affected the LAPD's treatment of undocumented immigrants, see Maya 2001; Papazian 2011. See also Andrews 2018, who found "modes of control" to be far more accommodating toward immigrants in Los Angeles than in North County San Diego.

33. Regarding the downgrading of public drinking in Los Angeles to a civil infraction, see https://www.nbclosangeles.com/news/local/LA-Downgrades-Low-Level -Crimes-to-Infractions-218433751.html.

34. On drinking-time rituals, see Gusfield 1987.

35. In an offhand but revealing comment, political economist Michael Piore drew a connection between drinking and the development of migrant communities, especially as it relates to changing orientations toward work: "The men, living impersonally side by side, take off a Saturday night to get drunk; the drunk extends into Sunday morning and begins to conflict with some of the extra work. Or people begin to sacrifice overtime work for companionship of their fellow men to have time occasionally to drink in the evening, to play cards or dominoes" (1979, 62).

Chapter Four

1. Collins 2008.

2. See Anderson 1999; Auyero and Kilanski 2015; Bourgois 1995; Contreras 2013; Jones 2009; Suttles 1968; but also see Garot 2007, 2009; Krupnick and Winship 2015; Lee 2009; Chan Tack and Small 2017.

3. On fighting strangers, see Conley 1999; Copes, Hochstetler, and Forsyth 2013; Jackson-Jacobs 2013; Tomsen 1997; Weenink 2015.

4. While I learned about the men's actions in this case from secondhand information, the outlines of the incident were confirmed by multiple actors and seemed reasonable given what I observed in the park and elsewhere.

5. Trouille and Tavory 2019.

6. Other researchers have made this same observation. See, for example, Collins 2008; Emerson 2015; Katz 1988.

7. Goffman 1967.

8. As Goffman 1961 observed, interactions in such situations become "flooded out" and no longer playful.

9. See Krupnick and Winship 2015 for a comparable case of "symbolic substitutions" that work to prevent street violence. See also Lee 2009.

10. Collins 2008; Emerson 2015; Jackson-Jacobs 2013; Katz 1988; Luckenbill 1977; Weenink 2014.

11. Gould 2003.

12. Collins 2008. See also Felson 1982; Jackson-Jacobs 2004, 2013; Lee 2009; Luckenbill 1977.

13. See Katz 1988 on "righteous slaughters."

14. Other researchers have made a similar point about the strategic uses of fighting in ice-hockey. See, for example, Colburn 1986; Faulkner 1974.

15. Anderson 1999; Papachristos 2009.

16. Jackson-Jacobs 2004.

17. Connell 1995; Messerschmidt 1993.

18. Anderson 1999, 68.

19. Out of concerns over embarrassing this research subject, I have elected, in this case, to use a pseudonym.

20. Geertz 2000.

Chapter Five

1. On the value of studying the "paired experiences" of wealthy clients and the working poor, see Farrell 2020. See also Bearman 2005; Hondagneu-Sotelo 2001; Sherman 2007; Rollins 1985.

2. On immigrant labor in private homes, see López-Garza 2001; Ramirez and Hondagneu-Sotelo 2009; Valenzuela 2003.

3. See, for example, Brown 2011; Glenn 1986; Hondagneu-Sotelo 2001; Rollins 1985; Romero 1992.

4. But see Chávez and Altman 2017; Huerta 2007; Lemus 2017; Pisani and Yoskowitz 2005, 2006; Ramirez 2011; Ramirez and Hondagneu-Sotelo 2009. On the "migrant handyman phenomenon" in the United Kingdom, see Kilkey and Perrons 2010.

5. Bean et al. 2012; Hagan, Hernández-León, and Demonsant 2015; Mahler 1995; Sassen 1991; Waldinger and Lichter 2003; Zlolniski 2006.

6. On Latino immigrant labor in restaurants, see Gomberg-Muñoz 2011; Wilson 2020.

7. Regarding the uncertainties and abuses faced by migrant day laborers, see Fussell 2011; Quesada et al. 2014; Walter, Bourgois, and Loinaz 2004.

8. See, for example, Malpica 2002; Ordóñez 2015.

9. See Kusenbach 2003 on the "go along" as an ethnographic research tool.

10. Romero 1988.

11. On immigrant skills and entrepreneurship, see Hagan, Hernández-León, and Demonsant 2015; Ramirez and Hondagneu-Sotelo 2009; Valdez 2011; Valenzuela 2001.

12. Regarding apprenticeship processes in Latino immigrant gardening, see Ramirez and Hondagneu-Sotelo 2009.

13. For a discussion of the informal economy, see Portes, Castells, and Benton 1989; Sassen 2000; Venkatesh 2008.

14. Catanzarite 2000.

15. On the power of referrals in predominately immigrant workforces, see Waldinger and Lichter 2003.

16. For other examples of people withholding support to non-reciprocators, see Dominguez and Watkins 2003; Stack 1974.

17. For examples of how workers draw prestige from their higher-status clientele in other settings, see Bearman 2005; Sherman 2007.

18. As Hagan 1998 and Hondagneu-Sotelo 2001 point out, domestic workers face similar challenges.

19. Granovetter 1977.

20. By contrast, see García 2019 on strategies used by undocumented Latino immigrants in cities in San Diego County hostile to immigrants to *reduce* their visibility in an attempt to pass as Mexican Americans.

21. Cranford 2005; Hondagneu-Sotelo 1994; Waldinger and Lichter 2003.

22. On the emergence of "extras" in gardening work, see Ramirez and Hondagneu-Sotelo 2009.

23. See Ramirez and Hondagneu-Sotelo 2009 for a similar finding.

24. Regarding the "skills of the unskilled," see Hagan, Hernández-León, and Demonsant 2015.

25. Regarding labor market competition in Los Angeles, see Light 2006.

26. On the "functional deficiencies" within job referral networks of African Americans, see Smith 2005. See also Royster 2003.

27. Regarding how nannies also congregate in parks to socialize and combat the isolation of their work, see Armenta 2009; Brown 2011; Hondagneu-Sotelo 2001.

28. On the "rise of polarized and precarious employment," see Kalleberg 2011. In a different work context, see Grazian 2019 on the importance of meeting places in the digital age.

29. See Liebow 1967 for a comparable case of outsiders misdiagnosing people's employment situation.

30. On the stigma associated with "brown-collar occupations," see Catanzarite 2000.

31. See Armenta 2009; Brown 2011.

32. Cited in English translation by Borjas 2016.

Conclusion

1. President Trump interviewed by Jonathan Karl on an ABC news program on October 31, 2018.

2. See Trouille 2014 for a more detailed analysis of the controversy concerning the field's fencing.

3. For a description of L.A.'s Park Advisory Boards, see https://www.laparks.org/info/volunteer/pab-member.

4. As part of the Proposition K project—a thirty-year, $776 million tax measure to improve the city's parks and recreational facilities—Mar Vista was earmarked for

$1 million for "outdoor sports field improvements and fencing." (Regarding park funding in Los Angeles, see Pincetl 2003; Wolch, Wilson, and Fehrenbach 2005.) After some debate, community members decided to use the majority of the funds for a "multi-use" sports field. Having recently brought an outdoor hockey rink to the park, Park Advisory Board (PAB) members were confident they could do something "big," as one member recalled. The project was supported by park officials, who by then were convinced of the value of artificial turf playing surfaces. PAB members also had the backing of their city councilperson, who helped pushed through the plans.

5. Despite repeated requests, I was unable to interview the previous park director.

6. Around the same time, conflict over installation of a skateboard park at nearby Stoner Recreation Center provides a stark contrast in terms of whose voices are included in community discussions. In that case, advocates in favor of the facility—primarily White skateboarders backed by middle-class capital and connections to corporations eager to profit from the project—were directly involved in the deliberations that eventually led to its construction (Snyder 2017).

7. Klinenberg 2018, 5.

8. Anderson 2015; Mitchell 1995; Smith 1996.

9. Klinenberg 2018, 5.

10. Jacobs 1961, 92.

11. Hagan 1998; Hondagneu-Sotelo 2017; Schmalzbauer 2014; but see Armenta 2009; Zentgraf 2002.

12. Connell 1995; Messner 1992.

13. Lopez 2007.

14. See García 2019 on the uneven burden of "illegality." See also Andrews 2018; Armenta 2017; Armenta and Rosales 2019; Papazian 2011; Romero 2006; Varsanyi et al. 2012.

15. Fink 2003; Mohl 2003.

16. Deeb-Sossa and Mendez 2008; Prieto 2018.

17. Sadon 2017; Wong 2014.

18. DeLand 2013.

19. As one barometer of political identification, 83 percent of the residents living in the neighborhood directly north of the park—home to the most active critics of the field—voted for Hillary Clinton in the 2016 presidential election. Only 11 percent voted for Donald Trump.

20. On sanctuary cities, see Delgado 2018.

21. Indeed, as I was finishing my book in August 2019, mass shooters targeted Latinos in El Paso, Texas, and in Gilroy, California. Many commentators linked these deadly attacks to President Trump's anti-Latino, anti-immigrant rhetoric.

22. Borjas 2016; Cornelius 1998; Piore 1979; Waldinger and Lichter 2003.

23. Kasinitz et al. 2009; Portes and Rumbaut 2001; Smith 2006.

24. Lofland 1998.

25. Bobo et al. 2000; Davis 2006; Fulton 1997.

26. Piore 1979.

27. On solidarity in the research process, see Kelley, Amariglio, and Wilson 2018.

REFERENCES

Abbott, Andrew. 1997. "Of Time and Space: The Contemporary Relevance of the Chicago School." *Social Forces* 75 (4): 1149–82.

Abrego, Leisy Janet. 2006. "'I Can't Go to College Because I Don't Have Papers': Incorporation Patterns of Latino Undocumented Youth." *Latino Studies* 4 (3): 212–31.

Abrego, Leisy Janet. 2014. *Sacrificing Families: Navigating Laws, Labor, and Love Across Borders.* Stanford University Press.

Abrego, Leisy Janet, and Leah Schmalzbauer. 2018. "Illegality, Motherhood, and Place: Undocumented Latinas Making Meaning and Negotiating Daily Life." *Women's Studies International Forum* 67 (March–April): 10–17.

Alarcón, Rafael, Luis Escala, and Olga Odgers. 2016. *Making Los Angeles Home: The Integration of Mexican Immigrants in the United States.* University of California Press.

Allison, Anne. 1994. *Nightwork: Sexuality, Pleasure, and Corporate Masculinity in a Tokyo Hostess Club.* University of Chicago Press.

Anderson, Elijah. 1978. *A Place on the Corner.* University of Chicago Press.

Anderson, Elijah. 1990. *Streetwise: Race, Class, and Change in an Urban Community.* University of Chicago Press.

Anderson, Elijah. 1999. *Code of the Street: Decency, Violence, and Moral Life of the Inner City.* W. W. Norton.

Anderson, Elijah. 2011. *The Cosmopolitan Canopy: Race and Civility in Everyday life.* W. W. Norton.

Anderson, Elijah. 2015. "The White Space." *Sociology of Race and Ethnicity* 1 (1): 10–21.

Anderson, Nels. 1923. *The Hobo: The Sociology of the Homeless Man.* University of Chicago Press.

Andrews, Abigail Leslie. 2018. *Undocumented Politics: Place, Gender, and the Pathways of Mexican Migrants.* University of California Press.

Armenta, Amada. 2009. "Creating Community: Latina Nannies in a West Los Angeles Park." *Qualitative Sociology* 32 (3): 279–92.

Armenta, Amada. 2017. *Protect, Serve, and Deport: The Rise of Policing as Immigration Enforcement.* University of California Press.

Armenta, Amada, and Rocío Rosales. 2019. "Beyond the Fear of Deportation: Understanding Unauthorized Immigrants' Ambivalence toward the Police." *American Behavioral Scientist* 63 (9): 1350–69.

Arreola, Daniel, ed. 2004. *Hispanic Spaces, Latino Places: Community and Cultural Diversity in Contemporary America.* University of Texas Press.

Auyero, Javier, and Kristine Kilanski. 2015. "From 'Making Toast' to 'Splitting Apples': Dissecting 'Care' in the Midst of Chronic Violence." *Theory and Society* 44 (5): 393–414.

Bashi, Vilna. 2007. *Survival of the Knitted: Immigrant Social Networks in a Stratified World.* Stanford University Press.

Bean, Frank D., Susan K. Brown, James D. Bachmeier, Zoya Gubernskaya, and Christopher Smith. 2012. "Luxury, Necessity, and Anachronistic Workers: Does the United States Need Unskilled Immigrant Labor?" *American Behavioral Scientist* 56 (8): 1008–28.

Bearman, Peter. 2005. *Doormen.* University of Chicago Press.

Becker, Howard. 1953. "Becoming a Marihuana User." *American Journal of Sociology* 59 (3): 235–42.

Bell, Michael Joseph. 1983. *The World from Brown's Lounge: An Ethnography of Black Middle-Class Play.* University of Illinois Press.

Ben-Porat, Amir. 2001. "'Biladi, Biladi': Ethnic and Nationalistic Conflict in the Soccer Stadium in Israel." *Soccer & Society* 2 (1): 19–38.

Ben-Porat, Amir. 2014. "'Who Are We? My Club? My People? My State?': The Dilemma of the Arab Soccer Fan in Israel." *International Review for the Sociology of Sport* 49 (2): 175–89.

Birrell, Susan. 1981. "Sport as Ritual: Interpretations from Durkheim to Goffman." *Social Forces* 60 (2): 354–76.

Bloom, Paul. 2017. *Against Empathy: The Case for Rational Compassion.* Random House.

Blumer, Herbert. 1969. *Symbolic Interactionism: Perspective and Method.* Prentice Hall.

Bobo, Lawrence, Melvin L. Oliver, James H. Johnson Jr., and Abel Valenzuela Jr., eds. 2000. *Prismatic Metropolis: Inequality in Los Angeles.* Russell Sage Foundation.

Bonilla-Silva, Eduardo. 2006. *Racism without Racists: Color-Blind Racism and the Persistence of Racial Inequality in the United States.* Rowman & Littlefield.

Borjas, George J. 2016. *We Wanted Workers: Unraveling the Immigration Narrative.* W. W. Norton.

Bourdieu, Pierre. 1990. *The Logic of Practice.* Stanford University Press.

Bourdieu, Pierre. 2000. *Pascalian Meditations.* Stanford University Press.

Bourgois, Philippe. 1996. *In Search of Respect: Selling Crack in El Barrio.* Cambridge University Press.

Bourgois, Philippe. 1998. "The Moral Economies of Homeless Heroin Addicts: Confronting Ethnography, HIV Risk, and Everyday Violence in San Francisco Shooting Encampments." *Substance Use & Misuse* 33 (11): 2323–51.

Boyd, Monica. 1989. "Family and Personal Networks in International Migration: Recent Developments and New Agendas." *International Migration Review* 23 (3): 638–70.

Brandes, Stanley H. 1975. "The Structural and Demographic Implications of Nicknames in Navanogal, Spain." *American Ethnologist* 2 (1): 139–48.

Brandes, Stanley H. 2010. *Staying Sober in Mexico City.* University of Texas Press.

Brissett, Dennis. 1978. "Toward an Interactionist Understanding of Heavy Drinking." *Pacific Sociological Review* 21 (1): 3–20.

Britton, Marcus. 2008. "'My Regular Spot': Race and Territory in Urban Public Space." *Journal of Contemporary Ethnography* 37 (4): 442–68.

Brooks, Scott N. 2009. *Black Men Can't Shoot.* University of Chicago Press.

Brown, Tamara Mose. 2011. *Raising Brooklyn: Nannies, Childcare, and Caribbeans Creating Community*. NYU Press.

Brown, Tamara M., and Joanna Dreby, eds. 2013. *Family and Work in Everyday Ethnography*. Temple University Press.

Burawoy, Michael. 2000. "Introduction: Reaching for the Global." In Michael Burawoy et al., *Global Ethnography: Forces, Connections, and Imaginations in a Postmodern World*. University of California Press.

Burawoy, Michael. 2003. "Revisits: An Outline of a Theory of Reflexive Ethnography." *American Sociological Review* 68 (5): 645–79.

Burn, Shawn Meghan. 2000. "'Heterosexuals' Use of 'Fag' and 'Queer' to Deride One Another: A Contributor to Heterosexism and Stigma." *Journal of Homosexuality* 40 (2): 1–11.

Cantú, Lionel. 2009. *The Sexuality of Migration: Border Crossings and Mexican Immigrant Men*. NYU Press.

Carrillo, Héctor. 2017. *Pathways of Desire: The Sexual Migration of Mexican Gay Men*. University of Chicago Press.

Catanzarite, Lisa. 2000. "Brown-Collar Jobs: Occupational Segregation and Earnings of Recent-Immigrant Latinos." *Sociological Perspectives* 43 (1): 45–75.

Cavan, Sherri. 1963. "Interaction in Home Territories." *Berkeley Journal of Sociology* 5: 17–32.

Cavan, Sherri. 1966. *Liquor License: An Ethnography of Bar Behavior*. Aldine.

Chan Tack, Anjanette M., and Mario L. Small. 2017. "Making Friends in Violent Neighborhoods: Strategies among Elementary School Children." *Sociological Science* 4: 224–248.

Charles, Camille Zubrinsky. 2004. *Won't You Be My Neighbor? Race, Residence and Intergroup Relations in Los Angeles*. Russell Sage Foundation.

Chavez, Leo R. 1998. *Shadowed Lives: Undocumented Immigrants in American Society*. Harcourt Brace.

Chavez, Leo R. 2008. *The Latino Threat: Constructing Immigrants, Citizens, and the Nation*. Stanford University Press.

Chávez, Sergio. 2016. *Border Lives: Fronterizos, Transnational Migrants, and Commuters in Tijuana*. Oxford University Press.

Chávez, Sergio, and Claire E. Altman. 2017. "Gambling with Life: Masculinity, Risk, and Danger in the Lives of Unauthorized Migrant Roofers." *American Journal of Industrial Medicine* 60 (6): 537–47.

Clawson, Laura. 2005. "'Everybody Knows Him': Social Networks in the Life of a Small Contractor in Alabama." *Ethnography* 6 (2): 237–64.

Cobb, Jessica Shannon, and Kimberly Kay Hoang. 2015. "Protagonist-Driven Urban Ethnography." *City & Community* 14 (4): 348–51.

Colburn, Kenneth. 1986. "Deviance and Legitimacy in Ice-Hockey: A Microstructural Theory of Violence." *Sociological Quarterly* 27 (1): 63–74.

Collins, Randall. 2000. "Situational Stratification: A Micro-Macro Theory of Inequality." *Sociological Theory* 18 (1): 17–43.

Collins, Randall. 2004. *Interaction Ritual Chains*. Princeton University Press.

Collins, Randall. 2008. *Violence: A Micro-Sociological Theory*. Princeton University Press.

Conley, Carolyn. 1999. "The Agreeable Recreation of Fighting." *Journal of Social History* 33 (1): 57–72.

Connell, R. W. 1995. *Masculinities*. Polity.

Contreras, Randol. 2013. *The Stickup Kids: Race, Drugs, Violence, and the American Dream*. University of California Press.

Contreras, Randol. 2019. "Transparency and Unmasking Issues in Ethnographic Crime Research: Methodological Considerations." *Sociological Forum* 34 (2) 293–312.

Cook, Karen Schweers. 2005. "Networks, Norms, and Trust: The Social Psychology of Social Capital 2004 Cooley Mead Award Address." *Social Psychology Quarterly* 68 (1): 4–14.

Cooley, Charles Horton. 1908. *Social Organization: A Study of the Larger Mind*. New York: Charles Scribner's Sons.

Copes, Heith, Andy Hochstetler, and Craig J. Forsyth. 2013. "Peaceful Warriors: Codes for Violence among Adult Male Bar Fighters." *Criminology* 51 (3): 761–94.

Cornelius, Wayne A. 1998. "The Structural Embeddedness of Demand for Mexican Immigrant Labor: New Evidence from California." In *Crossings: Mexican Immigration in Interdisciplinary Perspectives*.

Coser, Rose Laub. 1959. "Some Social Functions of Laughter: A Study of Humor in a Hospital Setting." *Human Relations* 12 (2): 171–82.

Coutin, Susan Bibler. 2003. *Legalizing Moves: Salvadoran Immigrants' Struggle for US Residency*. University of Michigan Press.

Crabbe, Tim, John Solomos, and Les Back. 2001. *The Changing Face of Football: Racism, Multiculturalism, and Identity in the English Game*. Berg.

Cranford, Cynthia J. 2005. "Networks of Exploitation: Immigrant Labor and the Restructuring of the Los Angeles Janitorial Industry." *Social Problems* 52 (3): 379–97.

Cranz, Galen. 1982. *The Politics of Park Design: A History of Urban Parks in America*. MIT Press.

Crossley, Nick. 2010. "Networks and Complexity: Directions for Interactionist Research?" *Symbolic Interaction* 33 (3): 341–63.

Csikszentmihalyi, Mihaly. 1974. *Flow: Studies of Enjoyment*. University of Chicago Press.

Davis, Mike. 2001. *Magical Urbanism: Latinos Reinvent the US City*. Verso.

Davis, Mike. 2006. *City of Quartz: Excavating the Future in Los Angeles*. Reprint. Verso Books.

Deeb-Sossa, Natalia, and Jennifer Bickham Mendez. 2008. "Enforcing Borders in the Nuevo South: Gender and Migration in Williamsburg, Virginia, and the Research Triangle, North Carolina." *Gender & Society* 22 (5): 613–38.

Deener, Andrew. 2012. *Venice: A Contested Bohemia in Los Angeles*. University of Chicago Press.

DeLand, Michael. 2013. "Basketball in the Key of Law: The Significance of Disputing in Pick-Up Basketball." *Law & Society Review* 47 (3): 653–85.

DeLand, Michael. 2018. "The Ocean Run: Stage, Cast, and Performance in a Public Park Basketball Scene." *Journal of Contemporary Ethnography* 47 (1): 28–59.

DeLand, Michael, and David Trouille. 2018. "Going Out: A Sociology of Public Outings." *Sociological Theory* 36 (1): 27–47.

Delgado, Melvin. 2018. *Sanctuary Cities, Communities, and Organizations: A Nation at a Crossroads*. Oxford University Press.

Del Real, Deisy. 2018. "Toxic Ties: The Reproduction of Legal Violence within Mixed-Status Intimate Partners, Relatives, and Friends." *International Migration Review* 53 (2): 548–70.

Desmond, Matthew. 2007. *On the Fireline: Living and Dying with Wildland Firefighters.* University of Chicago Press.

Desmond, Matthew. 2012. "Disposable Ties and the Urban Poor." *American Journal of Sociology* 117 (5): 1295–335.

Dolgon, Corey. 2005. "Polo Ponies and Penalty Kicks." In *The End of the Hamptons: Scenes from the Class Struggle in America's Paradise.* NYU Press.

Dominguez, Silvia, and Celeste Watkins. 2003. "Creating Networks for Survival and Mobility: Social Capital among African-American and Latin-American Low-Income Mothers." *Social Problems* 50 (1): 111–35.

Donaldson, Mike, Raymond Hibbins, Richard Howson, and Bob Pease, eds. 2009. *Migrant Men: Critical Studies of Masculinities and the Migration Experience.* Routledge.

Douglas, Mary. 1966. *Purity and Danger.* Penguin.

Douglas, Mary. 1987. "A Distinctive Anthropological Perspective." In *Constructive Drinking: Perspectives on Drink from Anthropology.* Routledge.

Doyle, Jennifer. 2018. "Pitches Less than Perfect: Notes on the Landscape of Soccer in Los Angeles." In *LA Sports: Plays, Games, and Community in the City of Angels,* edited by Wayne Wilson and David K. Wiggins. University of Arkansas Press.

Dreby, Joanna. 2010. *Divided by Borders: Mexican Migrants and Their Children.* University of California Press.

Dreby, Joanna. 2015. *Everyday Illegal: When Policies Undermine Immigrant Families.* University of California Press.

Du Bois, William Edward Burghardt, and Isabel Eaton. 1899. *The Philadelphia Negro: A Social Study.* University of Pennsylvania.

Duneier, Mitchell. 1992. *Slim's Table: Race, Respectability, and Masculinity.* University of Chicago Press.

Duneier, Mitchell. 1999. *Sidewalk.* Farrar, Straus & Giroux.

Duneier, Mitchell, Philip Kasinitz, and Alexandra K. Murphy, eds. 2014. *The Urban Ethnography Reader.* Oxford University Press.

Duneier, Mitchell, and Harvey Molotch. 1999. "Talking City Trouble: Interactional Vandalism, Social Inequality, and the 'Urban Interaction Problem.'" *American Journal of Sociology* 104 (5): 1263–95.

Durand, Jorge, and Douglas S. Massey. 1992. "Mexican Migration to the United States: A Critical Review." *Latin American Research Review* 27 (2): 3–42.

Durkheim, Émile. (1912) 1995. *The Elementary Forms of Religious Life.* Free Press.

Eason, John M. 2017. "Privilege and Peril in Prison Town Studies: Power and Position in Fieldwork Encounters." *Sociological Focus* 50 (1): 81–98.

Edgerton, Robert B. 1979. *Alone Together: Social Order on an Urban Beach.* University of California Press.

Emerson, Robert M. 2015. *Everyday Troubles: The Micro-Politics of Interpersonal Conflict.* University of Chicago Press.

Emirbayer, Mustafa, and Jeff Goodwin. 1994. "Network Analysis, Culture, and the Problem of Agency." *American Journal of Sociology* 99 (6): 1411–54.

Enriquez, Laura E. 2020. *Of Love and Papers: Forming Families in the Shadows of Immigration Policy.* University of California Press.

Erikson, Kai T. 1961. "Notes on the Sociology of Deviance." *Social Problems.* 9: 307.

Estrada, Emir. 2019. *Kids at Work: Latinx Families Selling Food on the Streets of Los Angeles.* NYU Press.

Farrell, Justin. 2020. *Billionaire Wilderness: The Ultra-Wealthy and the Remaking of the American West.* Princeton University Press.

Faulkner, Robert R. 1974. "Making Violence by Doing Work: Selves, Situations, and the World of Professional Hockey." *Sociology of Work and Occupations* 1 (3): 288–312.

Feld, Scott L. 1981. "The Focused Organization of Social Ties." *American Journal of Sociology* 86 (5): 1015–35.

Felson, Richard B. 1982. "Impression Management and the Escalation of Aggression and Violence." *Social Psychology Quarterly* 45 (4): 245–54.

Fernández, Matías. 2018. "Hanging Out Together, Surviving on Your Own: The Precarious Communities of Day Laborers." *Journal of Contemporary Ethnography* 47 (6): 865–87.

Figueroa, Arturo. 2003. "Community Identity and Sports: A Social History of Soccer in Salinas, California." *Culture, Society and Praxis* 2 (1): 5.

Fine, Gary Alan. 1979. "Small Groups and Culture Creation: The Idioculture of Little League Baseball Teams." *American Sociological Review* 44 (October): 733–45.

Fine, Gary Alan. 1987. *With the Boys: Little League Baseball and Preadolescent Culture.* University of Chicago Press.

Fine, Gary Alan. 2002. *Shared Fantasy: Role-Playing Games as Social Worlds.* University of Chicago Press.

Fine, Gary Alan. 2009. *Morel Tales: The Culture of Mushrooming.* Harvard University Press.

Fine, Gary Alan. 2012. *Tiny Publics: A Theory of Group Action and Culture.* Russell Sage Foundation.

Fine, Gary Alan. 2015. *Players and Pawns: How Chess Builds Community and Culture.* University of Chicago Press.

Fine, Gary Alan. 2019. "Relational Distance and Epistemic Generosity: The Power of Detachment in Skeptical Ethnography." *Sociological Methods & Research* 48 (4): 828–49.

Fine, Gary Alan, and Ugo Corte. 2017. "Group Pleasures: Collaborative Commitments, Shared Narrative, and the Sociology of Fun." *Sociological Theory* 35 (1): 64–86.

Fine, Gary Alan, and Michaela De Soucey. 2005. "Joking Cultures: Humor Themes as Social Regulation in Group Life." *Humor: International Journal of Humor Research* 18 (1): 1–22.

Fine, Gary Alan, and Sherryl Kleinman. 1983. "Network and Meaning: An Interactionist Approach to Structure." *Symbolic Interaction* 6 (1): 97–110.

Fink, Leon. 2003. *The Maya of Morganton: Work and Community in the Nuevo New South.* University of North Carolina Press.

Fischer, Claude S. 1982. *To Dwell among Friends: Personal Networks in Town and City.* University of Chicago Press.

FitzGerald, David, and John D. Skrentny, eds. 2021. *Immigrant California: Understanding the Past, Present, and Future of U.S. Policy.* Stanford University Press.

Flores, Glenda M. 2016. "Discovering a Hidden Privilege: Ethnography in Multiracial Organizations as an Outsider Within." *Ethnography* 17 (2): 190–212.

Flores, René D., and Ariela Schachter. 2018. "Who Are the 'Illegals'? The Social Construction of Illegality in the United States." *American Sociological Review* 83 (5): 839–68.

Flores, William Vincent, and Rina Benmayor, eds. 1997. *Latino Cultural Citizenship: Claiming Identity, Space, and Rights*. Beacon Press.

Flores-Yeffal, Nadia Yamel. 2013. *Migration-Trust Networks: Social Cohesion in Mexican US-Bound Emigration*. Texas A&M University Press.

Flores-Yeffal, Nadia Y., and Maria Aysa-Lastra. 2011. "Place of Origin, Types of Ties, and Support Networks in Mexico–U.S. Migration." *Rural Sociology* 76 (4): 481–510.

Foer, Franklin. 2004. *How Soccer Explains the World*. HarperCollins.

Fulton, William. 1997. *The Reluctant Metropolis*. Solano Press.

Fussell, Elizabeth. 2011. "The Deportation Threat Dynamic and Victimization of Latino Migrants: Wage Theft and Robbery." *Sociological Quarterly* 52 (4): 593–615.

Fussell, Elizabeth, and Douglas S. Massey. 2004. "The Limits to Cumulative Causation: International Migration from Mexican Urban Areas." *Demography* 41 (1): 151–71.

Gans, Herbert. 1962. *Urban Villagers: Group and Class in the Life of Italian Americans*. Free Press.

García, Angela S. 2019. *Legal Passing: Navigating Undocumented Life and Local Immigration Law*. University of California Press.

García, Robert, Erica S. Flores, and Elizabeth Pine. 2002. *Dreams of Fields: Soccer, Community, and Equal Justice*. Center for Law in the Public Interest.

Gardner, Carol Brooks. 1995. *Passing By: Gender and Public Harassment*. University of California Press.

Garfinkel, Harold. 1967. *Studies in Ethnomethodology*. Prentice Hall.

Garot, Robert. 2007. "Non-Violence in the Inner City: 'Decent' and 'Street' as Strategic Resources." *Journal of African American Studies* 10 (4): 94–111.

Garot, Robert. 2009. "Reconsidering Retaliation: Structural Inhibitions, Emotive Dissonance, and the Acceptance of Ambivalence among Inner-City Young Men." *Ethnography* 10 (1): 63–90.

Geertz, Clifford. 2000. "Deep Play: Notes on the Balinese Cockfight." In *Culture and Politics: A Reader*, edited by Lane Crothers and Charles Lockhart. Palgrave Macmillan.

Gibson, David R. 2005. "Taking Turns and Talking Ties: Networks and Conversational Interaction." *American Journal of Sociology* 110 (6): 1561–97.

Glenn, Evelyn Nakano. 1986. *Issei, Nisei, War Bride: Three Generations of Japanese American Women in Domestic Service*. Temple University Press.

Goffman, Alice. 2015. *On the Run: Fugitive Life in an American City*. Picador.

Goffman, Alice. 2019. "Go to More Parties? Social Occasions as Home to Unexpected Turning Points in Life Trajectories." *Social Psychology Quarterly* 82 (1): 51–74.

Goffman, Erving. 1961. *Encounters: Two Studies in the Sociology of Interaction*. Bobbs-Merrill.

Goffman, Erving. 1967. *Interaction Ritual: Essays on Face-to-Face Behavior*. Anchor Books.

Goffman, Erving. 1981. *Forms of Talk*. University of Pennsylvania Press.

Goffman, Erving. 1983. "The Interaction Order: American Sociological Association, 1982 Presidential Address." *American Sociological Review* 48 (1): 1–17.

Golash-Boza, Tanya, and Pierrette Hondagneu-Sotelo. 2013. "Latino Immigrant Men and the Deportation Crisis: A Gendered Racial Removal Program." *Latino Studies* 11 (3): 271–92.

Gomberg-Muñoz, Ruth. 2011. *Labor and Legality: An Ethnography of a Mexican Immigrant Network*. Oxford University Press.

Gomberg-Muñoz, Ruth. 2017. *Becoming Legal: Immigration Law and Mixed-Status Families*. Oxford University Press.

Gonzales, Roberto G. 2015. *Lives in Limbo: Undocumented and Coming of Age in America*. University of California Press.

Goodman, Cary. 1979. *Choosing Sides: Playground and Street Life on the Lower East Side*. Schocken Books.

Gould, Roger V. 2003. *Collision of Wills: How Ambiguity about Social Rank Breeds Conflict*. University of Chicago Press.

Gouldner, Alvin W. 1960. "The Norm of Reciprocity: A Preliminary Statement." *American Sociological Review* 25 (2): 161–78.

Granovetter, Mark S. 1977. "The Strength of Weak Ties." In *Social Networks: A Developing Paradigm*, edited by Samuel Leinhardt. Academic Press.

Grasmuck, Sherri. 2005. *Protecting Home: Class, Race, and Masculinity in Boys' Baseball*. Rutgers University Press.

Grazian, David. 2019. "Thank God It's Monday: Manhattan Coworking Spaces in the New Economy." *Theory and Society*: 1–29. https://doi.org/10.1007/s11186-019 -09360-6.

Guenther, Katja M. 2009. "The Politics of Names: Rethinking the Methodological and Ethical Significance of Naming People, Organizations, and Places." *Qualitative Research* 9 (4): 411–21.

Gusfield, Joseph R. 1987. "Passage to Play: Rituals of Drinking Time in American Society." In *Constructive Drinking: Perspectives on Drink from Anthropology*, edited by Mary Douglas. Routledge.

Gutmann, Matthew C. 2006. *The Meanings of Macho: Being a Man in Mexico City*. University of California Press.

Hagan, Jacqueline Maria. 1998. "Social Networks, Gender, and Immigrant Incorporation: Resources and Constraints." *American Sociological Review* 63 (1): 55–67.

Hagan, Jacqueline Maria, Rubén Hernández-León, and Jean-Luc Demonsant. 2015. *Skills of the Unskilled: Work and Mobility among Mexican Migrants*. University of California Press.

Hall, Edward T. 1959. *The Silent Language*. Doubleday.

Halle, David. 1984. *America's Working Man: Work, Home, and Politics among Blue-Collar Property Owners*. University of Chicago Press.

Hamilton, Nora, and Norma Stoltz Chinchilla. 2001. *Seeking Community in a Global City: Guatemalans and Salvadorans in Los Angeles*. Temple University Press.

Hardy, Stephen. 1981. "The City and the Rise of American Sport: 1820–1920." *Exercise and Sport Sciences Reviews* 9 (1): 183–220.

Haynes, Chris, Jennifer Merolla, and S. Karthick Ramakrishnan. 2016. *Framing Immigrants: News Coverage, Public Opinion, and Policy*. Russell Sage Foundation.

Hendricks, T. S. 2006. *Play Reconsidered: Sociological Perspectives on Human Expression*. University of Illinois Press.

Hernández-León, Rubén. 2008. *Metropolitan Migrants: The Migration of Urban Mexicans to the United States*. University of California Press.

Hjelte, George. 1977. *Footprints in the Parks*. Public Service Publications.

Hoang, Kimberly Kay. 2015. *Dealing in Desire: Asian Ascendancy, Western Decline, and the Hidden Currencies of Global Sex Work*. University of California Press.

Holmes, Seth. 2013. *Fresh Fruit, Broken Bodies: Migrant Farmworkers in the United States*. University of California Press.

Hondagneu-Sotelo, Pierrette. 1994. "Regulating the Unregulated? Domestic Workers' Social Networks." *Social Problems* 41 (1): 50–64.

Hondagneu-Sotelo, Pierrette. 1995. "Beyond 'The Longer They Stay' (and Say They Will Stay): Women and Mexican Immigrant Settlement." *Qualitative Sociology* 18 (1): 21–43.

Hondagneu-Sotelo, Pierrette. 2001. *Doméstica: Immigrant Workers Cleaning and Caring in the Shadows of Affluence.* University of California Press.

Hondagneu-Sotelo, Pierrette. 2014. *Paradise Transplanted: Migration and the Making of California Gardens.* University of California Press.

Hondagneu-Sotelo, Pierrette. 2017. "Place, Nature and Masculinity in Immigrant Integration: Latino Immigrant Men in Inner-City Parks and Community Gardens." *NORMA* 12 (2): 112–26.

Hondagneu-Sotelo, Pierrette, and Ernestine Avila. 1997. "'I'm Here, but I'm There': The Meanings of Latina Transnational Motherhood." *Gender & Society* 11 (5): 548–71.

Horowitz, Ruth. 1983. *Honor and the American Dream.* Rutgers University Press.

Huerta, Alvaro. 2007. "Looking Beyond 'Mow, Blow and Go': A Case Study of Mexican Immigrant Gardeners in Los Angeles." *Berkeley Planning Journal* 20 (1): 1–23.

Huizinga, J. 1949. *Homo Ludens: A Study of the Play-Element in Culture.* Routledge.

Hunter, Marcus Anthony, Mary Pattillo, Zandria F. Robinson, and Keeanga-Yamahtta Taylor. 2016. "Black Placemaking: Celebration, Play, and Poetry." *Theory, Culture & Society* 33 (7–8): 31–56.

Jackson-Jacobs, Curtis. 2004. "Taking a Beating: The Narrative Gratifications of Fighting as an Underdog: Introduction: Culture, Criminology, and Brawling in Tucson." In *Cultural Criminology Unleashed*, edited by Jeff Ferrell, Keith Hayward, Wayne Morrison, and Mike Presdee. Routledge-Cavendish.

Jackson-Jacobs, Curtis. 2013. "Constructing Physical Fights: An Interactionist Analysis of Violence among Affluent, Suburban Youth." *Qualitative Sociology* 36 (1): 23–52.

Jacobs, Jane. 1961. *The Death and Life of Great American Cities.* Random House.

Jerolmack, Colin. 2009. "Primary Groups and Cosmopolitan Ties: The Rooftop Pigeon Flyers of New York City." *Ethnography* 10 (4): 435–57.

Jerolmack, Colin. 2013. *The Global Pigeon.* University of Chicago Press.

Jerolmack, Colin, and Shamus Khan. 2014. "Talk Is Cheap: Ethnography and the Attitudinal Fallacy." *Sociological Methods & Research* 43 (2): 178–209.

Jerolmack, Colin, and Shamus Khan. 2017. "The Analytic Lenses of Ethnography." *Socius* 3.

Jerolmack, Colin, and Alexandra K. Murphy. 2017. "The Ethical Dilemmas and Social Scientific Trade-Offs of Masking in Ethnography." *Sociological Methods & Research* 48 (4): 801–27.

Jimerson, Jason B. 1996. "Good Times and Good Games: How Pickup Basketball Players Use Wealth-Maximizing Norms." *Journal of Contemporary Ethnography* 25 (3): 353–71.

Joassart-Marcelli, Pascale. 2010. "Leveling the Playing Field? Urban Disparities in Funding for Local Parks and Recreation in the Los Angeles Region." *Environment and Planning A* 42 (5): 1174–92.

Jones, Nikki. 2009. *Between Good and Ghetto: African American Girls and Inner-City Violence.* Rutgers University Press.

[218]   REFERENCES

Kalleberg, Arne L. 2011. *Good Jobs, Bad Jobs: The Rise of Polarized and Precarious Employment Systems in the United States, 1970s–2000s.* Russell Sage Foundation.

Karp, Ivan. 1980. "Beer Drinking and Social Experience in an African Society: An Essay in Formal Sociology." In *Explorations in African Systems of Thought,* edited by Ivan Karp and Charles S. Bird. Indiana University Press.

Kasinitz, Philip, John H. Mollenkopf, Mary C. Waters, and Jennifer Holdaway. 2009. *Inheriting the City: The Children of Immigrants Come of Age.* Russell Sage Foundation.

Katz, Jack. 1988. *Seductions of Crime: Moral and Sensual Attractions in Doing Evil.* Basic Books.

Katz, Jack. 2001. "From How to Why: On Luminous Description and Causal Inference in Ethnography (Part I)." *Ethnography* 2 (4): 443–73.

Katz, Jack. 2019. "Hot Potato Criminology: Ethnographers and the Shame of Poor People's Crimes." *Annual Review of Criminology* 2: 21–52.

Kefalas, Maria. 2003. *Working-Class Heroes: Protecting Home, Community, and Nation in a Chicago Neighborhood.* University of California Press.

Keller, Julie C. 2019. *Milking in the Shadows: Migrants and Mobility in America's Dairyland.* Rutgers University Press.

Kelley, Robin D. G. 1996. *Race Rebels: Culture, Politics, and the Black Working Class.* Simon & Schuster.

Kelley, Robin D. G., Jack Amariglio, and Lucas Wilson. 2018. "'Solidarity Is Not a Market Exchange': An RM Interview with Robin D. G. Kelley, Part 1." *Rethinking Marxism* 30 (4): 568–98.

Kidder, Jeffrey L. 2017. *Parkour and the City: Risk, Masculinity, and Meaning in a Postmodern Sport.* Rutgers University Press.

Kilkey, Majella, and Diane Perrons. 2010. "Gendered Divisions in Domestic Work Time: The Rise of the (Migrant) Handyman Phenomenon." *Time & Society* 19 (2): 239–64.

Kingsdale, Jon M. 1973. "The 'Poor Man's Club': Social Functions of the Urban Working-Class Saloon." *American Quarterly* 25 (4): 472–89.

Klein, Alan M. 1993. *Sugarball: The American Game, the Dominican Dream.* Yale University Press.

Klinenberg, Eric. 2018. *Palaces for the People: How Social Infrastructure Can Help Fight Inequality, Polarization, and the Decline of Civic Life.* Crown.

Koren, John. 1899. *Economic Aspects of the Liquor Problem: An Investigation Made under the Direction of a Sub-Committee of the Committee of Fifty.* Houghton Mifflin.

Kornblum, William. 1974. *Blue Collar Community.* University of Chicago Press.

Krissman, Fred. 2005. "Sin Cayote Ni Patrón: Why the 'Migrant Network' Fails to Explain International Migration." *International Migration Review* 39 (1): 4–44.

Krupnick, Joseph, and Christopher Winship. 2015. "Keeping Up the Front: How Young Black Men Avoid Street Violence in the Inner City." In *The Cultural Matrix: Understanding Black Youth,* edited by Orlando Patterson. Harvard University Press.

Kusenbach, Margarethe. 2003. "Street Phenomenology: The Go-Along as Ethnographic Research Tool." *Ethnography* 4 (3): 455–85.

Lahman, Maria K. E., Katrina L. Rodriguez, Lindsey Moses, Krista M. Griffin, Bernadette M. Mendoza, and Wafa Yacoub. 2015. "A Rose by Any Other Name Is Still a Rose? Problematizing Pseudonyms in Research." *Qualitative Inquiry* 21 (5): 445–53.

Lancaster, Roger N. 1994. *Life Is Hard: Machismo, Danger, and the Intimacy of Power in Nicaragua*. University of California Press.

Lane, Jeffrey. 2018. *The Digital Street*. Oxford University Press.

Latham, Alan, and Jack Layton. 2019. "Social Infrastructure and the Public Life of Cities: Studying Urban Sociality and Public Spaces." *Geography Compass* 13 (7).

Lauria, Antonio. 1964. "Respecto or Relajo: Interpersonal Relations in Puerto Rico." *Anthropological Quarterly* 37 (2): 53–67.

Lee, Jooyoung. 2009. "Battlin' on the Corner: Techniques for Sustaining Play." *Social Problems* 56 (3): 578–98.

Lee, Jooyoung. 2016. *Blowin' Up: Rap Dreams in South Central*. University of Chicago Press.

LeMasters, E. E. 1975. *Blue-Collar Aristocrats: Life-Styles at a Working-Class Tavern*. University of Wisconsin Press.

Lemus, Sergio. 2017. "Performing Power en Las Yardas (at the Yards): The Body, Capitalist Discipline, and the Making of Mexican Yardero Lives in South Chicago." *Anthropology of Work Review* 38 (2): 104–12.

Liebow, Elliot. 1967. *Tally's Corner: A Study of Negro Streetcorner Men*. Little, Brown.

Liebow, Elliot. 1993. *Tell Them Who I Am: The Lives of Homeless Women*. Simon & Schuster.

Light, Ivan. 2006. *Deflecting Immigration: Networks, Markets, and Regulation in Los Angeles*. Russell Sage Foundation.

Light, Ivan. 2013. "The Migration Industry in the United States, 1882–1924." *Migration Studies* 1 (3): 258–75.

Limón, José E. 1989. "Carne, Carnales, and the Carnivalesque: Bakhtinian Batos, Disorder, and Narrative Discourses." *American Ethnologist* 16 (3): 471–86.

Limón, José E. 1994. *Dancing with the Devil: Society and Cultural Poetics in Mexican-American South Texas*. University of Wisconsin Press.

Lofland, Lyn H. 1973. *A World of Strangers: Order and Action in Urban Public Space*. Basic Books.

Lofland, Lyn H. 1998. *The Public Realm: Exploring the City's Quintessential Social Territory*. Routledge.

Lomnitz, Larissa Adler. 1977. *Networks and Marginality Life in a Mexican Shantytown*. Academic Press.

London, Jack. 1913. *John Barleycorn: Or, Alcoholic Memoirs*. Ameron House.

Lopez, Steve. 2007. "You Pay to Play in Posh San Marino." *Los Angeles Times*. December 17.

López-Garza, Marta. 2001. "A Study of the Informal Economy and Latina/o Immigrants in Greater Los Angeles." In *Asian and Latino Immigrants in a Restructuring Economy: The Metamorphosis of Southern California*, edited by Marta López-Garza and David R. Diaz. Stanford University Press.

Loukaitou-Sideris, Anastasia. 1995. "Urban Form and Social Context: Cultural Differentiation in the Uses of Urban Parks." *Journal of Planning Education and Research* 14 (2): 89–102.Low, Setha M. 2010. *On the Plaza: The Politics of Public Space and Culture*. University of Texas Press.

Low, Setha, Dana Taplin, and Suzanne Scheld. 2009. *Rethinking Urban Parks: Public Space and Cultural Diversity*. University of Texas Press.

Luckenbill, David F. 1977. "Criminal Homicide as a Situated Transaction." *Social Problems* 25 (?): 176–86.

Lurie, Nancy Oestreich. 1971. "The World's Oldest On-Going Protest Demonstration: North American Indian Drinking Patterns." *Pacific Historical Review* 40 (3): 311–32.

Lyman, Stanford M., and Marvin B. Scott. 1967. "Territoriality: A Neglected Sociological Dimension." *Social Problems* 15 (2): 236–49.

MacAndrew, Craig, and Robert B. Edgerton. 1969. *Drunken Comportment: A Social Explanation.* Aldine.

Main, Kelly. 2013. "Planting Roots in Foreign Soil? Immigrant Place Meanings in an Urban Park." *Journal of Environmental Psychology* 36: 291–304.

Mahler, Sarah J. 1995. *American Dreaming: Immigrant Life on the Margins.* Princeton University Press.

Malpica, Daniel Melero. 2002. "Making a Living in the Streets of Los Angeles: An Ethnographic Study of Day Laborers." *Migraciones Internacionales* 1 (3): 124–48.

Mars, Gerald. 1987. "Longshore Drinking, Economic Security and Union Politics in Newfoundland." In *Constructive Drinking: Perspectives on Drink from Anthropology,* ed. Mary Douglas. Routledge.

Massey, Douglas S., Rafael Alarcón, Jorge Durand, and Humberto González. 1987. *Return to Aztlan: The Social Process of International Migration from Western Mexico.* University of California Press.

Mauss, Marcel. 1967. *The Gift: Forms and Functions of Exchange in Archaic Societies.* W. W. Norton.

May, Reuben A. Buford. 2001. *Talking at Trena's: Everyday Conversations at an American African Tavern.* New York University Press.

May, Reuben A. Buford. 2009. *Living through the Hoop: High School Basketball, Race, and the American Dream.* NYU Press.

Maya, Theodore W. 2001. "To Serve and Protect or to Betray and Neglect: The LAPD and Undocumented Immigrants." *UCLA Law Review* 49 (5): 1611–53.

Mazelis, Joan Maya. 2017. *Surviving Poverty: Creating Sustainable Ties among the Poor.* NYU Press.

McKinney, John C. 1966. *Constructive Typology and Social Theory.* Appleton-Century-Crofts.

Mead, George Herbert. 1934. *Mind, Self and Society.* University of Chicago Press.

Mears, Ashley. 2017. "Puzzling in Sociology: On Doing and Undoing Theoretical Puzzles." *Sociological Theory* 35 (2): 138–46.

Melchor, Leonard. 2014. "Mexican in Four Images: Cinema, Self and Soccer in the Creation of Real and Imagined Mexicans." PhD diss., UCLA.

Meneses, Guillermo Alonso, and Luis Escala Rabadan. 2015. *Offside/Fuera de Lugar Futbol y Migraciones en el Mundo Contemporáneo.* El Colegio de la Frontera Norte.

Menjívar, Cecilia. 2000. *Fragmented Ties: Salvadoran Immigrant Networks in America.* University of California Press.

Menjívar, Cecilia. 2006. "Liminal Legality: Salvadoran and Guatemalan Immigrants' Lives in the United States." *American Journal of Sociology* 111 (4): 999–1037.

Menjívar, Cecilia. 2016. "Immigrant Criminalization in Law and the Media: Effects on Latino Immigrant Workers' Identities in Arizona." *American Behavioral Scientist* 60 (5–6): 597–616.

Menjívar, Cecilia, and Leisy Abrego. 2012. "Legal Violence: Immigration Law and the Lives of Central American Immigrants." *American Journal of Sociology* 117 (5): 1380–421.

Messerschmidt, James W. 1993. *Masculinities and Crime: Critique and Reconceptualisation of Theory*. Rowman & Littlefield.

Messner, Michael A. 1992. *Power at Play: Sports and the Problem of Masculinity*. Beacon.

Mirandé, Alfredo. 2018. *Hombres y Machos: Masculinity and Latino Culture*. Routledge.

Mitchell, Don. 1995. "The End of Public Space? People's Park, Definitions of Public, and Democracy." *Annals of the Association of American Geographers* 85 (1): 108–33.

Mohl, Raymond A. 2003. "Globalization, Latinization, and the Nuevo New South." *Journal of American Ethnic History* 22 (4): 31–66.

Montes, Veronica. 2013. "The Role of Emotions in the Construction of Masculinity: Guatemalan Migrant Men, Transnational Migration, and Family Relations." *Gender & Society* 27 (4): 469–90.

Morrill, Calvin, David A. Snow, and Cindy H. White, eds. 2005. *Together Alone: Personal Relationships in Public Places*. University of California Press.

Müller, Floris, Liesbet van Zoonen, and Laurens de Roode. 2007. "Accidental Racists: Experiences and Contradictions of Racism in Local Amsterdam Soccer Fan Culture." *Soccer & Society* 8 (2–3): 335–50.

Myerhoff, Barbara. 1978. *Number Our Days: A Triumph of Continuity and Culture among Jewish Old People in an Urban Ghetto*. Touchstone.

Nelson, Lise. 2016. "Soccer and the Mundane Politics of Belonging: Latino Immigrants, Recreation, and Spaces of Exclusion in the Rural US South." In *Critical Geographies of Sport: Space, Power and Sport in Global Perspective*, edited by Natalie Koch. Routledge.

Nicolaides, Becky M. 2002. *My Blue Heaven: Life and Politics in the Working-Class Suburbs of Los Angeles, 1920–1965*. University of Chicago Press.

Oldenburg, Ray. 1999. *The Great Good Place: Cafés, Coffee Shops, Bookstores, Bars, Hair Salons, and Other Hangouts at the Heart of a Community*. Da Capo Press.

Ordóñez, Juan Thomas. 2015. *Jornalero: Being a Day Laborer in the USA*. University of California Press.

Pacewicz, Josh. 2016. *Partisans and Partners: The Politics of Post-Keynesian Society*. University of Chicago Press.

Papachristos, Andrew V. 2009. "Murder by Structure: Dominance Relations and the Social Structure of Gang Homicide." *American Journal of Sociology* 115 (1): 74–128.

Papazian, Steven. 2011. "Secure Communities, Sanctuary Laws, and Local Enforcement of Immigration Law: The Story of Los Angeles." *Southern California Review of Law & Social Justice* 21: 283.

Pascoe, Cheri J. 2011. *Dude, You're a Fag: Masculinity and Sexuality in High School*. University of California Press.

Patler, Caitlin. 2017. "'Citizens but for Papers:' Undocumented Youth Organizations, Anti-Deportation Campaigns, and the Reframing of Citizenship." *Social Problems* 65 (1): 96–115.

Pattillo, Mary. 2007. *Black on the Block: Politics of Race and Class in the City*. University of Chicago Press.

Pattillo-McCoy, Mary. 1999. *Black Picket Fences: Privilege and Peril among the Black Middle Class*. University of Chicago Press.

Perinbanayagam, Robert S. 2006. *Games and Sport in Everyday Life: Dialogues and Narratives of the Self*. Paradigm.

Pescador, Juan Javier. 2004. "¡Vamos Taximaroa! Mexican/Chicano Soccer Associations and Transnational/Translocal Communities, 1967–2002." *Latino Studies* 2 (3): 352–76.

Pickett, Justin T. 2016. "On the Social Foundations for Crimmigration: Latino Threat and Support for Expanded Police Powers." *Journal of Quantitative Criminology* 32 (1): 103–32.

Pincetl, Stephanie. 2003. "Nonprofits and Park Provision in Los Angeles: An Exploration of the Rise of Governance Approaches to the Provision of Local Services." *Social Science Quarterly* 84 (4): 979–1001.

Piore, Michael J. 1979. *Birds of Passage: Migrant Labor and Industrial Societies*. Cambridge University Press.

Pisani, Michael J., and David W. Yoskowitz. 2005. "Grass, Sweat, and Sun: An Exploratory Study of the Labor Market for Gardeners in South Texas." *Social Science Quarterly* 86 (1): 229–51.

Pisani, Michael J., and David W. Yoskowitz. 2006. "Opportunity Knocks: Entrepreneurship, Informality and Home Gardening in South Texas." *Journal of Borderlands Studies* 21 (2): 59–76.

Plankey-Videla, Nancy. 2012. "Informed Consent as Process: Problematizing Informed Consent in Organizational Ethnographies." *Qualitative Sociology* 35 (1): 1–21.

Poblete, Juan. 2015. "Latino Soccer, Nationalism, and Border Zones in the United States." In *Sports and Nationalism in Latin/o America*. Palgrave Macmillan.

Portes, Alejandro, Manuel Castells, and Lauren A. Benton, eds. 1989. *The Informal Economy: Studies in Advanced and Less Developed Countries*. Johns Hopkins University Press.

Portes, Alejandro, and Rubén G. Rumbaut. 2001. *Legacies: The Story of the Immigrant Second Generation*. University of California Press.

Portes, Alejandro, and Julia Sensenbrenner. 1993. "Embeddedness and Immigration: Notes on the Social Determinants of Economic Action." *American Journal of Sociology* 98 (6): 1320–50.

Powers, Madelon. 1998. *Faces Along the Bar: Lore and Order in the Workingman's Saloon, 1870–1920*. University of Chicago Press.

Pribilsky, Jason. 2012. "Consumption Dilemmas: Tracking Masculinity, Money and Transnational Fatherhood between the Ecuadorian Andes and New York City." *Journal of Ethnic and Migration Studies* 38 (2): 323–43.

Price, Marie, and Courtney Whitworth. 2004. "Soccer and Latino Cultural Space: Metropolitan Washington Fútbol Leagues." in *Hispanic Spaces, Latino Places: Community and Cultural Diversity in Contemporary America*. University of Texas Press.

Prieto, Greg. 2018. *Immigrants under Threat: Risk and Resistance in Deportation Nation*. NYU Press.

Prus, Robert. 1983. "Drinking as Activity. An Interactionist Analysis." *Journal of Studies on Alcohol* 44 (3): 460–75.

Purser, Gretchen. 2009. "The Dignity of Job-Seeking Men: Boundary Work among Immigrant Day Laborers." *Journal of Contemporary Ethnography* 38 (1): 117–39.

Quesada, James, Sonya Arreola, Alex Kral, Kurt C. Organista, and Paula Worby. 2014. "'As Good as It Gets': Undocumented Latino Day Laborers Negotiating Discrimination in San Francisco and Berkeley, California, USA." *City & Society* 26 (1): 29–50.

Quiroz Becerra, M. Victoria. 2014. "Performing Belonging in Public Space: Mexican Migrants in New York City." *Politics & Society* 42 (3): 331–57.

Radcliffe-Brown, Alfred R. 1940. "On Joking Relationships." *Africa* 13 (3): 195–210.

Ramirez, Hernan. 2011. "Masculinity in the Workplace: The Case of Mexican Immigrant Gardeners." *Men and Masculinities* 14 (1): 97–116.

Ramirez, Hernan, and Edward Flores. 2010. "Latino Masculinities in the Post-9/11 Era." In *Gender through the Prism of Difference*. 4th ed., edited by Maxine Baca Zinn, Pierrette Hondagneu-Sotelo, and Michael A. Messner. Oxford University Press.

Ramirez, Hernan, and Pierrette Hondagneu-Sotelo. 2009. "Mexican Immigrant Gardeners: Entrepreneurs or Exploited Workers?" *Social Problems* 56 (1): 70–88.

Rawls, Anne Warfield. 1987. "The Interaction Order Sui Generis: Goffman's Contribution to Social Theory." *Sociological Theory* 5 (2): 136–49.

Ray, Ranita. 2016. "Exchange and Intimacy in the Inner City: Rethinking Kinship Ties of the Urban Poor." *Journal of Contemporary Ethnography* 45 (3): 343–64.

Ray, Ranita, and Korey Tillman. 2019. "Envisioning a Feminist Urban Ethnography: Structure, Culture, and New Directions in Poverty Studies." *Sociology Compass* 13 (1): e12652.

Reich, Jennifer A. 2015. "Old Methods and New Technologies: Social Media and Shifts in Power in Qualitative Research." *Ethnography* 16 (4): 394–415.

Reid, Sarah Winkler. 2015. "Making Fun out of Difference: Ethnicity–Race and Humour in a London School." *Ethnos* 80 (1): 23–44.

Reyes, Victoria. 2018a. "Ethnographic Toolkit: Strategic Positionality and Researchers' Visible and Invisible Tools in Field Research." *Ethnography* (October).

Reyes, Victoria. 2018b. "Three Models of Transparency in Ethnographic Research: Naming Places, Naming People, and Sharing Data." *Ethnography* 19 (2): 204–26.

Rieder, Jonathan. 1985. *Canarsie: The Jews and Italians of Brooklyn against Liberalism*. Harvard University Press.

Riess, Steven A. 1989. *City Games: The Evolution of American Urban Society and the Rise of Sports*. University of Illinois Press.

Rios, Victor M. 2011. *Punished: Policing the Lives of Black and Latino Boys*. NYU Press.

Rios, Victor M. 2015. "Decolonizing the White Space in Urban Ethnography." *City & Community* 14 (3): 258–61.

Robins, Douglas M., Clinton R. Sanders, and Spencer E. Cahill. 1991. "Dogs and Their People: Pet-Facilitated Interaction in a Public Setting." *Journal of Contemporary Ethnography* 20 (1): 3–25.

Rollins, Judith. 1985. *Between Women: Domestics and Their Employers*. Temple University Press.

Romero, Mary. 1988. "Chicanas Modernize Domestic Service." *Qualitative Sociology* 11 (4): 319–34.

Romero, Mary. 1992. *Maid in the U.S.A.* Routledge.

Romero, Mary. 2006. "Racial Profiling and Immigration Law Enforcement: Rounding Up of Usual Suspects in the Latino Community." *Critical Sociology* 32 (2–3): 447–73.

Rosales, Rocío. 2020. *Fruteros: Street Vending, Illegality, and Ethnic Community in Los Angeles*. University of California Press.

Rosenzweig, Roy. 1983. *Eight Hours for What We Will: Workers and Leisure in an Industrial City, 1870–1920*. Cambridge University Press.

Roy, Donald F. 1959. "'Banana Time': Job Satisfaction and Informal Interaction." *Human Organization* 18 (4): 158–68.

Royster, Deirdre A. 2003. *Race and the Invisible Hand: How White Networks Exclude Black Men from Blue-Collar Jobs.* University of California Press.

Sacha, Jeffrey O. 2017. "Fighting Feelings: The Emotional Labor of 'Old Heads' in an Amateur Boxing Gym." *Sociological Perspectives* 60 (1): 77–94.

Sadon, Rachel. 2017. "On a Columbia Heights Soccer Field, the Effects of Gentrification Play Out." *dcist.* July 20. https://dcist.com/story/17/07/20/on-a-columbia-heights-soccer-field/.

Sandoval-Strausz, A. K. 2019. *Barrio America: How Latino Immigrants Saved the American City.* Basic Books.

Santa Ana, Otto. 2002. *Brown Tide Rising: Metaphors of Latinos in Contemporary American Public Discourse.* University of Texas Press.

Santos-Gómez, Hugo. 2017. "Leveling the Field: Soccer, Farmworkers, and Citizenship in the California San Joaquin Valley." *Human Organization* 76 (1): 28–37.

Sassen, Saskia. 1991. *The Global City: New York, Tokyo and London.* Princeton University Press.

Sassen, Saskia. 2000. "Informationalization: Imported through Immigration or a Feature of Advanced Economies?" *WorkingUSA* 30 (6): 6–26.

Scheper-Hughes, Nancy. 2000. "Ire in Ireland." *Ethnography* 1 (1): 117–40.

Schmalzbauer, Leah. 2014. *The Last Best Place? Gender, Family, and Migration in the New West.* Stanford University Press.

Schmitt, Raymond L., and Wilbert M. Leonard. 1986. "Immortalizing the Self through Sport." *American Journal of Sociology* 91 (5): 1088–111.

Schwartz, Barry. 1967. "The Social Psychology of the Gift." *American Journal of Sociology* 73 (1): 1–11.

Schwartz, Barry. 1975. *Queuing and Waiting: Studies in the Social Organization of Access and Delay.* Chicago: University of Chicago Press.

Scott, James C. 1990. *Domination and the Arts of Resistance: Hidden Transcripts.* Yale University Press.

Segura, Denise A., and Patricia Zavella, eds. 2007. *Women and Migration in the US-Mexico Borderlands: A Reader.* Duke University Press.

Sherman, Rachel. 2007. *Class Acts: Service and Inequality in Luxury Hotels.* University of California Press.

Silber Mohamed, Heather, and Emily M. Farris. 2020. "'Bad Hombres'? An Examination of Identities in US Media Coverage of Immigration." *Journal of Ethnic and Migration Studies* 46 (1): 158–76.

Skipper, James K. 1986. "Nicknames, Coal Miners and Group Solidarity." *Names* 34 (2). 134–45.

Small, Mario Luis. 2009. *Unanticipated Gains: Origins of Network Inequality in Everyday Life.* Oxford University Press.

Small, Mario L. 2015. "De-exoticizing Ghetto Poverty: On the Ethics of Representation in Urban Ethnography." *City & Community* 14 (4): 352–58.

Small, Mario Luis. 2017. *Someone to Talk To.* Oxford University Press.

Smith, Neil. 1996. *The Urban Frontier: Gentrification and the Revanchist City.* Routledge.

Smith, Robert. 2006. *Mexican New York: Transnational Lives of New Immigrants.* University of California Press.

Smith, Sandra Susan. 2005. "'Don't Put My Name on It': Social Capital Activation and Job-Finding Assistance among the Black Urban Poor." *American Journal of Sociology* 111 (1): 1–57.

Snyder, Gregory J. 2017. *Skateboarding LA: Inside Professional Street Skateboarding.* NYU Press.

Spicer, Paul. 1997. "Toward a (Dys)functional Anthropology of Drinking: Ambivalence and the American Indian experience with Alcohol." *Medical Anthropology Quarterly* 11 (3): 306–23.

Spradley, James P. 1970. *You Owe Yourself a Drunk: An Ethnography of Urban Nomads.* Waveland Press.

Stack, Carol B. 1974. *All Our Kin: Strategies for Survival in a Black Community.* Basic Books.

Strauss, Anselm L. 1978. *Negotiations: Varieties, Contexts, Processes, and Social Order.* Jossey-Bass.

Stuart, Forrest. 2016. *Down, Out, and Under Arrest: Policing and Everyday Life in Skid Row.* University of Chicago Press.

Stuart, Forrest. 2018. "Introspection, Positionality, and the Self as Research Instrument toward a Model of Abductive Reflexivity." In *Approaches to Ethnography: Analysis and Representation in Participant Observation*, edited by Colin Jerolmack and Shamus Khan. Oxford University Press.

Suttles, Gerald D. 1968. *The Social Order of the Slum: Ethnicity and Territory in the Inner City.* University of Chicago Press.

Tam, S. Ravi. N.d. *Distant Vistas: Exploring the Historic Neighborhoods of Mar Vista.* Mar Vista Historical Society. http://www.marvistahistoricalsociety.net/book.htm.

Tavory, Iddo, and Stefan Timmermans. 2009. "Two Cases of Ethnography: Grounded Theory and the Extended Case Method." *Ethnography* 10 (3): 243–63.

Tilly, Charles. 1990. "Transplanted Networks." In *Immigration Reconsidered: History, Sociology, and Politics*, edited by Virginia Yans-McLaughlin. Oxford University Press.

Timmermans, Stefan, and Iddo Tavory. 2012. "Theory Construction in Qualitative Research: From Grounded Theory to Abductive Analysis." *Sociological Theory* 30 (3): 167–86.

Tomsen, Stephen. 1997. "A Top Night: Social Protest, Masculinity and the Culture of Drinking Violence." *British Journal of Criminology* 37 (1): 90–102.

Topper, Martin D. 1985. "Navajo 'Alcoholism': Drinking, Alcohol Abuse, and Treatment in a Changing Cultural Environment." In *The American Experience with Alcohol: Contrasting Cultural Perspectives*, edited by Linda A. Bennett and Genevieve M. Ames. Springer.

Torres, Stacy. 2019. "On Elastic Ties: Distance and Intimacy in Social Relationships." *Sociological Science* 6 (10): 235–63.

Trouille, David. 2008. "Association Football to Fútbol: Ethnic Succession and Chicago-Area Soccer, 1890–1920." *Soccer & Society* 9 (4): 455–76.

Trouille, David. 2009. "Association Football to Fútbol: Ethnic Succession and Chicago-Area Soccer, 1921–2006." *Soccer & Society* 10 (2): 795–822.

Trouille, David. 2013. "Neighborhood Outsiders, Field Insiders: Latino Immigrant Men and the Control of Public Space." *Qualitative Sociology* 36 (1): 1–22.

Trouille, David. 2014. "Fencing a Field: Imagined Others in the Unfolding of a Neighborhood Park Conflict." *City & Community* 13 (1): 69–87.

Trouille, David, and Iddo Tavory. 2019. "Shadowing: Warrants for Intersituational Variation in Ethnography." *Sociological Methods & Research* 48 (3): 534–60.

Tuohy, Brian. 2018. "Mexican Chicago: Modes of Incorporation in a Mexican American Network." PhD diss., University of Chicago.

Turner, Ralph H. 1976. "The Real Self: From Institution to Impulse." *American Journal of Sociology* 81 (5): 989–1016.

Turnovsky, Carolyn Pinedo. 2006 "A la Parada: The Social Practices of Men on a Street Corner." *Social Text* 24 (3 [88]): 55–72.

Umemoto, Karen. 2006. *The Truce: Lessons from an L.A. Gang War.* Cornell University Press.

Valdez, Zulema. 2011. *The New Entrepreneurs: How Race, Class, and Gender Shape American Enterprise.* Stanford University Press.

Valenzuela, Abel, Jr. 2001. "Day Labourers as Entrepreneurs?" *Journal of Ethnic and Migration Studies* 27 (2): 335–52.

Valenzuela, Abel, Jr. 2003. "Day Labor Work." *Annual Review of Sociology* 29 (1): 307–33.

Valle, Victor M., and Rodolfo D. Torres. 2000. *Latino Metropolis.* University of Minnesota Press.

Varsanyi, Monica, Paul G. Lewis, Doris Marie Provine, and Scott Decker. 2012. "A Multilayered Jurisdictional Patchwork: Immigration Federalism in the United States." *Law & Policy* 34 (2): 138–58.

Venkatesh, Sudhir Alladi. 2008. *Off the Books.* Harvard University Press.

Villalón, Roberta. 2010. *Violence against Latina Immigrants: Citizenship, Inequality, and Community.* NYU Press.

Wacquant, Loïc. 2004. *Body & Soul: Notebooks of an Apprentice Boxer.* Oxford University Press.

Waldinger, Roger, and Mehdi Bozorgmehr, eds. 1996. *Ethnic Los Angeles.* Russell Sage Foundation.

Waldinger, Roger, and Michael I. Lichter. 2003. *How the Other Half Works: Immigration and the Social Organization of Labor.* University of California Press.

Waldinger, Roger, Eric Popkin, and Hector Aquiles Magana. 2008. "Conflict and Contestation in the Cross-Border Community: Hometown Associations Reassessed." *Ethnic and Racial Studies* 3 (5): 843–70.

Walford, Geoffrey. 2018. "The Impossibility of Anonymity in Ethnographic Research." *Qualitative Research* 18 (5): 516–25.

Walter, Nicholas, Philippe Bourgois, and H. Margarita Loinaz. 2004. "Masculinity and Undocumented Labor Migration: Injured Latino Day Laborers in San Francisco." *Social Science & Medicine* 59 (6): 1159–68.

Weenink, Don. 2014. "Frenzied Attacks. A Micro-Sociological Analysis of the Emotional Dynamics of Extreme Youth Violence." *British Journal of Sociology* 65 (3): 411–33.

Weenink, Don. 2015. "Contesting Dominance and Performing Badness: A Micro-Sociological Analysis of the Forms, Situational Asymmetry, and Severity of Street Violence." *Sociological Forum* 30 (1): 83–102.

Weibel-Orlando, Joan. 1985. "Indians, Ethnicity, and Alcohol: Contrasting Perceptions of the Ethnic Self and Alcohol Use." In *The American Experience with Alcohol: Contrasting Cultural Perspectives*, edited by Linda A. Bennett and Genevieve M. Ames. Springer.

Wilson, Eli Revelle Yano. 2020. *Front of the House, Back of the House: Race and Inequality in the Lives of Restaurant Workers.* NYU Press.

Wolch, Jennifer, John P. Wilson, and Jed Fehrenbach. 2005. "Parks and Park Funding in Los Angeles: An Equity-Mapping Analysis." *Urban Geography* 26 (1): 4–35.

Wong, Julia. 2014. "Dropbox, Airbnb, and the Fight Over San Francisco's Public Spaces." *New Yorker.* October 13.

Worby, Paula A., Kurt C. Organista, Alex H. Kral, James Quesada, Sonya Arreola, and Sahar Khoury. 2014. "Structural Vulnerability and Problem Drinking among Latino Migrant Day Laborers in the San Francisco Bay Area." *Journal of Health Care for the Poor and Underserved* 25 (3): 1291–307.

Whyte, William Foote. 1943. *Street Corner Society: The Social Structure of an Italian Slum.* University of Chicago Press.

Whyte, William Foote. 1994. *Participant Observer: An Autobiography.* Cornell University Press.

Wittel, Andreas. 2001. "Toward a Network Sociality." *Theory, Culture & Society* 18 (6): 51–76.

Zavella, Patricia. 2011. *I'm Neither Here nor There: Mexicans' Quotidian Struggles with Migration and Poverty.* Duke University Press.

Zentgraf, Kristine M. 2002. "Immigration and Women's Empowerment: Salvadorans in Los Angeles." *Gender & Society* 16 (5): 625–46.

Zepeda-Millán, Chris. 2016. "Weapons of the (Not So) Weak: Immigrant Mass Mobilization in the US South." *Critical Sociology* 42 (2): 269–87.

Zimmerman, Don H., and D. Lawrence Wieder. 1977. "You Can't Help but Get Stoned: Notes on the Social Organization of Marijuana Smoking." *Social Problems* 25 (2): 198–207.

Zlolniski, Christian. 2006. *Janitors, Street Vendors, and Activists: The Lives of Mexican Immigrants in Silicon Valley.* University of California Press.

Zukin, Sharon. 2009. *Naked City: The Death and Life of Authentic Urban Places.* Oxford University Press.

INDEX

Motor, 1–2, 15, 17, 51–52, 55, 58, 59,
    61, 63, 67, 68, 69, 71, 72, 76–77, 80,
    83, 85–86, 89, 93, 94, 95, 115, 120,
    121, 123–24, 131, 136–37, 140, 142,
    150, 151, 152, 154, 155, 156, 159,
    160, 161–162, 166, 167, 177, 186,
    203n13

nannies and childcare, 4, 13, 183, 144,
    170
neighbors. *See* Mar Vista neighbors and
    neighborhood
Nelson, 116–17, 118, 129, 132, 135,
    178, 179
networking and social ties: challenges to,
    8, 11–12, 23, 180, 184–88; through
    clients, 19, 157–61; from country of
    origin vs. post-migration ties, 7–9,
    10, 12, 157, 176, 198n25; drinking
    together (*see* drinking: for socializing,
    bonding, and networking); emotional
    support provided, 7, 8, 12, 35–36;
    through fights (*see* fighting: catalyst
    for bonding); among first-generation
    vs. second-generation immigrants, 93,
    187–88; through group activity and
    interactional rituals, 10–12; through
    humor and inside jokes (*see* jokes and
    humor: and social cohesion); as key
    to survival and success of newcom-
    ers, 7, 176, 179, 198n21; norms of
    behavior, 15, 22, 26, 36, 38, 40–42,
    45–46, 50, 79, 81, 87, 101, 105, 106,
    138, 169, 183, 187–88, 189, 204n23;
    resource exchanges, 7, 10, 11, 19,
    23, 149, 176, 179, 184, 186, 189;
    ritualistic encoding of relationships,
    11, 34, 35, 38, 64, 91, 96; shaped by
    social infrastructure and access to
    public space, 9, 13, 181, 186, 188,
    189; through shared language, cul-
    ture, and customs, 12, 15, 18, 20, 91;
    through shared past (*see* Mar Vista
    soccer players: histories, legacies, and
    heroes); social tying, 9, 10–12, 181,
    189; theories of, 7–10, 181, 198n25;
    of working-class immigrant men vs.
    White male professionals, 169, 180–

81, 186. *See also* immigrant labor:
    building reputations; reputation and
    respectability
nicknames, 2, 15, 17, 20, 34, 51, 58, 59,
    61, 62, 67, 68–69, 74, 75, 82, 89,
    90, 92, 97, 125, 143, 179, 199n49,
    200n66; alcohol-related, 90, 97, 112,
    179, 204n21; based on age, race,
    or physical traits, 2, 17, 40, 51, 52,
    57, 58, 60–61, 62, 68–69, 92, 124,
    129, 136; based on nationality, 17,
    40, 60–61, 62, 69, 83; based on
    occupation, 61, 125, 143; based on
    personality, 15, 51, 58, 82, 90, 97;
    based on quality of soccer play, 58,
    68–69, 74, 75, 89; based on relations
    with other players, 51, 58, 61, 67, 68;
    after famous soccer players, 58, 61,
    64, 69, 89; source of humor, 15, 34,
    59–61, 89, 179; used to mask identity
    of players, 20, 200n66
norms. *See* Mar Vista soccer players:
    norms of behavior; networking and
    social ties: norms of behavior

Oscar, 57–58, 59, 62, 67, 73

Pachanga, 76–77, 86, 90, 96–97, 153,
    204n21
Park, Robert, 6
Park Advisory Board, 43, 173, 174,
    201n69, 207n3, 207n4. *See also* Mar
    Vista Recreation Center: community
    meetings
Pasmado, 68, 71, 79, 80, 92, 96, 134,
    155
Payaso, 59, 61, 68
Penmar Park, 8, 198n27
photographs and photography, 20, 36,
    43, 69, 71, 102, 108–15, 172, 176,
    200n62, 200n63, 201n69, 201n70
pickup games. *See under* soccer play
Pikachu (park player), 83, 124
Pinocho, 92, 94, 96, 137, 139–40
Piore, Michael, 8, 205n35
Pisa Muerto, 120, 135, 143
police, 2, 12, 18, 26, 43, 45, 49, 80, 85,
    88, 90, 99–103, 107, 169, 171, 183,

Titi, 1, 2, 58–59, 98, 111, 142–43, 147, 148, 149, 150–51, 154, 158, 159, 160, 161, 162–63, 165–66, 167

Trump, Donald, 4, 5, 100, 171, 186, 189, 208n19; demonization of Latino immigrants, 4, 5, 171, 186, 208n21

trust, 10–11, 72, 95, 98, 106, 140, 149, 154, 169

Tulio, 30, 57–58, 76

UCLA, 3, 18, 168

Valderrama, 2, 11, 34–35, 66, 69, 96–97, 101, 102, 112, 117, 125–26, 135, 136, 142, 148, 149, 151, 152, 153, 155, 158, 160, 161, 163, 166, 169, 186

Vino Tinto, 84, 90, 112

Virginia (state), 184, 186

Westdale, 12–13. *See also* Mar Vista neighbors and neighborhood

West Los Angeles, 1, 12, 13, 19, 21, 25, 91, 99, 144, 146, 174, 176, 178, 187, 201n1, 202n5

Whiteness and White privilege, 3, 5, 12, 13, 19, 22, 27, 35, 42, 44, 45, 61, 102, 155, 156, 162, 169, 174, 183, 185, 189–90, 197n11, 208n6. *See also* class; race and racism

Whyte, William Foote: *Street Corner Society*, 6

Zapata, 25, 31, 49, 71, 79, 88, 90, 110, 177, 187

Zurdo, 68, 70–71, 73, 105, 113

Made in the USA
Monee, IL
18 August 2023

41224104R00136